Differentiating
Reading
Instruction

How to Teach Reading To Meet the Needs of Each Student

Laura Robb

Foreword by Carol Ann Tomlinson

 SCHOLASTIC

New York • Toronto • London • Auckland • Sydney
Mexico City • New Delhi • Hong Kong • Buenos Aires

Dedication

For my students and all the teachers I've coached and trained, with deepest thanks and respect for all you've taught me about reading.

With love for my grandchildren, Lucas Benjamin and Helena Sylvie-Rose.

"Hey" by David Harrison from CONNECTING THE DOTS: POEMS OF MY JOURNEY by David Harrison published by Wordsong, an imprint of Boyds Mills Press, 2004. Reprinted by permission of Boyds Mills Press, Inc. Text copyright © 2004 by David L. Harrison.

"The Party" by Pam Muñoz Ryan. Text copyright © 2001 by Pam Muñoz Ryan. Used with permission of the Author and BookStop Literary Agency. All rights reserved.

Cover Design: Jorge Namerow
Cover Photo: Bonnie Jacobson
Interior Design: LDL Designs
Interior Photos: Bonnie Jacobson

ISBN-13: 978-0-545-02298-9
ISBN-10: 0-545-02298-3

Copyright © 2008 by Laura Robb
All rights reserved. Published by Scholastic Inc.
Printed in the U.S.A.

1 2 3 4 5 6 7 8 9 10   23   13 12 11 10 09 08

Contents

Acknowledgments 5

Foreword 7

Introduction 9

Chapter 1: Differentiating Reading Instruction:
Reaching All Learners With Best Practice Teaching 11

Chapter 2: Routines, Assessment, and Planning:
Building the Foundation for Differentiating Reading Instruction 31

Chapter 3: Read Alouds and Differentiation:
Bridging Learning Gaps While Engaging Readers 65

Chapter 4: Whole-Class Instructional Reading and Differentiation:
Differentiated Whole-Class Instruction That Matches
Students and Books 99

Chapter 5: Small-Group Reading Instruction and Differentiation:
Supporting Students With Teacher-Led Reading Groups 139

Chapter 6: Independent Reading and Differentiation:
Developing Students' Stamina and Personal Reading Lives 169

Chapter 7: Writing and Differentiation:
Using Writing to Support Comprehension for Every Student 203

Chapter 8: Professional Development and Differentiated Reading Instruction:
Guidelines and Suggestions for Getting Started 247

Appendices

A: "The Party" 259

B: Choosing "Just-Right" Books for Independent Reading 262

C: Sample Schedules for Differentiated Whole-Class Instruction 263

D: Sample Schedules for Small-Group Instructional Reading 264

E: Book Log 265

F: Eleven Questions About Reading 266

G: Interest Inventory for Grades 4 and 5 267

H: Interest Inventory for Grades 6 and up 268

I: Reading Strategy Checklist 269

J: Reading Strategy Lesson: Drawing Conclusions 270

K: Reading Strategy Lessons: Using Context Clues 272

L: QtA Queries 273

M: Explanations of Nonfiction Text Features 274

N: Open-Ended Genre Discussion Questions 275

O: Book Review Guidelines 278

P: Book Review: Fiction 279

Q: Book Review: Nonfiction 281

R: Sample Journal Entries 282

S: Guidelines for Summarizing Fiction and Nonfiction Texts 283

T: List of Words That Describe Personality Traits 284

U: Mentor Text for Letters Between Two Characters 285

Bibliography of Professional Books 287

Bibliography of Children's Books 295

Index 299

Acknowledgments

There are three powerful forces that helped me see the need for differentiating reading instruction for adolescent learners. The first force is the students I have taught. Observing them I learned so much about the need to support all levels of readers to improve their reading and thinking skills. Moreover, it's my students who helped me refine the components of a differentiated approach to whole-class instructional reading (in which each student reads a different book) and teacher-led strategic reading groups. I am grateful for their honesty and for their willingness to work through strategies and provide invaluable feedback about organization, scheduling, and reading choices. They also pointed me in a direction beyond my personal literacy experiences that enabled me to respect their diverse literacy interests, knowledge, and abilities.

The second force that influenced this book are the teachers I coach and train in my school and in schools around Virginia and other parts of the country. These teachers want to reach each child in their classes, but their training doesn't adequately prepare them to meet the diverse reading and writing levels they encounter. Questions teachers posed pushed me to develop workshops in which teachers assumed the roles of students so they could experience differentiated reading instruction firsthand. The feedback I gathered from the debriefings after these workshops—and from teachers' e-mails, overflowing with management questions—enabled me to find ways to make differentiating reading instruction clearer for them. My deepest thanks go to all these teachers who recognize that "one size doesn't fit all."

The third force is an educator, researcher, and writer, Carol Ann Tomlinson, whose work on differentiating instruction across the curriculum supplied me with rich background knowledge and enlarged my mental model of what differentiation could and would look like in a reading workshop.

To my editor, Virginia Dooley, I offer sincerest thanks for pointing the way and helping me see the need for making a complex topic simple by explaining the process with clarity and examples and for giving me the time I needed to write and revise.

Virginia's questions and conversations enabled me to rethink and revise the book's organization and content. With her gentle and nurturing guidance, a book emerged that I hope teachers will find useful and practical.

My thanks to Terry Cooper and Gloria Pipkin who read the first two chapters and weighed in with suggestions that made them clearer and easier to read. My thanks as well to Joanna Davis-Swing for her thoughtful insights and revision suggestions.

Finally, to my husband Lloyd, my loving thanks for always encouraging me to write, write, write, and maintain the momentum of the emerging book.

— *Laura Robb*

Foreword

By Carol Ann Tomlinson, Ed.D.
The University of Virginia

*D*ifferentiation is little more than the common sense of teaching. Any of us who have taught for more than a day know that the students we teach learn on different timetables and in different ways; they have different interests and motivations and have different ways of "coming at" assignments.

We know, too, that it's essential for a teacher to have a clear vision of what students should know, what they should understand, and what they should be able to do as a result of a year spent with us, at the end of a unit of study, and at the end of day in our classroom. And we know that careful alignment of teaching and learning plans with rich and explicit learning goals is necessary for success.

Because we know some students will learn more rapidly and deeply than we had envisioned and that some will begin early on to lag behind, we see that continually assessing a student's status relative to essential goals is non-negotiable for a success-oriented teacher. And we know that what we learn from ongoing assessment is only of value if it helps us do a better job of teaching a wide variety of students.

Furthermore, we know that there are certain fundamental skills, such as reading and writing, which are prerequisites for student growth in any subject. We know from our own observations as well as from time-tested research that students who do not read and write proficiently are at an enormous disadvantage in school—that they are on a collision course with academic failure. These students are also, of course, greatly impaired when the schoolhouse door closes behind them for the last time and they enter the larger world to make their way.

We cannot possibly spend our days in the midst of young learners and not know these things. And yet, many of us teach as though all of our students are essentially alike. We struggle to move beyond teaching a set of prescribed standards to ensure that our learning goals are coherent, connected, and rich. We still use assessment data as filler for grade books, more than we use it to help us re-craft the way we will work with students tomorrow or the next day. And beyond the earliest grades in school, we still act as though the teaching of reading and writing is someone else's job.

I am a teacher, and despite this somber analysis, I believe in teachers. Over several decades, my colleagues have taught me through their daily actions that teachers care about their work and about students. I don't think our failure to modify our teaching habits and practices to serve increasingly diverse learners is the result of our failure to see the need for differentiation, or the result of our being unconcerned or unwilling to re-invent ourselves. I think we persist in old habits because we do not know what the new ones look like— because we do not know how to move ourselves from Point A to Point B.

I see *Differentiating Reading Instruction* as a guidebook for those of us who want to ensure that an avid reader or writer doesn't have to "regress" in order to learn. This book is for teachers who want to guarantee that a struggling reader or writer can find support for developing the skills that are necessary for academic and life success. In this book, I hear the voice of a teacher who knows experientially how to teach "older" students to grow as readers and writers—wherever they are on the achievement spectrum. This teacher does not assign the responsibility to a colleague, nor does she blame a past teacher. Laura Robb has figured out how to establish classroom routines that allow her to teach where her students are, even while she unites them in shared conversation and inquiry.

She shows us how to do what many of us want to do: support a broad range of learners in becoming more confident and competent readers and writers. Her clarity, practicality, detail, and examples provide us with images of an academically responsive teacher and with the tools necessary to begin creating those images in our own work.

I am excited for the teachers for whom this book will be a bridge to a more dynamic way of teaching—and for their students.

Introduction

Several years have passed since I wrote *Teaching Reading in Middle School (2000)* and *Teaching Reading in Social Studies, Science, and Math* (2003), and I continue to learn from the students I teach at Powhatan School as well as from the students I work with at public schools in Virginia and across the country. It is students who push me to deepen my understanding of teaching reading—students like Justine, an eighth grader, who wrote in September, "I HATE READING!!!!!" on her survey, or Ben who noted that the first word that popped into his mind when he thought about reading was "annoying," or John who wrote "ow, man" indicating the pain he associated with reading.

When I work with different schools, I often notice how teachers and administrators struggle to meet the needs of students who read two or more years below grade level. It was my own teaching and my work with teachers of readers who struggle that started me on my personal journey of exploring the research on differentiating instruction. I started by reading Carol Ann Tomlinson, moved to enlarging my knowledge of brain research with David Sousa as my guide, and then explored Howard Gardner's theory of different intelligences. I began to think about how I could use this knowledge as I taught reading—and this book is the result of my journey.

As you review the table of contents and dip into various chapters, you'll see many teaching practices that you probably already include in your daily instruction, such as independent reading, small-group reading instruction, and one-on-one reading conferences. But my goal is for you to see these practices in a new way—through the lens of differentiation.

My hope is that as you differentiate reading instruction by implementing some of the strategies in this book, you will be able to support and improve the reading of the struggling, reluctant, grade-level, and proficient readers who are in your classes.

Chapter 1

Differentiating Reading Instruction

Reaching All Learners With Best Practice Teaching

Before I coach a teacher, I always set aside time to observe him or her teaching the same class for two or three consecutive days. It was during one of these observations that I realized the importance of helping teachers learn to differentiate reading instruction. I was observing a sixth-grade teacher, Ms. Hayes (a pseudonym), who had a class of 30 students. The instructional reading levels in her class ranged from mid-third grade to seventh grade. For 30 minutes, Ms. Hayes read aloud from *Lyddie* by Katherine Paterson (Dutton, 1991). Each student had a copy of the book and was told to follow along as the teacher read. After the read aloud, Ms. Hayes spent ten minutes asking questions that prompted students to recall what they had heard. Watching these students each day revealed much about the level of learning in this class. The same six students dominated the question/answer period. Eight students spent the class with their heads on their desks. Fourteen slouched in their seats, looking at the floor, the ceiling, the door—anything but the book. Out of 30, only 8 students appeared to be following the lesson.

After the third day of observation, I met with Ms. Hayes. The purpose of this first meeting was purely investigative. When I asked Ms. Hayes why her reading class consisted of reading *Lyddie* aloud and then checking students' recall of details by asking questions that focused on the plot, she said, "This is a required book for sixth grade. Only a handful of students can read it, so I decided to read the book aloud." She told me that some teachers on her team purchased an audio recording of *Lyddie*. "Students listen to that every day."

Next, I asked, "How do you feel about this accommodation?"

"Frustrated and bored, " she said. Ms. Hayes felt frustrated because she recognized that students reading below a sixth-grade level couldn't really follow along. "Those [students] get turned off to reading. They tell me class is 'boring.'" Ms. Hayes admitted that she felt as bored as her students because each day was the same, and the discussions were uninspiring.

Unfortunately, accommodations like the ones Ms. Hayes and her team made are all too common in classes I visit around our country. Recently, at a training session on guided reading in Winchester, Virginia, a teacher told me that she and her colleagues were required to teach every student the lesson from the grade-level basal anthology before moving to guided reading groups. "How am I supposed to help a child reading on a second-grade instructional level complete a fifth-grade selection and related worksheets?" the teacher asked me. Unfortunately, the only strategies teachers use are reading the text aloud or having students listen to the books on tape.

These accommodations reveal how hard teachers work to meet district and state requirements—requirements that often mandate one novel, one grade-level basal, or one content textbook for everyone. But these accommodations can't and don't support learners in classes that have inclusion students or students who read on a wide range of instructional levels (Allington, 2006b; Tomlinson, 1999). When teachers have to make these kinds of accommodations, it means that students who read below grade level aren't learning to apply strategies and skills at their instructional levels. Day after day, those who need the best instruction and the most practice with reading, sit passively in classes, heading backward in skill and attitude (Allington, 2001, 2002, 2006a, 2006b; Allington & Cunningham, 2002; Anderson, 1992). So what can we do to effect meaningful change—change that reaches every learner, all day long? The answer is to differentiate reading instruction in language arts classes and in every content class students take (Allington, 2006b; Tomlinson, 1999).

As You Continue to Read . . .

First, we'll look at the core principles of a differentiated approach to teaching. Next you'll step inside my eighth-grade classroom, where you can observe some elements of differentiation in action as I teach reading. With a clearer mental model of differentiation, we'll look at its research base. I've also included suggestions for integrating issues into your units of study. The chapter closes with an exploration of how differentiation works within the three-part reading framework (before, during, and after).

What Is Differentiated Instruction?

Differentiation is a way of teaching; it's not a program or a package of worksheets. It asks teachers to know their students well so they can provide each one with experiences and tasks that will improve learning. As Carol Ann Tomlinson has said, differentiation means giving students multiple options for taking in information (1999). Differentiating instruction means that you observe and understand the differences and similarities among students and use this information to plan instruction. Here is a list of some key principles that form the foundation of differentiating instruction.

- **Ongoing, formative assessment:** Teachers continually assess to identify students' strengths and areas of need so they can meet students where they are and help them move forward.
- **Recognition of diverse learners:** The students we teach have diverse levels of expertise and experience with reading, writing, thinking, problem solving, and speaking.

Ongoing assessments enable teachers to develop differentiated lessons that meet every students' needs.

- **Group work:** Students collaborate in pairs and small groups whose membership changes as needed. Learning in groups enables students to engage in meaningful discussions and to observe and learn from one another.

- **Problem solving:** The focus in classrooms that differentiate instruction is on issues and concepts rather

Group work allows students to observe and learn from one another.

than "the book" or the chapter. This encourages all students to explore big ideas and expand their understanding of key concepts.

- **Choice:** Teachers offer students choice in their reading and writing experiences and in the tasks and projects they complete. By negotiating with students, teachers can create motivating assignments that meet students' diverse needs and varied interests.

From this list you can see that differentiating instruction asks teachers to continually strive to know and to respond to each student's needs to maximize learning. I want you also to understand why educators like Carol Ann Tomlinson, Richard Allington, and me strongly believe that instruction in reading should be differentiated. To deepen your understanding, let me share information with you that explains this strong commitment to differentiated learning.

DATA THAT SUPPORTS DIFFERENTIATION IN READING

Most primary teachers differentiate reading instruction through guided reading (Fountas & Pinnell, 2001). However, the landscape often changes when students enter fourth grade. Studies show that these students' personal reading lives and their delight in reading start to wane, and by middle school, they read less on their own than they did in the early grades (Ruddell & Unrau, 1997). Add a diet of tough textbooks and less time for reading instruction to this diminished interest in personal reading, and the result is far too many students reading below grade level, struggling to learn. The U.S. Department of Education noted that more than 8 million students in grades 4 through 12 are struggling readers (2003). High school students in the lowest 25 percent of their class are 20 times more likely to drop out of school than excellent and proficient learners (Carnevale, 2001).

Gina Biancarosa and Catherine Snow (2004), authors of *Reading Next*, point to a statistic that should cause all middle grade, middle school, and high school educators to rethink their instructional practices. They noted:

> "A full 70 percent of U.S. middle and high school students require differentiated instruction, which is instruction targeted to their individual strengths and weaknesses." —*Reading Next*, page 8

Whether they come from middle- and upper-class income levels, from low-income households, from families living in poverty, or from families who are English language learners, 70 percent of adolescent learners will benefit from differentiated instruction. This is a powerful statistic that we teachers need to remember and act upon as we teach reading. Right now, too many middle schools place students in a curriculum in which everyone reads the same text and completes the same assignments. Unfortunately, this leaves too many students behind instead of moving them forward (Tomlinson, 2002).

You and I need to explore and try ways to teach our students at their instructional levels. This is the heart of differentiation, and this is the primary reason I have written this book. In it, you'll find the planning techniques, strategies, and organization and management suggestions I have developed and that my students have helped me refine. As Hannah, an eighth grader, noted in her evaluation of instructional and independent reading: "Give kids books they can read so they can learn. They might even like school because they can be part of a discussion."

Step Inside My Classroom

So what does differentiated reading instruction look like? I invite you to step inside my eighth-grade classroom at the beginning of my reading workshop. After a brief warm-up

exercise, and a read aloud for enjoyment, I introduce an essential component of my approach to
differentiated reading instruction—the teaching
read aloud. To be certain that I am reaching
every student in my class, I use the read aloud to
model how I apply reading strategies and to
show students how to use questioning, discussion, and writing to build comprehension and
new understandings while reading (Beck &

Reading Workshop

You'll read more about workshop in
Chapter 2. However, you can differentiate reading instruction in any teaching
framework as long as you include materials that meet the diverse reading levels
of your students.

McKeown, 1997, 2006; Robb, 2000, 2003). In fact, the read aloud has become the common
mentor or teaching text for my students, and a primary teaching tool. In addition, I use it as
a catalyst to raise students' awareness of issues and to build background knowledge.

As you observe lessons in my classroom, you'll also note that the reading strategies
I'm modeling relate to inferential thinking—using facts and details to discover unstated
meanings and new understandings. These are the important strategies that all students—not just proficient readers—need. Not only will these important strategies help
students do well on tests, but—even more gratifying—they will make reading joyful and
exciting. My experiences with teaching students who are reading below grade level continue to show me that although these students may have difficulty reading, they are
capable of inferring, drawing conclusions, and making connections to characters, events,
people, and information. My read aloud shows that struggling readers can think at high
levels. When I provide them with books at their instructional levels, they also know that
they can analyze and think while they read. Understandably, learners falter when teachers ask them to infer and analyze texts they can't decode and comprehend.

Stay longer in my classroom, and you would observe that writing has taken center
stage. During my read aloud, conferences, and small-group meetings, students write to
explore hunches, concepts, meaning, and connections. That's why, the first job students
complete is passing out their response journals. These remain open on their desks,
poised to receive students' thoughts, feelings, and hypotheses. This writing is critical in
a differentiated reading classroom. Reading students' writing helps me know what students understand and where they need more support.

You would also notice that I use multiple texts for my instructional reading lessons. Sometimes, I use a whole-class instructional approach, where each student is reading a different text while exploring an issue or practicing the application of a reading strategy that I have modeled in my read aloud. Other times, students work in small groups. Within each group, members read the same book, and again they explore issues and practice the strategies I've modeled during the read-aloud lesson. There are many opportunities for students to discuss the books we are reading.

Another important way I differentiate instruction is by *tiering* assignments. Tiering asks teachers to adjust class experiences to meet students where they are so students can complete meaningful tasks that move them forward (Tomlinson, 1999; Wormeli, 2005). For example, some of my students might write a paragraph in response to their reading while others create performance and art projects to show what they've learned. Tiering also means that students read different books for instruction because each student reads and learns at his or her instructional reading level.

In addition, it's important for students to practice reading at school and at home, using books at their comfort levels (see appendix page 262). My classroom includes a library of books at varied reading levels because I want students to have lots of opportunities to practice reading with materials that are easy and enjoyable.

Ten Practices to Differentiate Reading Instruction

What you saw in your "visit" to my classroom are practical ways I differentiate to improve my students' literacy. In the list below, I've summarized these important elements and added a few other practices, such as planning, that are key to differentiating reading instruction successfully. In subsequent chapters of this book, we'll take a closer look at these elements and explore ways to integrate them into your lessons so you can support every student you teach.

1. **Make your read alouds a common teaching text.** In addition to being just for fun, read-aloud materials will become your common text, setting the stage for differentiation. Use them to build background knowledge and to show students how you

apply strategies (Beck & McKeown, 2006; Robb, 2008; Wilhelm, 2001, 2005). You can also use them to introduce issues and invite students to respond to these issues in their journals. Making your read aloud your teaching text will ensure that every student has access to the information and skills they need to become a better reader. See Chapter 3 for more on read alouds.

2. **Teach with diverse materials.** Avoid using one text for the entire class. Instead, use multiple texts at diverse reading levels for your units of study. This will enable every student to gather information from books and magazines they can truly read (Robb, 2003; Worthy et al., 1999).

3. **Organize for instruction so you meet all reading levels.** Whether you use a differentiated whole-class instructional approach or have students work in small groups, you'll need to organize each unit of study around a genre, issue, or topic—rather than teaching "the book." See chapters 4 and 5 for more on instructional reading.

4. **Value independent practice reading.** Set aside 15 to 30 minutes of class time, at least three times a week, for students to read books at their comfort levels—and these levels vary from student to student. See chapter 6 for more on independent reading.

5. **Tier your assignments.** The books students read and the assignments they complete should match their needs. Students who struggle might need scaffolded or supported tasks that enable them to improve their thinking and analytical skills to experience the success needed to rebuild self-esteem, self-confidence, and the motivation to work harder (Tomlinson, 1999, 2002).

6. **Show students how to construct meaning while reading.** Students can become better readers only if they understand how to construct meaning as they read. By modeling the ways you think about texts during your read alouds, while you work with small reading groups, and in your one-to-one instructional conferences with students, you are offering students multiple opportunities for learning how to construct meaning.

7. **Encourage discussion.** Discussion is especially important in a differentiated reading classroom because it provides a powerful way to build on every students' understandings and knowledge of facts. It also provides them with opportunities to clarify meaning and to build comprehension. By asking students to move beyond memorizing the facts to applying those facts to issues and problems through discussion, students deep-

en their understanding and recall. In-depth discussions among small groups, and with the entire class, can show students how their peers think and reason, can build background knowledge, and can make the facts relevant to their own lives.

8. **Write to explore, think, learn, and improve comprehension.** Learners can write only what they know and understand (Alvermann & Phelps, 1998; Robb, 2002; Self, 1987; Vaughan & Estes, 1986). If they haven't absorbed a lesson, they will have little to write. It's crucial for teachers to know that everyone in a class does not absorb the same information from a demonstration or a lesson (Clay, 1993). Reading students' journals can provide insights into whether students can think inferentially and analyze chunks of text. These insights support planning interventions for individuals, pairs, small groups, and, at times, the entire class. See Chapter 7 for more on writing.

9. **Use ongoing assessments to support each student.** Study the assessments students complete for a unit to discover their successes and their areas of need. Then support each student in your class by getting to know him or her so you can provide targeted instruction. Ongoing assessments allow you to do this. See Chapter 2 for more on assessments.

10. **Plan your units carefully.** Thinking through each unit of study enables you to understand what you want students to learn about a genre, an issue, and reading strategies (Tomlinson, 1999). It will also

Suggested Reading Related to Differentiation

Here are some seminal books on differentiation. Set aside time to reflect on the ideas in these texts, and then discuss what you've learned with colleagues. Continually ask, *How can this information support change in my teaching practices?* This question will start your differentiation journey. (See Chapter 8 for more suggestions on changing practice.)

Developing Students' Multiple Intelligences by Kristen Nicholson-Nelson, Scholastic, 1998

The Differentiated Classroom: Responding to the Needs of All Learners by Carol Ann Tomlinson, ASCD, 1999

Differentiation in Action by Judith Dodge, Scholastic, 2005

How the Brain Learns by David A. Sousa, Corwin Press, 2001

How to Differentiate Instruction in Mixed Ability Classrooms by Carol Ann Tomlinson, ASCD, 1995

Multiple Intelligences: The Theory in Practice by Howard Gardner, Basic Books, 1993

ensure that you have gathered reading materials that meet the needs of each student, as well as appropriate texts for your read alouds. See Chapter 2 for more on planning.

As you begin to embrace some of these differentiation practices, it's important for you to know the research that supports this kind of instruction. Knowing the research will enable you to select materials to read for building your own background knowledge and expanding your understanding of differentiation. I've included a list of other books you can study that relate to and highlight the need for differentiation in the box on page 19.

The Research Base for Differentiated Instruction

Several key researchers have pointed the way toward differentiating reading instruction. Carol Ann Tomlinson, Howard Gardner, David Sousa, Lev Vygotsky, and the schema theorists all contributed important thinking.

CAROL ANN TOMLINSON—DIFFERENTIATION

The person I turn to again and again when wanting to clarify my ideas and deepen my understanding of differentiation is Carol Ann Tomlinson. Tomlinson has dedicated her research and writing to supporting teachers as they move from one text for all to planning differentiated lessons and tiering learning experiences and assignments (Tomlinson, 1999; Tomlinson & Cunningham, 2003). Her books and professional articles are practical, showing teachers how to change their learning environment, and explaining the instructional strategies that support teaching the multilevels of learners in one classroom. Tomlinson sprinkles her chapters with literacy vignettes about teachers who differentiate instruction, making the process accessible to teachers and administrators.

HOWARD GARDNER—MULTIPLE INTELLIGENCES

The researcher of multiple intelligences, Howard Gardner, moved people away from thinking that intelligence was a single, inborn trait that could be measured by administering a test. Instead, he suggested that there are a variety of ways people are smart. Gardner's research on multiple intelligences helped educators understand that children take in and process information differently. For example, a student who has strong verbal-linguistic ability will take in and learn information through stories, drama, and words. A student whose strength is logical-mathematical will benefit from seeing models, blueprints, plans, and solutions to problems.

Note that Gardner cautions teachers about labeling students according to their dominant intelligence. Gardner explains that each one of us is a combination of these intelligences, even though one might be a strength, and that all the intelligences interact together as we read, write, think, and speak.

An understanding of multiple intelligences will help you address students' learning preferences as you design learning activities and develop assessments. Choices that attend to learning preferences can include designing a brochure or pamphlet, illustrating a text, writing a news article, performing an original Readers Theater script, or building a model.

> ## Gardner's Intelligences
>
> Note that we all have these traits, but often one stands out and becomes dominant.
> - verbal-linguistic
> - spatial
> - logical-mathematical
> - musical
> - interpersonal
> - bodily-kinesthetic
> - intrapersonal

DAVID SOUSA—BRAIN RESEARCH

David Sousa's research on how our brains learn best, also supports the notion of differentiating instruction. In a keynote speech at The Dodge Learning Conference in Perry, Georgia, in 2005, Sousa encouraged teachers to expand their knowledge of how the brain works so they can select learning strategies for students that will enable them to experience success. In his book *How the Brain Learns* (Corwin Press, 2001), and in his keynote, Sousa made the case for bringing issues, stories, and connections to learning. He explained that to learn information, we observe, identify patterns and generalize, then form conclusions based on patterns, and finally evaluate these conclusions using our observations and prior knowledge. Therefore, Sousa pointed out, memorizing facts and vocabulary for tests and quizzes without connecting these to stories, or other ideas, other books, movies, and so on, means learners won't retain the information.

Sousa also asks teachers to consider the difference between the "difficulty" and the "complexity" of an assignment. Instead of increasing the difficulty by asking students to read and write more, Sousa invites teachers to design activities that increase complexity. We teachers often ask proficient readers and writers to write three pages that relate to an issue, character, or theme in a book, whereas we ask struggling readers to write a paragraph. Using Sousa's concept of complexity, we might adjust this task by asking all students to write a paragraph. However, those who struggle will work on summarizing, which asks them to select details from their books, while those who are proficient learners may take a more complex approach, choosing a key event and showing how it affected the character's decisions and actions.

SCHEMA RESEARCHERS—READING RESEARCH

According to schema theory research, the brain stores all background knowledge and experiences in structures called schemata. Schema theory researchers pointed out that because all of our experiences differ, learners arrive at school with different sets of experiences and prior knowledge (Anderson, 1984; Clay, 1993; Duke & Bennett-Armistead, 2003; Duke & Pearson, 2002; Grolnick & Ryan, 1987; Marzano, 2004; Robb, 2000, 2008). Since learners' literacy experiences differ, what each student brings to his or her reading and writing to construct meaning will also differ. When you and I develop instructional practices that attend to these differences in prior knowledge and experiences, we are adjusting and differentiating instruction so all students can learn and progress.

LEV VYGOTSKY—LEARNING RESEARCH

Lev Vygotsky's view of teacher and peer experts as learning mediators also validates the case for differentiating reading instruction (1978). His research supports three elements that I consider essential aspects of differentiated reading instruction: meaningful discussion, learning at instructional levels, and scaffolding instruction.

Meaningful discussion: Vygotsky believed that children learn best in social situations in which they work alongside adults and peers who can help them accomplish a tough task. Classes rich in meaningful discussion about texts support what adolescents love to do: talk and interact with their peers (Bowers, 1995; Davies, 1996). In differentiated reading classes, students engage in small-group discussions, paired discussions, and confer with their teachers about strategies and books. In these classes, students who struggle with reading observe and learn more about how proficient readers summarize, pose questions, infer, synthesize information, and make connections.

Instructional learning levels: Vygotsky described three zones of learning: the *Zone of Actual Development*, where learners can complete tasks independently; the *Zone of Proximal Development*, where learners can accomplish a task only with the support of an expert; and the *Frustration Zone*, where the work is too difficult, even with the teacher's support. Continually learning in the *Frustration Zone* can diminish students' self-confidence, self-esteem, and reading skill (Schunk & Zimmerman, 1997; Wigfield, 1997).

The ideal teaching zone is the *Zone of Proximal Development*. However, what students in a class can learn with the support of an expert differs because students' instructional reading and writing levels differ. When teachers do what Carol Ann Tomlinson describes as "teach to the middle" by using one text for all students, only one group learns and progresses. "Teaching to the middle" also results in a group of students working at their independent learning level but *not* moving forward. A third group spends the year at their frustration level; they can't read texts or complete assignments. To support students in the teaching zone, the *Zone of Proximal Development*, we need to provide scaffolds or supports for each student with the goal of moving him or her to independence (see the chart on page 24).

Scaffolds and gradual release of responsibility: Teachers can scaffold learning by first modeling tasks and then supporting students as they attempt these tasks. Support is provided until the student is in the *Zone of Actual Development* and can accomplish the task independently. The most effective way to accomplish this is to gradually release the responsibility for learning from you to the student by first modeling, then supporting the student as he or she practices, and, finally, withdrawing support when the student demonstrates his or her ability to complete the task independently (Allington & Cunningham, 2002; Morrow, Gambrell, & Pressley, 2003; Robb, 2002).

Therefore, in Vygotskian terms, we can view learning as working on a tough task with the support of an expert. The goal is to enable the student to complete that tough

The Zone of Actual Development	The Zone of Proximal Development, or The Teaching Zone		The Zone of Actual Development
The Results of Scaffolding in the Zone of Proximal Development In this differentiated instructional model, the teacher supports each student with challenging but reachable tasks, so there is no frustration level. The cycle always returns to the Zone of Actual Development, and what the student can do independently grows throughout the school year.			
This is what each student can do on his or her own without any support.	Scaffolds	Gradual Release of Responsibility	The student has added the task to his or her repertoire of work that can be completed independently and without any support. Now the student is ready to work on a new, scaffolded task.
	The teacher or a peer expert supports the student.	Over time, the teacher releases the responsibility for completing the learning task to the student.	

task on his or her own by gradually giving the student more and more responsibility until the teacher's support is no longer necessary. To identify the learning tasks students can complete with scaffolds, ongoing assessment is vital.

Assessment, Tiering, and Discussion

Assessment, tiering, and discussion are integral to differentiating reading instruction. Let's take a closer look at each of them.

ASSESSMENT

Ongoing literacy assessment is the cornerstone of differentiating reading instruction. The only way to reach every learner and help him or her improve is to identify that student's strengths and his or her areas of need that require extra support. The ongoing assessments should include students' written work, oral presentations, quizzes, tests, conferences with students, and the observational notes you collect as students read, discuss, write, and speak (McTighe & O'Conner, 2006; Tomlinson, 1999, 2002). In Chapter 2, you will find more on assessment, including a chart that lists, in general terms, the kinds of assessments I recommend, along with student behaviors that indicate a need for support, and the kinds of teaching interventions you can try.

TIERING

As I mentioned earlier, matching texts to students' instructional reading levels is an example of tiering. Varying the number of instructional and independent reading books you expect students to complete is another example of tiering. When teachers use ongoing assessments, including their observations, to decide which reading strategy a student or a small group needs to practice and apply, this is another aspect of tiering.

Another element of tiering that relates to reading instruction is designing activities or tasks that students complete. When tiering these tasks, I like to ask all students to analyze and think at high levels. What differs is the complexity of assignments, and whether the project is oral, written, dramatic, or emphasizes drawing or movement. With each unit I develop, there are some required activities as well as a set of activities that students can

choose from. I find that students choose projects that they can complete well. If I feel that a student makes a poor choice, then I meet with that boy or girl outside of class and try to renegotiate the choice. If a weak student insists on sticking with a challenging project, let him or her, but make sure you offer support. If a top student chooses a project you consider "too easy," find out why the student made this choice. Sometimes a student has to care for

This student concentrates on a tiered project.

a sick family member, babysit, or prepare for a recital and feels pressed for time. Honor the student's choice and explain that you'll look forward to him or her choosing a more challenging project for the next unit.

To successfully plan learning activities and projects for a unit, you must be able to identify the understandings, the kinds of analytical thinking, and the skills you want all students to learn. In addition, you want to make sure that you don't tier by overloading your proficient readers with extra writing and longer projects (Sousa, 2001). You'll find examples of tiering when you review Big Picture Plans on pages 54–56 and in chapters 4, 5, and 6.

DISCUSSION

Discussions can help students and adults gather new information and understandings, see information and ideas from the perspectives of multiple reading texts, and share thoughts, data, and feelings about a topic or issue. When students read texts at their instructional or comfort levels, this diversity of materials means that every student can contribute ideas and information to the discussion and, at the same time, hear a variety of perspectives relating to a topic or theme.

Meaningful discussion, especially when the conversation moves beyond reciting the facts to linking the facts to issues, and to using the facts to solve problems and identify big ideas, is an analytical activity (Applebee et al. 2003). Research also shows that when students talk about their reading, they become more motivated to read (Guthrie et al., 1996). In my eighth-grade class, we were examining the issue of human rights, the abuse of power, and the need to control using *California Blue* by David Klass and *The Chocolate War* by Robert Cormier. Melissa was in the group of eight students reading *The Chocolate War*. Halfway through the book, I asked students to evaluate their discussions of the text in relation to issues. Here's what Melissa wrote in her journal:

> *I thought this [small-group discussions] would be silly—like what we did in second and third grade. But I find I can't wait for these discussions. They make me think about power and control in ways I wouldn't do, without discussing. I've learned that the line between violating human rights and doing something wrong like pushing someone in line is much clearer to me now.*

Bringing middle and high school students to Melissa's point, where they relish group discussions and recognize the benefit of thinking about books, takes time and practice. Students have to be able to read and comprehend a text, and the text should be worth thinking about for several weeks. So, though my students enjoy Meg Cabot's books for independent reading, for sustained group or individual investigations, I want them to choose from texts that provoke deep thinking about life and world issues (Rosenblatt, 1978).

Recently, I taught two eleventh-grade classes at Lee High School in Staunton, Virginia. In that school, the majority of teachers had students sitting in traditional rows, and students worked alone. After completing a 90-minute lesson in each of two English sections, where I had groups of four to five students discuss either poems that dealt with justice and injustice or science fiction stories that warned humankind about too much technology, I asked students to evaluate their feelings about small-group discussions. Their written responses made me sad, for I had not realized the extent of isolation and separation these students felt. Here are some statements written by these students:

Andrew: *I like working in a group because it lets you see other people's ideas and opinions rather than just your own. It's also nice because you don't feel so alone.*

Jess: *I like working together because I could talk to people I wouldn't normally talk to.*

Sharon: *Hearing thoughts and ideas from our group gives me more ideas, doesn't make me feel* <u>*isolated*</u> [student's underlining], *lonely.*

Organizing Instruction Around Issues

Because this idea is so crucial to differentiating reading instruction, I feel it's worth repeating here that having every student read the same book, no matter what accommodations you make, means that many students won't have an opportunity to improve their reading skills. But how do you move away from "one-book-for-all" teaching? At a differentiation workshop I facilitated with English, special education, and reading resource teachers at Lee High School, Katie, a ninth-grade teacher, shared that teaching *The Odyssey* did not work with a class of students whose reading levels ranged from fourth to ninth grade. "The majority hated it [*The Odyssey*] and couldn't read it, so I read it out loud."

When I asked, "Why did you choose to do that book?"

"It was in the anthology," Katie replied. "Now I have to teach *To Kill a Mockingbird*," she said, "but I don't think it's going to work either. What can I do?" I asked Katie to tell me what she wanted her students to get out of this book. She thought for a few minutes and then told me and her colleagues, "I want them to understand what life in the South was like for children and adults before civil rights legislation."

Do I Need a Special Schedule?

You can differentiate reading even if you have 40- to 50-minute daily classes in which to teach reading and writing. You'll find suggestions for organizing differentiated reading instruction in short blocks of time, or in longer, 90-minute blocks of time on pages 263–264.

I wanted to dance, to sing, to shout huzzah! Katie hit a bull's-eye! Once her thinking moved to issues and ideas, Katie could think about differentiating instruction because her purpose was no longer teaching *the one book*. After the workshop, we browsed through the reading resource room and added these books to her unit: *Roll of Thunder, Hear My Cry*, *The Friendship*, and *The Gold Cadillac*, all by Mildred Taylor. Not only did students read and discuss books at their instructional levels, but as Katie explained, "They learned about life then [pre-civil rights legislation] from African-American perspectives, and it made the unit richer and more enjoyable. Also, every student read, learned, and contributed to the discussions."

Instead of considering *the one book* as the heart of instruction, think of issues, themes, topics, and genres as the organizing elements for integrating multiple texts into a unit of study. (See Chapter 3 for more about issues and chapters 4 and 5 for more about using multiple texts.)

Differentiate Reading Instruction Within the Three-Part Framework

About a week before March exams, my second-block eighth-grade class marched into the room grumbling and complaining about having to again memorize more than 50 items for their science and history exams, as well as a long list of words, names, and events. "Why do we forget them?" Grace asked. "We've had quizzes on all these words, yet I can only remember the meaning of about ten," she added. Shouts of "yeah" and "count me in" peppered the room. Like me, you might be wondering, *What's wrong with this kind of teaching?*

Memorizing does not mean that students understand vocabulary or new information (Alvermann & Phelps, 1998; Beck et al., 2002; McKeown et al. 1993; Robb, 2000, 2003). If not understood, memorized information is not stored in the brain's schemata. Whether teachers construct a traditional or differentiated learning environment, they can build students' understanding of new terms and facts and bolster recall by teaching reading strategies, vocabulary, issues, and topics within the three-part framework: before, during, and after learning. Using this research-tested framework slows down the learning. It offers students repeated exposure to vocabulary, text structure, issues, and new information, that enables them to make sense of information, create new understandings, and connect ideas and concepts (Dowhower, 1999; Gillet & Temple, 2000; Tierney & Readence, 2000; Vaughan & Estes, 1986).

Before reading or starting a unit, reserve time and provide plenty of opportunities for students to engage in experiences that activate and build upon their prior knowledge. This prepares students for all the learning that follows. Asking students to share their prior knowledge and experiences with one another can enlarge everyone's background knowledge.

During reading, show students how to apply strategies that build comprehension so students learn how to select important details, make connections, and synthesize information, as well as continually strive to understand. In addition, explain that there will be times when words and passages in a text are confusing; offer students fix-up strategies such as rereading and close reading so they can solve problems encountered while reading, and move to independence.

After reading, help students savor and process their reading by inviting them to discuss, write in their journals, and complete tiered activities to share with classmates. Vaughan and Estes (1986) call this third part "contemplation." During and after completing contemplation activities, learners have multiple opportunities to connect and process ideas and to create new, meaningful, and lasting understandings.

Pause, Reflect, and Consider Six Questions . . .

Teaching is an art and a profession that invites hard work as you and I strive to reach all students in our classes, providing instruction and scaffolds that meet each child where he or she is and inch them forward. I find that using these questions as a springboard for conversations with yourself and with colleagues can recharge your teaching batteries and focus your energies on differentiating instruction, as you plan units of study and connect students to issues that enable them to think, write about, and discuss texts.

- Am I balancing both reading instruction and independent reading?
- Do my students have access to books in my class—books they can read?
- Do my students read and learn with books at their instructional levels?
- Do I model and think aloud to show students my expectations and my process?
- Do I encourage discussions that ask students to use issues and information to problem solve, create new understandings, and enlarge their prior knowledge of a topic?
- Am I teaching within the research-tested three-part framework so students can recall information and construct new understandings?

Routines, Assessments, and Planning

Building the Foundation for Differentiating Reading Instruction

"*B*ut workshop is so loose." "Kids do what they want." Two teachers blurted out these statements at the same time during a training session for middle school teachers on differentiating reading instruction. Why do teachers often feel this way? I believe their concerns emerge from the word *workshop*. Teachers unfamiliar with this organizational framework, and those who don't have a mental model of it in action, often picture students constantly talking, doing their own thing, and not much learning taking place because of noise levels and lack of structure.

When I think of a reading workshop, I'm transported back in time to an artist's studio in the Renaissance period. I watch the master painter guiding and giving advice to his apprentices. Each day, as the master paints, a few of his apprentices work on sections of the canvas. Several times during the day the master gathers his apprentices and explains how to paint the color of the skin, or the velvet cloth or the pearls the model wears. I notice that apprentices chat and support one another. Newcomers observe both the master and the experienced apprentices to internalize technique and craft; the master offers newcomers tasks that they can do and provides support with tougher assignments.

A reading workshop is similar to an artist's workshop. Your class, like the painter's workshop that had apprentices at differing levels of expertise, has students who have a diverse range of reading, critical thinking, and writing levels. Students observe your demonstrations to learn more about reading; they practice with texts that they *can* read and think with; they support one another through paired and small-group discussions and think alouds; they have multiple opportunities to read independently, confer with you, and write about their reading. Sometimes, you group students and work with them on applying a strategy or connecting details from a book to an issue, such as peer pressure. All the time, your overarching goals are to develop learners' reading skills and their stamina, and to inspire their desire to read for pleasure.

Whether you choose to organize your lessons around a reading workshop (Atwell, 1987, 1999; Calkins & Harwayne, 1991; Robb, 2000), or choose to construct another learning environment, there are various experiences that I recommend you include as you teach reading because they support differentiation. In the chapters that follow, you will explore, in depth, the following learning experiences, each one a building block of differentiation:

- instructional read alouds
- differentiated whole-class instructional reading
- small-group instructional reading
- independent reading
- writing to improve reading

For me, a workshop approach is ideal for differentiating. But, no matter which approach you take, you will need to prepare your students for the learning experiences listed above. You will also need to assess students to discover their instructional reading levels and get to know them as readers, writers, and thinkers. Such thoughtful and careful preparation will ensure that you are meeting all the needs of your students.

As You Continue to Read . . .

This chapter contains foundational material that can support you as you begin to differentiate reading instruction. First, you'll review the routines you need to establish with students in the first three or four weeks of school. Then we'll explore the assessments you need to administer to discover students' instructional reading levels. Since assessment drives instruction and makes differentiation possible, I've included a set of assessments that you can use to monitor students in the differentiated whole-class or small-group instructional models (see chapters 4 and 5). Each assessment includes student behaviors to look for so you can decide whether to confer with a student and offer extra support.

Next, you'll explore ways to plan your units of study by reviewing sample Big Picture Plans I created, which include call-outs that explain my thinking and decision-making process (see pages 54–56). You'll also review the framework that I use for planning reading lessons (see page 50). The chapter closes with a description of a six-week unit of study on the oceans for a fifth-grade class so you can see a unit in action.

Routines

"I started a differentiated unit of study at the end of the first week of school, and it flopped. My students talked all the time. They read little; their journal work was more doodling than writing. I'll never do this again." Can you hear the frustration in these words? Believe me, you can avoid developing these feelings by designing your Big Picture Plans before the unit starts (see pages 54–56). I use the first three to four weeks of school to introduce and practice the basic routines students need, and to administer assessments that enable me to identify my students' strengths and needs (see pages 38–41). During the fourth week, I begin writing up plans for my first instructional unit.

PREPARING STUDENTS FOR A DIFFERENTIATED UNIT OF STUDY

Listed below are five reoccurring routines that I introduce during the three to four weeks before I launch my first unit of study. These routines form the foundation of differentiated reading instruction. Once students experience the routines and understand how they support learning, they will be ready to work in pairs or small groups during your instructional units, freeing you to confer and to scaffold students' learning. Here are the routines listed in the order in which I use them:

1. **Post a daily class schedule.** On the chalkboard, write the date and a list of activities you hope to cover that day, and quickly read them to the class. If there's time, you can write the schedule before class or while students arrive. The schedule benefits both you and your students. It helps keep you focused on planned instruction and lets students know what to expect. However, if responding to students' needs means that you have to depart from the schedule, do that. Here's a sample schedule from the first week of school for my eighth-grade class:

   Reading, September 8
   - Warm-up: explain antagonistic forces
   - Read aloud for fun: *Carver: A Life in Poems* by Marilyn Nelson (Front Street, 2001)
   - Instructional read aloud: introduce the issue of power and control with *The Yellow Star* by Carmen Agra Deedy (Peachtree, 2000)
   - Journaling: write about shifts in power and control with *The Yellow Star*
   - Independent reading [while students read, I do three teacher-student conferences and assessments]
   - Copy homework: read 30 minutes

2. **Give out and prepare response journals.** Assign monitors to quickly give out students' response journals that you've organized class by class in a carton, a plastic crate, or on a bookshelf. At the end of class, monitors can collect and return the journals to the same storage space. Write the journal heading format you want students to follow on the chalkboard for them to copy. I always include name, date, and the title of the journal response. The first activity I ask students to complete in their journals is the warm-up. During class, I invite students to respond to the read

aloud in their journals (see pages 88–90 and Chapter 7 on writing). Make sure that students understand that writing helps them clarify understandings and explain what they know.

3. **Provide a daily warm-up activity.** This is a brief activity that takes two to three minutes for teachers to explain and students to complete. I prefer warm-ups that review material I've recently introduced or that refresh students' memories on material completed in previous weeks. Warm-ups at the start of class focus students on your subject. The teacher writes the activity on the chalkboard, and students complete it in their journals immediately after the bell rings. Then, the teacher explains the answer and students correct their work. This is a quick review and should stay within the two- to three-minute time limit.

4. **Present daily read alouds.** The read aloud develops students' listening skills and is your tool for explicitly modeling how to apply strategies, how to think about an issue or themes, as well as how to complete journal entries. (See Chapter 3 for more on using the read aloud to teach.) During the first three or four weeks of school, your read aloud should introduce students to the genre, theme, topic, or issue of your first unit of study—a differentiated whole-class instructional workshop (see box below). Continue this modeling throughout the unit of study, for the read aloud is your instructional tool.

5. **Have students read independently.** After your read aloud, use the remaining class time to teach students the routines and behaviors necessary for independent reading. Begin by showing them how to choose a book at their comfort level (see appendix page 262), and then how to complete and store their reading logs (see appendix page 265). Next, I invite students to find a comfortable place to read during this time. At the end of the first week, I

> ### Starting With Differentiated Whole-Class Instruction
>
> I recommend that, after you've established routines and assessed your students at the start of the year, you use a differentiated whole-class instructional approach for your first unit rather than starting with small-group instruction. Why? In my experience, this instructional approach is easier to implement and manage. It requires less preparation on your part and more time to confer with students. (See Chapter 4 for more on differentiated whole-class instruction.)

invite students to set behavior guidelines for sustained silent reading. Here are the behavior guidelines set by my sixth-grade class:

Behavior Guidelines for Independent Reading
- Come to class with your independent reading materials.
- Settle down for silent reading quickly.
- Talk briefly and quietly if you want to share a great or funny passage.
- Respect the space of others.

I reserve about five minutes, twice a week, for students to update their reading logs, which they staple to the back of their reading-writing folders. Folders are standard filing folders with students' names printed on the tabs. I store these with each class's stack of response journals.

FOUR LAYERS OF DISCUSSION SUPPORT DIFFERENTIATING READING INSTRUCTION

As I mentioned in Chapter 1, discussion is an important part of differentiating reading instruction. To build students' discussion stamina—the ability to sustain meaningful conversations about literature, magazines, or news articles—I recommend that you implement the four layers of discussion that follow, beginning in the first three or four weeks of school. Ultimately, the goal is for students to question as they read independently and to have rich discussions with one another—and within themselves.

1. Discussions and the Teacher's Role

Before students can lead in-depth discussions, they need to observe questioning techniques and prompts that move discussions forward; in other words, build and enlarge their mental model of what productive discussions look like. Using your read aloud, model raising interpretive, open-ended questions that stir divergent ideas. Call attention to the prompts you use to move discussions forward, like the ones that follow, by writing them on a chart.
- Does anyone see this differently?
- Does anyone have something to add?
- Does anyone have a related point to make?

By modeling what you're doing and explaining why it's helpful, you are enabling students at all reading levels to learn how to maintain discussions that move beyond spouting the facts to thinking, drawing conclusions, and making connections with them.

2. Paired Discussions

Paired discussions are particularly important for students who have had little experience with meaningful conversations. With partners, listening can improve, and you can set up the guidelines so that both students contribute ideas (Alvermann & Phelps, 1998). In a group, a shy, tentative, or unprepared student may remain silent, and more often than not, the teacher won't know, especially if the class is large.

3. Small-Group Discussions

I recommend that teachers lead small groups before inviting students to organize groups and create their own questions and agendas. When you lead small groups, you can help students practice their behavior guidelines, show them how to use prompts to maintain discussions, and help them see the benefits of having an issue or problem to

> ### Use These Verbs to Pose Open-Ended Questions
>
> | | | |
> |---|---|---|
> | analyze | categorize | compare |
> | contrast | connect | design |
> | evaluate | examine | show |
> | hypothesize | judge | persuade |

solve while discussing their texts (Adler & Rougle, 2005; Day et al., 2005; O'Flavahan et al., 1992). In the box above are verbs students can use to help them pose open-ended questions that lead to rich discussions.

4. Discussions With Oneself

During whole-class, paired, and small-group discussions, continually remind students that you're hoping they will have internal discussions while reading. Students who don't do this while reading cannot enjoy even the simplest text because they don't know how to connect to and bond with their reading. Demonstrating what goes on in your mind, either while reading aloud or while working with pairs and groups, can support the development of internal conversations and visualizations.

As you begin to establish routines and encourage rich discussions in these early weeks of school, I find it helpful to invite students to create a chart of behavior guidelines that support the meaningful exchange of ideas. At right is an example of what such a chart might look like.

Behavior Guidelines for Discussions

- Come prepared: complete the reading, bring your journal.
- Be a good listener.
- Value and encourage diverse thinking with support from texts.
- Ask probing follow-up questions.

Assessment

The first several weeks are important not only for establishing routines, but also for making initial assessments of your students. In a differentiated classroom, ongoing assessments are key. They allow you to target students' needs and to help them grow as readers.

ASSESS STUDENTS DURING THE FIRST WEEKS OF SCHOOL

Use the first three or four weeks of school to get to know your students. If you get to know them as readers and people, you will not only understand their attitudes toward reading but will learn about their strengths and their ability to use fix-up strategies to solve reading problems. Remember, the more you know about your students' reading lives and achievement, the better equipped you are to estimate their instructional reading levels and recommend texts for independent reading that interest them.

You don't have to complete all the suggestions that follow. I recommend that you study standardized test patterns and compare them to students' daily achievement. Have students complete an interest inventory and the eleven questions about reading. If you spread the following assessments over three to four weeks, students can complete most of them, providing you with data needed to estimate instructional reading levels.

Eleven questions about reading. You'll find these questions on appendix page 266. Show students how to respond to these eleven questions using a think-aloud and noting on chart paper your responses to each one. Respond to a few questions each day, over a period of three days. Then invite students to write about their reading lives; completion time will vary. Students can work on these questions during independent reading and writing time.

Interest inventory. Interest inventories for two different grade levels are on pages 267–268. I find that students are honest, and their responses let me know their attitudes toward reading, their favorite genres and authors, their knowledge of strategies, and their television habits. Knowing this enables you and the school librarian to suggest books and magazines on topics students care deeply about.

What's easy? What's hard? Show students how you complete a "What's easy? What's

---

WHAT'S EASY? WHAT'S HARD?

Name Bobby L. _____ Date Sept. 15 _____

What's Easy About Reading? Why?

free reading books
magazines & like
retelling

What's Hard About Reading? Why?

summaries
history book – words to hard
learning vocab. 20+ words
science – to many new words

FIGURE 2.2: Note how honestly Bobby answered these questions.

Interest Inventory for Grades 6 and up

Name Tanisha W. _____ Date March 21

Complete this survey so your teacher and school librarian can help you find books you will want to read.

1. What do you enjoy doing most in your free time? playing hoops

2. What sports do you enjoy playing? Explain why. basketball and tennis

3. What sports do you love to watch? Explain why. basketball and soccer

4. What is your favorite subject? Why do you enjoy it? Chorus. I like to sing.

5. Do you have any hobbies? List a few, and then write about your favorite one. listening to music

6. Do you have a favorite author? If so, can you explain why you love to read his/her books?

7. If you could travel back in time, where would you go? Explain your answer.

8. Do you read comic books and magazines? Which ones do you enjoy most? Yeah. Teen magazines + Romance mags

9. What kinds of music do you enjoy? Do you have a favorite group? Instrument? Musician? Name these. Rap, Rock, + Show tunes

10. What kinds of books do you enjoy the most when you read on your own? Use the list below to help you choose the genres you enjoy. don't read much

(mystery)   historical fiction   science fiction
(romance)   biography/autobiography   diaries
realistic fiction   series books   letters
information books   folktales   (suspense)
fantasy   short stories   myths and legends
funny stories   history   graphic novels

FIGURE 2.1: Tanisha's interest inventory shows a preference for magazines and shows me the kinds of free reading I'll suggest to her at first.

hard?" exercise about reading. Help them understand that there are times when reading is tough for you. Then ask students to reflect on their reading strengths and needs by explaining "What's easy? and What's hard?" for them about reading. This can provide you with insights into how students perceive themselves as readers. Use these clues at a conference to explore ways you can support each student.

Standardized test scores. Review all of students' standardized test scores and any reading reports that may have been completed by a resource teacher. Studying a range of standardized test scores can show you whether students are improving or scoring lower each year. Sometimes students' achievement on tests is much lower or higher than in their daily work. In either of these cases, you will want to probe further with either an abbreviated informal reading inventory or a retelling conference (see pages 115–120).

Reading strategy checklist. Ask students to complete the "Reading Strategy Checklist" on appendix page 269. The list can give you insights into what students know about the three-part reading framework, and which strategies they use before, during, and after reading.

Conferences. Hold brief chats in a quiet place away from the rest of the class. Students need to feel safe when talking about their reading lives. Not every student willingly discusses his or her reading strengths and needs. The challenge for you and me is to help students verbalize what they can and cannot do so we can support reading and learning. Start a conference by discussing data gained from the interest inventories and the queries about reading. Encouraging students to discuss what they have written can lead to explanations of their needs. Next, share some details about your reading life. Then invite students to explain what they do well, and elicit

---

Reading Strategy Checklist

Name __Jen__   Date __Sept. 06__

Put a checkmark next to the strategies you use.

BEFORE READING . . .
- ✓ I skim, looking at and thinking about the pictures, photos, graphs, and charts.
- ____ I read headings and captions.
- ✓ I read the book's back cover and/or print on the inside flaps of the jacket.
- ____ I use the three-finger method to see if the book is just right for me.
- ____ I ask questions.
- ✓ I make predictions.

WHILE READING . . .
- ✓ I make mental pictures.
- ____ I identify confusing parts and reread these.
- ____ I use pictures, graphs, and charts to understand confusing parts.
- ____ I identify unfamiliar words and use context clues to figure out their meanings.
- ____ I stop and retell to see what I remember. If necessary, I reread.
- ✓ I predict and then adjust or confirm.
- ____ I raise questions and read on to discover answers.
- ____ I jot down a tough word and the page it's on and ask for help.

AFTER READING . . .
- ✓ I think about the characters, settings, events, or new information.
- ✓ I discuss or write my reactions.
- ____ I reread parts I enjoy.
- ____ I skim to find details.
- ____ I reread to find support for questions.

Comments: _Jen has strategies for fiction. We need to work on informational text features & structures w/strategies._

FIGURE 2.3: Jen also needs to work on self-monitoring strategies.

Differentiating Reading Instruction

ways that you can help them improve. Young adolescents are honest; react positively to their candid answers and use what they say to frame your lessons and instructional decisions.

Struggling and reluctant readers often couch their feelings toward reading in tough language. They might write or say in a conference: "Reading is dumb"; or "Reading is useless"; or "Books are boring"; or "You can't make me read." Try to move beyond these comments and the anger they can stir within you. These students are sending you an

Analyzing These Assessments

Review all of these assessments to estimate the instructional reading levels of each one of your students. This will be your starter list for gathering instructional reading materials.

Assess and evaluate students each time they complete a unit of study because students' instructional reading levels will change as they improve. You will probably need to adjust your first estimates as you work with students.

Also teach the three-finger method to assist them in their selection of independent reading materials (see appendix page 262).

important message about their reading lives: We need your support.

Assess students' oral reading. Do this only when you are unsure of a student's instructional level. First, choose the book that you feel is appropriate, and then do the following:

a. Have the student read two pages aloud. Listen for errors that can affect meaning such as omitting a key word, substituting a word, or mispronouncing a word.

b. Ask the student to reread the passage silently and then retell it, following the guidelines for a narrative or informational text (see pages 115–121 for more on retellings). Retellings are a measure of readability because students retell what they comprehend. A rich retelling for fiction includes the main character's name, mention of other characters, plot details in sequence, and some personal connections. For nonfiction, retellings include specific details about the information in the text.

c. If the student's retelling is detailed, and if the student makes no more than five errors that affect meaning, then the book is probably a good instructional choice. If the book is too hard, repeat the procedure using an easier realistic novel. (See *Teaching Reading in Middle School*, pages 248–253, for a more detailed discussion of conducting an oral reading analysis.)

ONGOING PERFORMANCE-BASED ASSESSMENTS

In *Reading Next*, authors Catherine Snow and Gina Biancarosa call for key instructional practices that can improve adolescent literacy. In addition to using diverse multiple texts to differentiate reading instruction, they also explain the importance of "Ongoing Formative Assessment of Students."

> "This element is included under instructional improvements because the best instructional improvements are informed by ongoing assessment of student strengths and needs. Such assessments are often, but not exclusively, informal and frequently occur on a daily basis, and therefore are not necessarily suited to the summative task of accountability reporting systems. . . These formative assessments are specifically designed to inform instruction on a very frequent basis so that adjustments in instruction can be made to ensure that students are on pace to reach mastery targets" (page 19).

Like Snow and Biancarosa, I agree that frequent assessment of students should drive instruction and interventions. As I work with teachers in school districts around the country and at conferences, I find that there's more interest in assessments for establishing grades than in assessments that inform instruction and the choice of materials that students can read. Of course, assessments can be used for grading. But to differentiate instruction, assessments should also enable teachers to respond to the diverse academic and emotional needs of a class of students.

As soon as assessment becomes the force that drives instruction and the choice of learning materials, teachers can plan instruction that meets each student's needs (McTighe & O'Conner, 2006; Shepard, 2006; Tomlinson, 1999). As you review the categories I've included in the assessment charts on pages 43–47, consider adding ideas that work for you and your students. Jot these down, for time has a way of helping us forget these important and informative details.

I have introduced all but two of the terms in the assessment charts that follow on pages 43–47. Both terms relate to writing, and I've briefly explained each one below. **Criteria for writing:** These are the standards or expectations for content, style, and writing conventions that teachers establish with students. Criteria often emerge from a series

Interpreting Assessments to Differentiate Your Lesson Plans

Assessment	Student Behavior	Interventions/Scaffolds
Observation of independent reading	• Has difficulty choosing a book. • Chooses books that are too hard to read. • Takes a long time to settle down and read. • Chats during silent reading times. • Leafs through materials but avoids reading.	• Confer to discover interests. • Find materials student cares about and let him or her read those. • Help student learn how to decide if materials are readable. • Make sure materials student chooses are topics he or she has background knowledge for. • Find computer games with text that interests the student, and start here.
Observations during small-group lessons	• Comes unprepared, has not read the pages. • Does not volunteer ideas. • Writes little in journal. • Has difficulty using text details to support ideas.	• Ask student why he or she has not read the pages. Perhaps you need to transfer student to another group. • Ask why student doesn't participate in discussions. Help student prepare a question and answer to build self-confidence. • Meet one-on-one to model, and think aloud to show student how to skim to find details. Continue to practice and gradually release responsibility to student. • Model and think aloud during your read aloud to show how you use story details to support ideas. • Invite student to talk to you before writing, to show the link between talking and writing. If necessary, jot down what the student says to create a visual link between talking and writing. Gradually release responsibility. • Model the connections between internal talking and writing.

Assessment	Student Behavior	Interventions/Scaffolds
Observations during teacher read alouds	• Appears inattentive. • Reads under desk. • Does homework. • Tries to chat with a classmate. • Avoids writing in journal or writes very little. • Doesn't volunteer to read journal. • When volunteers to read, doesn't look at journal. What student says is more detailed and longer than journal entry.	• Confer to find out why the student appears inattentive or is doing other work. Negotiate ways to support student such as move student closer to you; periodically discuss your homework policy with the class; explain how your read alouds include modeling and instruction; ask how you can help student listen better. • Use scaffolds for students' journal writing. • Ask student to add all the terrific ideas you heard to his or her journal response. • Ask student to read what they've written.
Observations of group project work	• Does not take notes in journal. • Does not participate in group discussions. • Is not part of an oral presentation. • Contributes little to nothing for a written project.	• Provide groups with specific guidelines that show students how to divide work equitably. • Monitor groups carefully by observing and asking them to turn in or show their notes with a series of deadline dates. • Support student who has difficulty contributing by working one-on-one and by helping that student find work he or she can do.
First draft writing	• Makes many errors with usage. • Makes writing convention errors. • Has many spelling errors. • Needs work with paragraphing. • Writing plan does not meet pre-established criteria. • Writing plan is fine; draft doesn't follow plan.	• Ask student to read the piece out loud, and try to detect usage and convention errors. • Help student adjust plan. • Review and/or reteach rules for starting new paragraphs. Refer to teacher's guidelines and student's writing plan to see how paragraphing was built into the writing guidelines. • Meet with student and help him or her edit for one convention at a time. • Show student how to check draft against criteria and against the approved, completed writing.

Assessment	Student Behavior	Interventions/Scaffolds
First draft writing (cont'd)		• Work with pairs or individuals who have difficulty planning their writing, and support them during this stage to improve first drafts. • Teach students to peer edit early drafts for one convention at a time.
Final draft writing	• Has many usage and convention errors. • Does not follow the suggestions made on student's first draft.	• Head this problem off by supporting student at the drafting stage. • Work one-on-one and have student read small sections out loud; help student hear and see editing needs. • Ask student why he or she did not refer to suggestions and notes from conference to craft final draft. • Work one-on-one and show student how to use comments and suggestions on first draft to integrate revisions into the final draft.
Inferential thinking	• Finds literal meanings. • Struggles with personal connections to characters. • Doesn't create mental and sensory images • Has difficulty deciding which details are important and which are not. • Has a tough time drawing conclusions about events, people, or characters. • Has trouble finding themes. • Has little prior knowledge to bring to a text. • Says text is too difficult to read.	• Find a readable text on the topic you're studying. • Build background knowledge by reading aloud picture books, showing photographs, and looking at video clips. • Think aloud to show student that inferring means you find unstated meanings using text details. Use data in nonfiction. Use what a character says, does, thinks, and feels, as well as conflicts, inner thoughts and interactions with others in fiction. • Study author tags in dialogue such as "wept, screamed," or "ranted." • Show student how you set purposes to determine important details in a text. • Show students how issues and core questions can help determine importance and find big ideas. • Ask student to move from the literal, *What does it say?* to inferring with, *What does it mean?*

Assessment	Student Behavior	Interventions/Scaffolds
Writing about strategies	• Unable to define a strategy. • Unable to tell when to use the strategy. • Unable to explain how to apply the strategy. • Doesn't know how the strategy improves constructing meaning.	• Reteach strategy and ask student to observe you applying it. Do this a few times or until student can describe what you're doing and why it helps. • Provide time for guided practice that asks student to apply the strategy to an easy text so the focus is on the strategy and not on the struggle to read. • Work with a pair or small group that would benefit from a quick review and one to two guided practice sessions. • Pair up students who need a bit more practice discussing the strategy and applying it, and have them work together. • Review how the strategy supports readers to ensure that students understand how it can improve their reading comprehension.
Paired and small-group discussions	• Does not actively discuss because he or she is unprepared. • Does not actively discuss, even though he or she has completed the work or reading. • Raises hand enthusiastically but then "forgets" response. • Blurts out answer before being recognized. • Dominates the discussion. • Does not discuss topic, issue, or question but creates own agenda.	• Ask student why he or she is unprepared. Help student find ways to complete assigned reading; reading in class is one way. Ask student to read the required pages and then join his or her group. • Explain to your class that it's important to have wait time before answering. Some students can respond immediately; others need a minute or two to gather thoughts. • Show students how to jot down notes to prepare for a discussion (see pages 185–187). With notes, starting a discussion is easier. • Explain to pairs/small groups that they will share with the entire class the points discussed. You can keep students on track. You can also sit in to help pairs/groups stay focused. • Help all students understand that blurting out answers prevents others from participating and

Assessment	Student Behavior	Interventions/Scaffolds
Paired and small-group discussions (cont'd)		also creates frustration for those students who need more wait time before answering. • Try to find out why a student who is prepared avoids sharing ideas. First, try to gather suggestions from the student. You can also set him or her up for success by giving the topic for his or her next paired/group discussion and helping the student prepare a response.
Whole-class discussions	• Blurts out answers. • Does not participate. • Doesn't relate answers to the topic.	• Help students who blurt out answers understand that you applaud their enthusiasm, but that you need their help to make sure everyone has a chance to answer. • Explain that some students need wait time, and help these students understand the importance of wait time.

of mini-lessons. An example of content criteria is having details from the text to support a position. Criteria for style include varying sentence openings and writing with a strong voice. An example of writing convention criteria is writing with complete sentences.

Writing plan: Once students understand the writing assignment and have brainstormed lists of ideas, they can create a writing plan that contains the points they'll make and the support for each point, or a plan that explains what ideas will be included in the introduction, the body, and the conclusion. For narratives, students can name and discuss their characters, identify the key problem the characters will face, and list a few possible outcomes.

Forms for Assessing Students' Work in Order to Differentiate Instruction

It's helpful to have forms that you can quickly complete—forms that enable you to determine which students need reteaching and/or scaffolding and which ones can work independently. I've included three forms, one for assessing instructional reading (see page 51) and two for assessing students' writing convention needs (see pages 52–53).

With the reading form, you can assess students who are near or at the same instructional level, whether you're differentiating reading instruction in a whole-class setting (see Chapter 4) or in small, teacher-led groups (see Chapter 5). The purpose of completing this form is not to assign a grade but to support your instructional decisions and move every learner forward.

Besides reading students' journal entries to better understand their

> **Collect Feedback for Writing Convention Mini-Lessons**
>
> **Method of Assessment: Check the kind(s) of writing on the list below that you are using to evaluate progress.**
> ____ Journal entry
> ____ First draft of a paragraph
> ✓ First draft of an essay
>
> List the names of students who need extra teaching, and then their writing convention needs.
>
> | Student's Name | Writing Convention Needs |
> | --- | --- |
> | Justine A. | - Marking #s
- run-on sentences |
> | Emily A. | |
> | Mary B. | - pronoun references |
> | Will D. | - subject/verb agreement |
> | Melissa F. | - pronoun references |
> | Luke H. | - run-on sentences; marking #s |
> | Grant J. | - run-on sentences; subj./verb agreement |
> | Jay L. | - marking #s |
> | Joe S. | - run-on sentences; upper case letters |
> | Rhett W. | - run-on sentences; commas-series |

FIGURE 2.4: This list enables me to group students and review or reteach lessons about writing conventions that each group needs.

thinking and their application of a reading strategy, I also note writing conventions that need reviewing or reteaching. Keep in mind that these responses are all first-draft writing and that you've invited students to focus on content, not usage, spelling, and punctuation. You'll definitely find writing convention errors in students' journal work and other writing: run-on sentences, misspellings, incorrect use of commas, or no commas at all. On the first form (page 52), you list the errors students make in their writing. The second form (page 53) enables you to make instructional decisions based on the list. You may be able to transform errors into mini-lessons that teach students how to apply what they've learned to their written work. Students need to use writing conventions correctly so they and others can understand their ideas.

Planning

Once you have estimated students' instructional reading levels, discovered their interests and attitudes toward reading, and gained insights into what they can do well, it's time to design your unit of study. To accomplish this, I find that planning is vital for enabling me to support students and help them progress (Pearson et al., 1992; Robb, 2008). The plan is dynamic, always responding to students whose work, discussions, and actions show me they need support or they can work independently. I can note changes and adjustments on the plan and use these thoughts as I create my next unit of study.

A FRAMEWORK FOR PLANNING UNITS OF STUDY

In my own school, and as I travel and work with schools around the country, I find that the culture of planning has waned. Teachers seem to resent having to hand in plans to administrators, many of whom don't want to review plans. When I coach a teacher, I require long-term planning and support the teacher through the process.

Thinking through and planning units of study focuses you on instructional goals and can improve your daily teaching and students' achievement. Why? Because instead of "winging it," you have carefully selected your read alouds, teaching texts, strategies, and assessments. Writing these units provides you with a resource that you can adjust as you monitor daily and weekly instruction and assessment. In addition, with long-term planning, you can reflect on the strategies and writing experiences students have absorbed, and on those that need revisiting during the next unit of study. It's a memory tool that prevents repetition—a dynamic memory tool with your jots that note adjustments you've made on specific activities and suggestions for upcoming units of study.

I've included two plans on pages 54–55. The plans can be adapted to small-group and differentiated whole-class instructional reading. The only difference in the planning process is in the materials you gather. For whole-class instructional reading, you'll offer students the opportunity to choose texts for a genre, topic, or theme that meet their instructional needs. So, in a class of 30, you may have 30 different books because each student may choose to read a different book. (See Chapter 4 for more on whole-class instructional reading.) For small-group instruction, you'll select three books that will enable you to meet the instructional needs of each group.

Once you've completed a draft of your Big Picture Plans, daily planning is easy because what you teach day by day comes from your unit plan. Here is the daily lesson plan framework that I use and pass on to teachers.

Goals of the lesson: what you hope to accomplish.

Learning experiences: what you and what students will do to accomplish the goals. This includes teacher read alouds, strategy lessons, students' completing guided practice, reading of texts at students' instructional levels, writing, and discussions.

Assessments: your observations, students' self-evaluations, journal responses, oral or written book reviews, conferences, essays, drama presentations or poetry performances, art projects, or tests. You need to offer or negotiate with students a range of assessments that differentiate and provide students with writing and projects they can learn from and do.

Note that the assessments for both units of study are performance-based and emerge from what students practice and learn during the unit. Note, too, that the range of assessments enables me to meet diverse learning levels.

Collect Feedback on Students' Understanding of Inferential Reading Strategies

Reading Strategy _____ Date Assessed _____

Names of Students Being Assessed:

Method of Assessment: Check those that you are using to evaluate progress.

_____ Bookmark

_____ Discussion during a conference

_____ Writing about a strategy

_____ Applying the strategy in a journal entry

_____ Applying the strategy during small-group lessons

Differentiating Instruction: List names of students under each heading whom you plan to support during sustained silent reading and/or while students work on writing.

Reteach One-on-One   Review and Offer Pairs Extra Practice

Review With Small Group   Organize Partners Who Can Support Each Other

Collect Feedback for Writing Convention Mini-Lessons

Method of Assessment: Check the kind(s) of writing on the list below that you are using to evaluate progress.

_____ Journal entry

_____ First draft of a paragraph

_____ First draft of an essay

List the names of students who need extra teaching, and then their writing convention needs.

Student's Name   Writing Convention Needs

Prioritize Students' Writing Convention Needs and Plan Intervention

Date Completed _____

1. Reread your list and choose key writing convention needs for your grade level and curriculum.
2. Collect students' names and list each one under the appropriate heading.
3. Support students during sustained silent reading and/or writing workshop time.

One-on-One Writing Convention Meeting   Small-Group Writing Convention Meeting

Mini-Lessons for Entire Class   Partners Who Can Support Each Other

Big Picture Plan for an Issues-Based Whole-Class Instructional Unit of Study: Grade Eight

Issue Human rights   **Estimated Time** Seven to eight weeks

Goals

- To develop an understanding of human rights
- To have students choose to read a text at their instructional level
- To confer with students to monitor their application of making connections, finding important information, and expanding their knowledge of human rights
- To show students how to discuss different texts around an issue and strategy
- To have students read two or more books at their recreational or comfort reading levels and complete a bookmark on one
- To enlarge vocabulary by using context clues and by teaching roots, prefixes, and suffixes
- Use school and class libraries to collect 40 books with readability levels ranging from grade 5 to grade 9.

Have students interview parents and peers to find other views of the issue; share these in class.

Monitor these one at a time to keep conferences short.

Read-Aloud Text *Chu Ju's House* by Gloria Whelan

- Think aloud to show how you pinpoint violations and repairs of human rights.
- Think aloud to share your emotional reactions to violations.

Reading Strategies

- Practice selecting important details from the text.
- Make connections between events in the text and human rights. Study violations, repairs, and honoring of human rights.

Review Strategy

- Questioning the Author

Writing to Improve Reading

- Bookmark based on Questioning the Author (see pages 233–234)
- Diary entries from a character's perspective on human rights

Use with only the read aloud; move from discussion to writing and get inside students' heads.

Assessments

- Bookmark
- Conferences
- Diary kept by a character discussing two events lived through and human rights
- Oral book talk on one of the two books completed
- Cartoon that illustrates a key problem and its solution
- Letters of advice written to a character
- Interview of two characters by two students
- Self-evaluations of journaling

Adjust assessments for students who read two to three years below grade level.

Ask students to help design oral book talk guidelines.

Big Picture Plan for a Genre Study for Small-Group Instructional Unit of Study: Grade Six

Genre Realistic fiction

Issue Problems surrounding growing up

Estimated Time Seven weeks

Goals

- To understand the structure of realistic fiction
- To relate these books to the issues that surround growing up
- To work with small groups on applying the reading strategies for this unit and discussing the struggles characters experience while growing up
- To help students use writing to clarify their thoughts and deepen their understanding of character, genre, and the issue of growing up

Materials

The Great Gilly Hopkins by Katherine Paterson

Miracle's Boys by Jacqueline Woodson

Crash by Jerry Spinelli

Read-Aloud Text *Somewhere in the Darkness* by Walter Dean Myers

- Ask students to write in their journals after I model journal responses.
- Use the read aloud to show the application of strategies.

Reading Strategies

- Drawing conclusions about characters and events
- Questioning the Author
- Vocabulary and context clues

Review Strategy

- Make connections

Journal Work: Double Entry

- Changes in character, and causes of changes
- Monitor what causes children to grow up.

Independent Reading Students will choose one realistic novel to read independently and will complete a book talk on this novel. Any additional books read will be listed in book logs.

Assessments: Note the range that helps me meet diverse learning needs and levels.

- Journal writing, which includes drawing
- Observations of students during discussions
- A news story or a Readers Theater script based on two related events
- Puppet show based on part of a text

> Weave justice and injustice into issues as these accompany growing up.

> This may run eight weeks depending on students' needs.

> I like to list the specific issues, reading strategies, journal entries, and assessments under separate headings. This enables me to think carefully about the teaching and learning elements in each unit of study.

> Revisit goals each week to adjust lessons and provide support for students who need it.

> All books meet the needs of different reading levels.

> Monitor the two students who you have bumped into the *Crash* group and make sure that with support they can move forward with this text.

> Review predict/support/adjust and retellings for those reading two to three-plus years below grade level.

> Spend time making connections to issues.

> Teach students to self-evaluate their entries; adjust last year's form.

> Use mentor texts written by former students and also a local newspaper.

> Art/drama projects can show fine thinking and tap into one of the multiple intelligences.

Big Picture Plan for Whole-Class Instructional Reading Unit on the Oceans

Topic The oceans

Estimated Time Six to seven weeks

Goals

- To introduce students to the oceans and ocean life
- To enlarge students' background knowledge of the oceans
- To teach thinking about texts through read-aloud lessons
- To teach note making
- To include whole-, small-group, and paired discussions
- To make writing an integral part of listening to read-aloud texts
- To enlarge students' vocabulary relating to the oceans

Materials

- Books about the oceans and ocean life at diverse reading levels

Read-Aloud Texts

- *All About Sharks* by Jim Arnosky
- *Follow the Water from Brook to Ocean* by Arthur Dorros
- *Hotel Deep: Light Verse from Dark Water* by Kurt Cyrus
- *Oceans: The Vast, Mysterious Deep* by David Harrison
- *Sponges Are Skeletons* by Barbara Juster Esbensen

Reading Strategy

- Questioning the Author (QtA)

Journaling

- Writing to clarify thinking and improve reading
- Note taking; using QtA to find big ideas from notes

Assessments

- Art projects
- Journal work
- Illustrating vocabulary and concepts
- Discussions
- Oral presentations
- Self-evaluation

DIFFERENTIATING READING INSTRUCTION IN ACTION: GRADE FIVE

Now I invite you to visit Norie Noll's fifth-grade classroom so you can see how differentiating reading instruction benefits a class that includes English language learners (ELL).

My primary goal for including literacy vignettes from a fifth-grade class with a wide range of instructional reading levels is to illustrate how both the assessment and the differentiated teaching and learning elements that I introduced in Chapter 1 and earlier in this chapter affect students' progress. I've included the assessments, the Big Picture Plan (see page 56), and discussion of the decision-making process that Norie Noll and I fashioned in order to meet a wide range of instructional needs. Some of the specific lessons that moved students forward with listening, reading, writing, and thinking are also included.

Norie Noll teaches at Virginia Avenue/Charlotte DeHarte Elementary School, and she uses and follows the district's mandated reading program: the *Open Court Reading Series*, a one-size-fits-all program. Since I wanted to differentiate reading instruction, I negotiated with Norie and Kathy Wetzel, the principal, for having students deepen their ability to construct meaning by reading diverse science trade books to learn about the oceans, a required unit of study.

Ms. Noll's class of 24 included 20 percent African American, 50 percent Hispanic, and 30 percent Caucasian students. Students' reading levels ranged from early first grade to tenth grade. The next closest reading level to tenth grade was seventh grade. Norie determined these instructional levels in March by using data gathered from guided reading groups, assessments completed by reading resource and ELL teachers, conferences, journal writing, and informal reading inventories.

The first differentiation challenge for me and Norie was to find books on the subject of the oceans to cover this wide range of reading levels so every student could read, think, learn, and share meaningful ideas with classmates. Norie collected books from her school library, and I gathered books from my school and personal library; together, we had more than 40 books spanning a reading range that met the needs of these students (Snow & Biancarosa, 2004). Norie and I had three texts on the ocean for students reading at an early first-grade level. We sat side by side with students and supported them when they read texts that were slightly more difficult. Next, we created the Big Picture Plan on page 56.

Norie and I used the read aloud to show how to apply a strategy to construct meaning while reading, and also model thinking and writing. My goal was to gradually release responsibility from me to students by inviting them to respond in think alouds. To build students' comprehension while reading or listening to texts, I chose *Questioning the Author* (Beck & McKeown, 2006). I showed Norie how I planned a reading strategy lesson with follow-up activities (see below). A written plan guarantees that I've carefully thought through the strategy, and the framework helps me focus and clarify my thoughts before presenting them to students. (I've also included two additional, fully developed strategy lessons on appendix pages 270–272.)

SAMPLE STRATEGY LESSON PLAN FOR QUESTIONING THE AUTHOR

PURPOSE To build comprehension while reading fiction or nonfiction

TIME 40 minutes

MATERIALS Informational chapter or picture books

HOW IT HELPS STUDENTS The strategy asks them to pause and question the author to figure out a tough word, a big idea, what the author wants them to think, and what the author means. It encourages making meaning while reading and helps students get important details as well as the author's message.

PRESENTING THE LESSON

1. Write the initiating and follow-up questions on chart paper (see appendix page 273).
2. Model with a read aloud. Think aloud and show students how you pause, query, and then answer by using specific details from the text.
3. Organize students into pairs. Read aloud and have them discuss the query, and then have one or two pairs share.

SUGGESTIONS FOR FOLLOWING UP

1. Organize students into pairs and invite them to use QtA with a short passage from the read aloud or an instructional book.
2. Circulate around the room and listen to pairs to see if any need your support.
3. Continue to differentiate instruction by supporting readers who struggle one-on-one or in pairs; show partners how they can support each other, and have them practice in front of you.

Now that we had working drafts of the Big Picture Plan and a detailed lesson plan for QtA, I was ready to introduce our six-week study of the oceans to fifth graders through whole-class read alouds.

My QtA Think-Aloud

I gathered students around me on a large rug in Norie's classroom. In a think aloud, I explained that Questioning the Author is a way of helping every student in the class deepen his or her understanding of books about the ocean. Students were unfamiliar with this strategy, so I modeled how it worked by reading aloud in the first four to five lessons. I divided each one-hour lesson into two parts: the first part lasted about 20 minutes, and I read aloud showing them how I paused to question the author after a small chunk of text. My goal was to turn thinking aloud using QtA over to students. During the remaining ten minutes, I invited students to listen to one another carefully as they shared one detail they recalled. Our meeting closed with students recording, for about 10 to 12 minutes, everything they remembered from my read aloud and from listening to classmates.

After the third meeting with students, I developed the read-aloud plan that follows.

- Gather students in a circle and have them bring a pencil and their journals so they can respond.
- Review the purpose of QtA with students.
- Model how to read a chunk of text, to pause, to question the author, and then to respond.
- Ask students, after the second to fourth read-aloud session, to respond to QtA in their journals. The timing of this depends on your students, so be flexible. To tier the response task, students can write, or draw, or write and draw and label their drawings.
- Here are the three QtA queries that I posted on the large whiteboard:
  - What does the author want me to think at this point?
  - Why does the author tell me this information or these details?
  - What big ideas does the author help me see with this information?
- Have students volunteer to share their QtA notes and invite the group to discuss these.
- Close the session by going around the circle and asking students to share some-

thing they learned that was memorable.

- Invite students to jot down all they recalled from the read alouds and the sharing session.
- Start the next day's lesson with students sharing one item from their list. This reinforces memory of details, provides an opportunity to flesh out big ideas, and segues into the next read aloud.

At our fourth meeting, I modeled the Questioning the Author strategy and my responses by thinking aloud, and then jotted down my ideas on a large whiteboard. Notice that I eliminated talking before writing, which is my usual way of structuring journal writing. My reason for turning immediately to writing while using QtA was to get into each student's head and monitor and analyze their thinking. Along with short conferences, this was another way to understand students' ability to construct meaning. It enabled me to pinpoint those who needed scaffolds to improve.

> ## Scaffolding Tip: Respond to the Special Needs of ELL Students
>
> With ELL students reading on an early first-grade level or with students who struggle with recall of a chunk of text during a read aloud, you can try some of the suggestions that follow.
>
> - Explain that you will reread the chunk of text one or two times and that you want the students to listen carefully because they will have to use the details for a QtA response.
> - Return to talking through the response. Once students explain with ease, invite them to write, or draw and write. Gradually remove the talking and explain that you want students to have internal conversations with authors.
> - Ask students to explain their response, and you jot it down in their journals. The purpose of this strategy is to model the connection between talking and writing. For each time you do this, explain that your goal is for the student to have the conversation inside his or her head, and then write and draw.

QtA and Journal Responses

In think alouds, I showed students how I responded to a QtA question, using Arthur Dorros's *Follow the Water From Brook to Ocean*. As I stopped and questioned the author, students observed my thinking. By the middle of the book, the QtA process was in students' hands, and they were responding in their journals. Tiering responses by allowing students to draw or write enabled Osiris Ortiz, who's learning English, to show what he's thinking and understanding with pictures; and Rebecca Cain, one of Norie's top students, to use words and one illustration.

Chatting with Osiris informed me that he understood that water from ponds, rivers, and lakes finds its way to the ocean. His illustrations show that he knows that fish populate the ocean. Note how Rebecca has begun to pick up the language of QtA in her responses.

Moreover, her last paragraph illustrates her pin-

FIGURE 2.5: Osiris shows that water from rivers, ponds, and streams finds its way to the ocean.

pointing of the big ideas the author showed her. She also explained vocabulary that emerged from the book and discussions.

Follow-up conferences and/or inviting students to share what they've written is another way to learn what kinds of responses students can complete on their own. Besides helping me gain insights into students' thinking, sharing helps move students forward, as they see

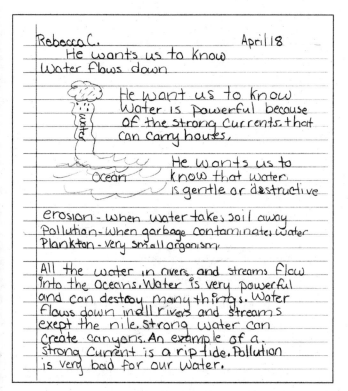

FIGURE 2.6: Rebecca explains with words and includes one illustration to show the path of water moving to the ocean.

and hear what others write. Look at how sharing and conferring improved Osiris's journal response several weeks later. He draws a detailed illustration with some labeling of a tidal pool. In addition, he voluntarily copied down words from the whiteboard that the class discussed. And he was able to use words to answer this query: *What does the author want us to understand about tidal pools?* "Many different animals" was Osiris's reply, which illustrates how much he has comprehended. Conferences also enable me and Norie to celebrate students' progress and set goals for their next response.

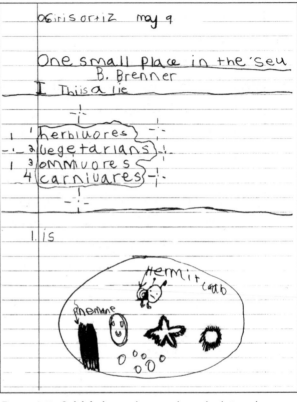

FIGURE 2.7: Osiris's journal several weeks later shows labels with pictures.

Having Students Work in Pairs

Once students showed that they were able to respond to queries in their journals, Norie and I invited them to read books with a partner and take notes using QtA. Multiple texts gave all students a chance to read, take notes, and bring a variety of information about the ocean to the class through discussions and by sharing journal entries.

Norie paired students so they could support each other while reading and taking notes. Partners' reading levels were fairly close, so that one student did not dominate another and the collaboration was meaningful and productive. Norie and I supported several ELL students who could not read most of the books.

As part of our plan to differentiate reading and note taking, Norie modeled for students two ways to take notes and asked students to choose the one they felt at ease with. One way was to use a double-entry technique, in which students listed main points on the left-hand side and questioned the author on the right-hand side, using the details to find

Differentiating Reading Instruction

big ideas. Alonso used this model to write and think about the sculpin fish. The second technique was for students to stop at the end of a page, and in their own words, jot down what they learned, reread their notes, and think of the big idea(s) the author wanted them to

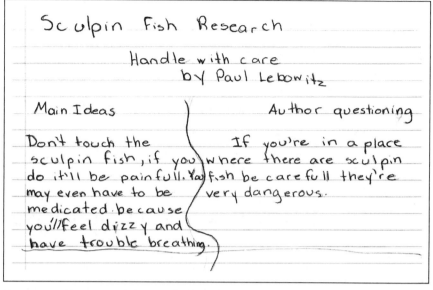

FIGURE 2.8: Alonso used QtA to find the big ideas in a book about sculpin fish.

know. By the end of May, students' journals illustrated their ease with taking notes and using QtA to figure out big ideas. Norie and I agreed that this was the ideal time to invite students to self-evaluate QtA in their journals.

Students Self-Evaluate Questioning the Author

After lots of practice using QtA during my read alouds, after reading and taking notes on ocean texts, and after continually applying the strategy to parts of their independent reading, fifth graders were asked this self-evaluation question: *Does QtA help you? Explain why.* Here is a sampling of students' responses:

MARIA: I think it [QtA] does help me because I could understand more and could get more information. I talked with my older brother about Questioning the Author when we're reading and why the author is giving us the information and what's the big idea of the book.

CHEVELLE: I got pretty good at Questioning the Author. I even used it for some of the SOL's [state tests] that I took. So if I pass, 40 percent goes to you.

TANESHIA: When you would read us a story and you would ask us a question and we
write, it has been really fun.

TYLER: I like it [QtA and writing] because I think it gets things stuck in your head.

Students' self-evaluations showed that many of them were using the strategy to pause and reflect by asking the author a question, and then were using the details to think, move beyond the facts, and construct meaning.

Pause, Reflect, and Consider Nine Questions . . .

I want you to think of moving to differentiating reading instruction as a gradual process—much like building a house, starting with the basement, the floors, the frame, room divisions, siding, a roof, and then adding wallboards, paint, bathroom fittings, and kitchen appliances. Builders construct a house, section by section. I want you to add differentiation techniques, section by section, and always monitor your comfort level. Use the questions that follow to think about or to discuss with a colleague how you organize instruction and the role of preparation, planning, and assessing in your teaching life.

- How can I add differentiation to my teaching framework?
- Have I incorporated differentiation strategies into my instruction?
- Am I using the read aloud as a common teaching text?
- Am I preparing students for differentiated reading instruction by establishing daily learning routines?
- Do I use students' assessments to inform instructional decisions?
- Have I thought through my unit and written Big Picture Plans?
- Have I developed ongoing formative assessments that drive differentiated instruction?
- Are my assessments responding to what students can successfully do?
- Do I ask students to self-evaluate so they understand their progress?

Chapter 3

Read Alouds and Differentiation

Bridging Learning Gaps While Engaging Readers

I'm with a group of 22 sixth graders in a middle school near Ann Arbor, Michigan. As part of my consulting for several school districts, I've been asked to teach these students reading during their geography and language arts classes. In geography, students use a grade-level textbook; in language arts, a grade-level basal anthology. The literacy coach asked me to focus on geography. My purpose for this demonstration lesson is to show teachers how the read aloud can become their common teaching text.

I have two hours to show the 30 teachers and the principal, who observe me in the back of the classroom, how I structure reading to meet the needs of every learner. Instructional levels in this sixth-grade class start at second grade, with pairs or small groups reading at each grade level through seventh grade. Students have just completed studying the concept of culture in geography, so I decided to use folktales from Europe and South America and brought six different folktales to match the six instructional levels of students in this class.

Since students showed me, during a discussion, that they understood a great deal about the folktale's structure, I moved into the heart of the lesson: I wanted students to explore in their folktale the characters' values as well as what they valued. For a culminating experience, students would help me construct a chart that would showcase the values in each folktale to see if there were any values common to two or more stories.

Groups spent about ten minutes figuring out an explanation of values, who affected their values, and what they valued. Asia and Mauricio expressed a concern that many of their classmates had: "We can figure out our values, but we don't know what to do in a story." Anticipating this kind of question, I began to read aloud a short German folktale, "Tante Tina," retold by Ruthilde Kronberg and Patricia C. McKissack in *A Piece of the Wind* (HarperCollins, 1990). In this story, Tante Tina sacrifices her home by setting it on fire to warn people about an approaching storm. Halfway through the story, I paused to think aloud, making inferences to show students how I figured out Tante Tina's values. When I continued reading and got to the paragraph on page 14 (see below), several students raised their hands and together blurted out, "We know, we know. Can we say it?"

> *Suddenly her heart grew calm and she knew what to do. She crept out of her bed and went over to the stove, where she grabbed a piece of burning wood and hurled it into her bed. Almost immediately the straw mattress exploded into flames.*

Here's what students shared:

"She cares about the people."

"She values others more than her house 'cause it'll burn."

"She put her life in danger. She'd rather see lots [of people] live more than herself."

"She values life more than things."

Wow! I thought to myself, and mentally waltzed around the room. Yes, these students "got it." Yes, I experienced a surge of excitement the moment my modeling clicked; I always do. And from the point when students asked to participate, I turned thinking aloud over to them because I know that each read-aloud lesson starts with the teacher modeling and thinking aloud and eventually moves to the students' sharing their thinking.

Choose a motivating and engaging read aloud, and when students show you they're ready to participate, invite them into the process. If they don't "get it," model again with another text or more of the original text. Continue modeling until students show that they grasp the lesson. When students take over the thinking, they send the message that they are ready to apply what they've observed and absorbed to their instructional reading texts.

As You Continue to Read . . .

As you continue to read this chapter, you will explore multiple ways to use the read aloud as your common text for the entire class, setting the stage for differentiation. Like me, you'll eventually find rich and favorite books and articles for read alouds that you can use each year for multiple purposes. Your read alouds are the key to being able to differentiate. Once your read aloud becomes the common teaching text, you gain the freedom to move away from having all students read the same book for reading instruction. Instead, you can match students with books at their instructional-reading levels so they can truly read them and learn from them (see chapters 4 and 5).

How Read Alouds Help You Set the Stage for Differentiation

- They help all students enlarge their prior knowledge.

- They ensure that all students learn to apply reading strategies and explore issues and themes.

- By making read alouds your teaching text, students can then read other texts at their instructional level.

Rethinking the Role of the Read Aloud

In addition to the traditional read aloud that opens a class, I use read alouds for the following purposes:

- to build background knowledge

The Power of the Traditional Read Aloud

Reading aloud every day—poems, stories, and books you love—transmits to your students the passion and joy you have for reading. Reading aloud strengthens students' listening skills and also tunes their ears to the music in our language, and their minds to the visions the text conjures up. Alter the timbre of your voice as you become different characters; vary the pace and dynamics of your voice. Help your students create the smell of Jesse Aaron's kitchen (*Bridge to Terabithia* by Katherine Paterson, Crowell, 1997). Invite them to hear Jesse's heart pound as he races with his friends at recess, and feel and taste the anger and bitterness of Jesse's pain when he learns his beloved friend Leslie is dead. These daily read alouds nurture your soul. But even more important, reading aloud every day can transform the blank landscape of the minds of the struggling readers who feel nothing and see nothing when they read, into a pageant of pictures, emotions, and sensory perceptions. The cadence and rich tones of your voice can draw students into a text and grip their imaginations, enabling them to enter into the story, become a character, and live in that character's world.

For those students who heard few stories before entering school and who may not be bonding to books while in school, your daily read alouds can awaken their torpid imaginations and replace "nothing" with myriad sensory images, colors, and emotions (Laminack & Wadsworth, 2006). At the 2006 Culham Writing Conference in Sun Valley, Idaho, author Lester Laminack proposed that teachers read aloud several times a day. In self-contained classes, teachers can read aloud in the morning, before and after lunch, and at the end of the day; they can read a short poem to transition from one subject to another. In middle and high school, teachers can read aloud at the start and end of class and transition from reading to writing workshop with a poem. The point is that one read aloud a day is not enough to build and strengthen students' imaginations.

- to model the application of reading strategies
- to teach narrative story elements
- to teach informational text features
- to use as a catalyst for teaching unfamiliar themes

- to teach different kinds of journal responses
- to help students explore issues and themes for pinpointing big ideas in texts

All the time, just as with a traditional read aloud, you're asking students to listen, so you're strengthening their listening skills. Whether you have a 90-minute block or a 45-minute class period, you can set aside enough time for five- to ten-minute teaching and modeling lessons with read-aloud texts. (See appendix pages 263–264 for sample schedules.)

Read Aloud to Build Background Knowledge

I'm in a sixth-grade classroom and the teacher introduces a unit of study on women's suffrage by asking her students to complete a fast-write on what they know about the topic. As the teacher and I circulate, we notice that students write little. More than half the class starts their piece with "What's suffrage?" This literacy vignette spotlights how important it is for teachers to prepare for students learning. If comprehending or constructing meaning while reading a text depends on the background knowledge and experiences learners bring to the reading, then discovering what students know before plunging into a topic or issue is a key step in the reading process (Beers, 2002; Braunger & Lewis, 2006; Dowhower, 1999; Duke & Pearson, 2002; Robb, 2000, 2003, 2008; Tierney & Readence, 2000).

Obviously, these students did not have the background knowledge necessary to start this unit. So the teacher and I visited the school and public libraries and found *Rabble Rousers: 20 Women Who Made a Difference* by Cheryl Harness (Dutton, 2003). This text's two-page biographies, rich with illustrations, were ideal for enlarging students' knowledge in a short time. We started with a piece on Elizabeth Cady Stanton and then followed it with one about Alice Paul. By reading aloud and discussing each text in two consecutive classes, we provided every student with background information that could improve their comprehension of instructional books. Spending from 20 to 30 minutes a day enlarging students' background knowledge made the difference in students' comprehension and their ability to recall, connect to, and think with details. Enlisting the help of your school and public librarians can make the task of finding poems, short texts, and magazines rich in photographs, such as *National Geographic*, an easy one.

Read Aloud to Model How You Apply Strategies

You can introduce a strategy through a read aloud, using the same passages you used to build background knowledge. The strategic read aloud is one of three strategic reading layers you'll use as you move students toward independent strategy use. First, you model for students. Next, you support them as they practice applying the strategy to their instructional reading. Finally, they use the strategy as they read independently.

The power that strategic read alouds unleash is that they provide you with multiple opportunities to show students how you apply a comprehension-building strategy before, during, or after reading. The repeated modeling keeps students focused on the strategy and can enhance and deepen their understanding of how the strategy works to their advantage. Here are two examples of how I planned and delivered a strategic read aloud in both a sixth-grade and an eighth-grade class.

STRATEGIC READ ALOUD: GRADES SIX AND EIGHT

PURPOSE To introduce a strategy to students; to show how to apply a specific strategy while reading and how it helps students

TIME 10–15 minutes for preparation; 6–7 minutes for presentation

MATERIALS A short selection from a picture or chapter book, or an article or a passage from your read-aloud text

HOW IT HELPS STUDENTS Modeling the application of a strategy during read alouds helps students build their prior knowledge of the strategy and how it works. Modeling during your read aloud for several days offers students multiple opportunities for observing how you apply the strategy to build comprehension.

I recommend that you continue modeling the strategy, using the five steps described on pages 71–72, two or three times a week. In addition to deepening students' understanding of how a specific strategy supports constructing meaning from a text, you will be introducing students to picture books or magazine and newspaper articles they might not choose to read on their own. I store my modeling materials in a crate or on a bookshelf and encourage students to dip into these during independent reading. I find that many students check out these texts later on because the short read aloud aroused their interest and curiosity.

PREPARING THE LESSON

The first time you try this type of lesson, you are apt to feel uncomfortable; I did. My tongue thickened, and the words sounded awkward. Practice will eliminate these feelings, and you'll easily and fluently present lessons like this.

1. Decide on the strategy you'll focus on. For this three-week unit on suffrage, the teacher and I focused on drawing conclusions about a person's character. The goal was to help students understand the personality traits needed to create lasting change.

2. Select a text. The text we used in this lesson is "Elizabeth Cady Stanton" from *Rabble Rousers: 20 Women Who Made a Difference* by Cheryl Harness.

3. Write the five steps you will follow on chart paper.
   - Name the strategy.
   - Explain how to do it, why it helps, and when it works.
   - Summarize, if necessary, the key points of any text you have previously read.
   - Read the passage aloud.
   - Think aloud during and after the reading to show how you apply the strategy.

4. Explicitly state the steps as you model so students can follow the lesson with ease. This also provides students with a process for doing partner think alouds with the strategy later on in the unit (see pages 73–75).

PRESENTING THE LESSON

1. **Name the strategy.** I tell students:

   Today I'm going to show you how I draw conclusions about Elizabeth Cady Stanton's personality.

2. **Explain how to do it, why it helps, and when it works.** Here's my think aloud:

   When you draw conclusions about a person, you use what you learn about them to infer what they were like. Doing this helps you understand the person's decisions, actions, and words. Use this strategy with biography, fiction, interviews, and news stories. Today I'm going to read a section of this short biography about Elizabeth Cady Stanton, select some details, and then use these to figure out her personality traits.

3. **Summarize the key points of any text you have previously read.**

   When Elizabeth Cady Stanton married, like other women who lived in the 19th century, she had no rights. If she worked, or inherited land or money, her husband owned it all. Children belonged to her husband. She couldn't serve on a jury, sign a contract, or vote. Lizzie and her friend Susan B. Anthony worked together for a woman's right to vote and own property.

4. **Read the passage aloud.**

   "Lizzie and Susan (Susan B. Anthony), the tireless traveling speaker, aimed their souls at reforming the world. 'I forged the thunderbolts,' said Lizzie, and Susan fired them. They worked for temperance (against drunkenness) and abolition. They got New York lawmakers to give married women equal rights to their own wages and children. They faced many set backs and mixed blessings in their battles for suffrage—the right to vote. The 15th Amendment to the Constitution allowed black men to vote—glorious day! Women could not." (from *Rabble Rousers: 20 Women Who Made a Difference*, pp. 20–21)

5. **Show how you apply the strategy.** Here's what I say:

   The quotation, "I forged the thunderbolts," tells me that Lizzie thought her ideas were as strong, loud, and incisive as thunderbolts. I also learned that she and Susan were determined to never give up or give in because they got New York lawmakers to give women the right to keep their wages and control of their children. I also learned that she cared about racial prejudice because she and Susan worked for abolition of segregation and for temperance. If either woman drank alcohol and became drunk, it would have had a negative impact. I also learned that although both women worked for the right to vote, the 15th Amendment didn't include them. This leads me to infer that women's position in society was still very low. Note that I use details from the paragraph to support my inferences and ideas.

SUGGESTIONS FOR FOLLOWING UP

1. Invite students to pair up, choose a section from an instructional reading text, and think aloud using the five steps you've written on chart paper. Pairs can use the same or different texts. If they use the same text, have them choose different passages. Do this after two to three weeks of your modeling so students have had time to observe and understand the process.

2. Circulate and listen to the think alouds of three to four pairs each day. Support them by helping them follow the steps. Note students who can't work independently.

3. Add the strategy as a review lesson to your next unit of study if you've observed that many students have not absorbed the strategy. You might find that the entire class needs the review, or only a small group.

Differentiating Reading Instruction

Partner Think Alouds in Action

So you can hear the voices of students thinking aloud to demonstrate their understanding of a reading strategy, I've included the conversation of two pairs of students: a pair of eighth graders who have absorbed the process, and a pair of sixth graders whose inability to offer story details shows that they need extra support. These conversations come from notes I took while listening to students.

Both partners experience the role of listener and speaker. The listener reminds the speaker to use the five steps written on the chart as a road map through the process.

Partner Think Aloud: Grade Eight

TEXT: *Red Scarf Girl: A Memoir of the Cultural Revolution* by Ji Li Jiang (HarperCollins, 1997)

STRATEGY: Drawing conclusions about a person's character, events, words, or actions

REBECCA'S PAGES: 161–162

REBECCA'S THINK ALOUD: In this part I see that the government is brainwashing Ji Li and her classmates. They have to repeat sayings like "Down with Imperialism" and "Down with Revisionism." I can conclude that many students don't take these chants seriously when they make fun of the teacher and turn a phrase into "beef crackling" instead of "New Tzars." I know Ji Li is distracted and bored in the class because she looks out the window and dreams about a class where she learns science. I can infer that she enjoys physics, chemistry, and biology and dislikes these classes with slogan chanting and worksheets that spout Communist agendas like farming and industry.

EMILY'S RESPONSE: I noticed that you used the details on these pages to support your conclusions. Can you explain why math didn't change under Mao?

REBECCA: I guess they [Communist Party] couldn't think of anything to replace math with that was practical and part of the economy.

EMILY'S PAGES: 165 to third paragraph on 166

EMILY'S THINK ALOUD: I can conclude that winter coming fast and making Ji Li shiver is like the winter that's come to her family. Her dad has to go to political study class. Her aunt and uncle are in trouble. I can see that this confuses and worries Ji Li. She loves her family, but they're in trouble with the government. I can conclude that the Communists were hard on people who were rich and made money. They [government] made her confess that he committed crimes. I know Ji Li's dad is nervous and anxious—he comes home and smokes and never smiles. What I think is that the Chinese government wants Ji Li and other teens to go against their families and follow Mao.

REBECCA'S RESPONSE: That's all scary. And you proved everything. How do you think Ji Li feels when she clenches her fist and says that her family's problems grew worse no matter what she did?

EMILY: I think she felt discouraged and helpless. I think she was angry when she clenched her hands and wondered why the government hates the family she loves.

ROBB'S OBSERVATIONS: Both girls were able to use text details to draw conclusions and infer. They have learned to listen carefully to each other and raise questions that allow them to revisit every key detail in the book. Both Emily and Rebecca can be peer helpers, supporting classmates who are still learning how to apply the strategy.

Partner Think Aloud: Grade Six [Students' names here are pseudonyms.]

TEXT: "Seventh Grade" in *Baseball in April: And Other Stories* by Gary Soto (Odyssey Books, 1990)

STRATEGY: Cause/effect/make an inference

CHARLIE'S PAGES: 66

CHARLIE'S THINK ALOUD: The cause is Michael learning to scowl from looking at photos in *GQ* magazine. The effects are that Michael scowls all the time, and Michael says Belinda Reyes looked at him because he scowled.

DAVID'S RESPONSE: Yeah, that's good.

DAVID'S PAGES: bottom of 71 to top of page 72

DAVID'S THINK ALOUD: The cause is that Victor tries to speak French to impress Teresa. The effects are he makes up French words. Victor turns red. The teacher goes on with showing students how to say French words.

CHARLIE'S RESPONSE: Sounds right to me.

ROBB'S OBSERVATIONS: Both boys can identify a cause and provide the effects. All the effects are stated in the text. Neither student attempted to make an inference that would explain what he had learned about Victor, Michael, or the teacher.

POSSIBLE SCAFFOLDS FOR CHARLIE AND DAVID: First, I will ask the boys why they didn't infer. Perhaps they forgot to do this. If they struggled to infer, then I'll try these interventions. (1) Work one-on-one with each boy and practice figuring out what the author was telling him about a character. (2) Pair each boy up with a student who is proficient in the strategy and have them practice together. (3) Try Questioning the Author (QtA) prompts: *What do the cause and effects tell you about_____? What do the cause/effects tell you about the character's feelings? What kind of a person is he/she?*

Knowing When Students Have Absorbed a Reading Strategy

One question teachers repeatedly ask is, *How do I know when a student has absorbed a strategy?* Here are some assessments you can use to evaluate students' progress.

Talk about the strategy. Sit with a small group and listen carefully as they tell you everything they know about the strategy.

Ask them to write what they know about the strategy. For example, ask students to write everything they know and understand about drawing conclusions.

Listen to pairs think aloud, or invite a student to think aloud for you. Using your read aloud text or their independent reading book, have students use the five steps in a think aloud. The think aloud will provide insights into their ability to apply the strategy.

Complete a strategy bookmark. Have students monitor their ability to apply a strategy by answering questions on a bookmark about an independent reading book (see pages 230–234 for more on these bookmarks).

Remember to continue to read aloud and model with the common text to show students how you use a strategy to improve comprehension and make connections. It's the layers of practice, year after year that eventually enable students to internalize, understand, and regularly use a strategy. Each student's timetable for absorbing a strategy will differ, which is why you need to model, model, model.

Read Aloud to Teach Narrative Story Elements

"Explaining antagonistic forces and finding the climax of a story always confuses me. My memory of learning these [narrative elements] was that we memorized a list and definitions, and then took a test. It's hard for me to connect stuff like exposition, conflict, climax, theme to a book or short story." These words, spoken by Danielle, a seventh grader, reflect the confusions of many adolescent readers. A positive and enjoyable way to simplify the process for Danielle and her peers is to teach narrative story elements through read alouds. Equally important is that when students understand the structure of narratives, they can transfer their learning to their own writing.

How you structure and pace the lessons is important. Here's the process I use.

- Choose narrative poems and/or a very short story to read aloud. I like to start with a poem and then move to the story.
- Read the text and think aloud until students raise their hands to share or they tell you, "I can do this."
- Once you have seen that students can identify the elements you're focusing on, invite pairs to talk after a read aloud, and ask them to pinpoint the element. Then ask volunteers to share with the rest of the class.

Teach These Narrative Story Elements

These are the narrative elements I teach during read alouds:

- exposition
- setting
- protagonist
- rising action (plot)
- theme
- dialogue

- antagonist
- conflict
- problem
- climax & denouement
- foreshadowing
- inner thoughts

PLAN A LESSON THAT TEACHES NARRATIVE STORY ELEMENTS: GRADE SEVEN

PURPOSE To build students' knowledge and understanding of narrative story elements

TIME 15–20 minutes

MATERIALS A narrative poem. I use "Hey" from *Connecting Dots: Poems of My Journey* by

David Harrison (Boyds Mills, 2004), a resource you'll turn to again and again.

> *I'm thirteen. Many of my friends from Oak Grove Elementary are now going to Jarrett Junior High School, too. But unless we're in the same classes, it's hard to keep in touch. Jarrett's a big place.*

Hey
At lunch today I see Billy.
"Hey," we say:
"How's it going?"
We don't stop to say more.
Can't think of anything.
From third grade on
we were best friends,
sleeping over
at each other's house.

Rode horses,
teased his sister . . .
I think of the night
we laughed so hard
he fell out of bed.

Now he's in homeroom 106.
I'm in 107.
And all we can say,
when we meet at lunch is,
"Hey, how's it going?"

HOW IT HELPS STUDENTS It's important for students to understand the story elements in narrative texts so they can explore meaning, make inferences, and build new understandings by reflecting on each element. During a conference, Meg, an eighth grader, expressed the importance of understanding narrative elements: "They're [the narrative elements] like having a map that helps with the reading. I'm looking for problems, conflicts, inner thoughts, and dialogue to understand the main character and to figure out the theme. It makes the reading comfortable and lets me think right away 'cause I know what to expect."

Presenting the Lesson

1. Write a short narrative poem on chart paper or make an overhead transparency of it to share with students.

2. Read the poem aloud twice.

3. Reread the poem a third time. Explain that you will show how you connect narrative structure terms to the poem. For students in grades seven and up, tell them that you will ask them to explore themes in this poem by thinking about what the boys say, do, and think. Offer this option to younger students if they have had past experience with theme.

4. Have pairs or small groups discuss theme.

5. After I read "Hey" twice and then partners read the poem, I present this think aloud to seventh graders:

   Robb's think aloud: *The short poem has all the elements of a narrative. First, setting—in the school cafeteria, at school near their homerooms, and in each other's homes when they were in third grade. The settings help readers see the change in the boys' relationships from third grade to middle school. Second, characters—the narrator is the protagonist, and Billy is an antagonist. Third, the problem—their friendship has faded, and they have little to say to each other.*

6. Have groups of students discuss the themes in the poem. Here are some thoughts about themes that groups of seventh graders reported after discussing "Hey" for several minutes. I had asked students to support their theme with details from the poem. One member of each group responded for that group. Three out of five groups had different themes.

   Danny's group: If a friendship is shallow, it won't last when the friends separate. When the boys were in separate rooms at school, they went their separate ways. They no longer had anything to talk about.

   David's group: When you grow up, you can grow out of being friends. The boys were best friends in third grade. Now they hardly speak. They're in middle school 'cause it says homeroom, and also the note above the poem tells that it's junior high. What could have happened is that they're interested in different things, so they don't hang out.

TONY'S GROUP: Growing apart happens to some friends as they get older. We thought that when the author wrote, "Hey, how's it going?" and said that's all they had to say, the author was telling us that they no longer had anything in common—anything to talk about. We concluded that now their lives must be very different.

SUGGESTIONS FOR FOLLOWING UP

1. Teach narrative elements with short stories. Choose stories that you can complete in two to three days so students can recall the plot and use narrative elements to think and deepen their understanding of setting, problems, and theme.

2. Select novels with short chapters so you can read two chapters a day. If you're passionate about a longer novel with lengthy chapters, go ahead and read it, presenting one chapter a day. Your love for a book is sure to rub off on your students.

3. As you read aloud short stories or chapters in a novel, share your thoughts about narrative elements halfway through the text and again at the end. Sometimes I pause briefly while reading to share an emotion, a prediction, or an image.

I present numerous lessons on narrative elements to be sure students absorb them. But I'm going to fast-forward through these lessons and show you what the read aloud looks like when I turn exploring story elements over to students—or gradually release responsibility to them. I always tell students to listen carefully as they will have to think along with the story and recall details. If your students have not experienced enough read alouds and are unused to listening carefully, you might have to read a section of short text twice.

More Narrative Poems That Work

"Madam and the Rent Man" by Langston Hughes

"Bishop Hatto" by Robert Southey

"The Highwayman" by Alfred Noyes

"The Wreck of the Hesperus" by Henry Wadsworth Longfellow

"The Ballad of the Oysterman" by Oliver Wendell Holmes

"Incident" by Countee Cullen

Traditional ballads such as "Lord Randall," "Greensleeves," "John Henry," "Barbara Allen," and "Edward, Edward"

The lesson that follows asks students to teach about story elements by thinking aloud after the story "The Party" by Pam Muñoz Ryan has been read. Both the read aloud and the students' think alouds take place during the same class. (You'll find this story on pages 259–261 of the appendix.)

PLAN A LESSON THAT INVITES STUDENTS TO TEACH STORY ELEMENTS: GRADE EIGHT

PURPOSE To observe how students connect narrative elements to a short story

TIME 10–15 minutes for students' preparation; 15 minutes presentation

MATERIALS I use "The Party," a short story by Pam Muñoz Ryan, but you can use any short story you have read aloud.

HOW IT HELPS STUDENTS Inviting groups of students to showcase their knowledge of short-story elements by connecting these to a read aloud lets you know whether students understand these elements and are able to connect them to their instructional texts independently. Students also gain experience with jigsaw, a learning strategy that divides the work among groups and asks each group to teach the rest of the class.

Asking students to present their findings offers you a chance to listen carefully to each group's presentation as well as the follow-up comments from members of other groups. From these presentations, you will know if you need to continue to think aloud about specific terms, if you need to work with a small group while others work on their own, or if you can move the entire class to independence.

PREPARING THE LESSON

1. On a separate index card, print each narrative element found in the box on page 76.
2. On chart paper, write these guidelines for students' presentations:
   - Define each term.
   - Connect each term to the read-aloud story by choosing story details that help you and others understand the term in relation to the text.
   - Raise questions if the term or the story details confuse you.

PRESENTING THE LESSON

1. Review the guidelines you've written on chart paper. Call for questions to clarify students' understandings.

2. Hold index cards face down and have a student from each group choose two. These will be the terms the group teaches. (For "The Party," I replace *exposition* with *ambiguous* ending.)

3. Explain that groups will have 10 to 15 minutes to define each term and connect it to the story.

4. Take three minutes and invite students to retell the story so you are sure every student knows the plot details and characters' names. I suggest that you note the names of the characters on the chalkboard. If students can't retell the text, then reread it.

5. Circulate and listen to discussions. Add extra time if you sense that students need it.

6. Ask each group to divide their presentation this way: two students each define a term; two connect a term to the story. If your groups are larger, it's effective for them to choose two spokespersons to present; rotate the positions of spokespersons so all students experience this job.

7. Give clear time limits for groups to choose presenters. I tell them that they have two minutes. If they haven't made a choice by then, I assign jobs. Since students prefer—and I prefer—that they make their own choices, they learn to choose quickly the next time.

8. Explain to students these teacher guidelines for presentations:
   - Students define one term and connect it to the story.
   - The teacher asks other group members if they have anything to add.
   - The teacher asks other students in the class if they have comments or ideas. I usually limit these to one or two because of time.
   - Repeat the above for each term.

Here's what eighth graders presented for *theme* and *ambiguous endings*.

HATTIE ON THEME: Our group thought that the author was saying that it's okay to be in the "out-group." We also thought that the author was talking about the power and control popular kids have over those who aren't accepted when it [the story] says maybe she'll invite you. I thought that the story also showed that you can want to be "in" so badly that it takes over your mind.

JOE ON AMBIGUOUS ENDINGS: At the end of the story, the author doesn't tell you if the narrator took the invitation. She leaves that up to you. Three in our group decided that she [the narrator] didn't take it. From the last words, "And then, I smiled," we inferred that she didn't take it, and felt good about her decision. We felt if she had taken it, that would have happened right away. But she [the narrator] kept thinking about her decision. We felt the smile showed that she saw how shallow and manipulative Bridget was.

RHETT ON THE ENDING: I thought she [the narrator] took it. Through the whole story that's all she wanted. Even if she's an "afterthought," the drive to be at the party, to be part of what happens, and to be with the in-group would make her take it.

SUGGESTIONS FOR FOLLOWING UP

1. Have pairs or groups read a short story at their instructional level and present the narrative elements.

2. Encourage creativity and ask students for ideas about how they might show an understanding of narrative elements. Eighth graders made these suggestions: a journey through a short story, highlighting the narrative elements found in the box on page 76; a Readers Theater, with the terms as characters; a dramatization of the story focusing on the elements.

3. Evaluate students' ability to define the terms and connect them to a story by giving a test. Use a story that your weakest reader can comprehend or select two to three stories that students can read independently.

4. Continue to support students who need extra help while others read or complete a journal entry.

Dip Into These Collections of Short Stories

Baseball in April: And Other Stories by Gary Soto (Odyssey Book, 1990)

Dirty Laundry: Stories About Family Secrets, Lisa Rowe Faustino, editor (Viking, 1998)

El Bronx Remembered by Nicholasa Mohr (HarperCollins, 1975)

Past Perfect, Present Tense: New and Collected Stories by Richard Peck (Dial, 2004)

Salsa Stories by Lulu Delacre (Scholastic, 2000)

Teaching Powerful Writing by Bob Sizoo (Scholastic, 2001)

Visions: Nineteen Short Stories by Outstanding Writers for Young Adults, Donald R. Gallo, editor (Bantam Doubleday Dell, 1997)

Zlateh the Goat and Other Stories by Isaac Bashevis Singer (HarperCollins, 1994)

You'll also find short texts to read in magazines such as *Storyworks* (Scholastic).

Read Aloud to Teach Informational Text Features

When you read aloud informational texts, such as picture and chapter books, and magazine and newspaper articles, students will need to see the text features that you are thinking about, such as sidebars, diagrams, captions, graphs, and the index. I suggest that you choose two or three features to focus on for each read aloud and explain the purpose of each one. Sidebars, for example, contain extra information about a topic—details that don't work in the main text but are so fascinating that the author includes them. (In the appendix on page 274, you will find a list of informational text features and explanations of how each one helps readers.)

The lesson that follows contains some suggestions that will help familiarize your students with these features.

PLAN A LESSON THAT BUILDS STUDENTS' KNOWLEDGE OF NONFICTION TEXT FEATURES: GRADE FIVE

PURPOSE To introduce and familiarize students with nonfiction text features

TIME 5–10 minutes for teacher preparation; 5–10 minutes to deliver to class

MATERIALS One of the nonfiction texts from the box on page 84, or one you choose; transparencies of the table of contents and a sidebar, or photocopies of them for students

HOW IT HELPS STUDENTS A deep understanding of nonfiction text features enables students to better navigate these texts and construct meaning while reading. Using these features to preview a book or magazine article before reading can enlarge students' knowledge of the topic. For example, learners who have little background about a topic can study features such as captions, photographs, and sidebars to gain background knowledge and improve their comprehension and recall.

Make sure students understand that writers may include excerpts from letters, diaries, and newspapers, as well as interviews and first-person accounts of events. The award-winning book *Through My Eyes* by Ruby Bridges (Scholastic, 1999) is a text you can use to show students how effective these features are and how they breathe warmth and humanity into a text.

PREPARING THE LESSON

1. Choose a nonfiction text. I use *The World of Castles* by Philip Steele (Kingfisher, 2005). I do not read the entire text, but I use a few pages to focus on features. Because this whets their curiosity, many students later check out the book to read during independent work times.

2. Decide on the features you will focus on that day. For this lesson, I chose the table of contents and the sidebar.

3. Make an overhead transparency of the table of contents and the sidebar.

4. If you don't have an overhead projector, provide each student or pair of students with photocopies of the pages you will be using.

PRESENTING THE LESSON

1. On the overhead projector, place the table of contents transparency and ask students, "What do you notice?"

   Fifth graders pointed out that in the table of contents, the headings told them that they could learn about building a castle, defending a castle, daily life in a castle, and what a castle town was like. They also noticed that the book included a glossary. The class wanted to see what the glossary was like: "Is it just a list of words like our

Ten Informational Picture Books for Reading Aloud

These books are great read alouds and ideal for teaching informational text features. Explain to students that they won't find every feature in one book. Writers choose to include only those features that enhance their topic and purposes for writing.

All About Sharks by Jim Arnosky (Scholastic, 2003)

CAPITAL! Washington D.C. from A to Z by Laura Krauss Melmed, illustrated by Frane Lessac (HarperCollins, 2003)

Crossing the Delaware: A History in Many Voices by Louise Peacock, illustrated by Walter L. Krudop (Simon & Schuster, 1998)

Egypt: In Spectacular Cross-Section by Stephen Biesty (Scholastic, 2004)

Forest Explorers: A Life-Size Field Guide by Nick Bishop (Scholastic, 2004)

Following the Coast by Jim Arnosky (HarperCollins, 2004)

Hurricanes: Earth's Mightiest Storms by Patricia Lauber (Scholastic, 1996)

Snapshots: The Wonders of Monterey Bay by Celeste Davidson Mannis (Viking, 2006)

Promises to Keep: How Jackie Robinson Changed America by Sharon Robinson (Scholastic, 2004)

The World of Castles by Philip Steele (Kingfisher, 2005)

Differentiating Reading Instruction

science textbook?" asked Michael. [Even though I hadn't planned on discussing the glossary, I grasped this teachable moment and went with it.] I walked around the room and let each group study the glossary, which included illustrations. Michael and others loved the illustrations. Students agreed that the detailed illustrations made them want to read those entries.

2. Read aloud pages 4–6. Then place the transparency of the sidebar on the overhead projector and ask students, "What do you notice?"

    John immediately pointed to the King John's seal and said, "It's cool that messages were marked by pressing the royal seal in wax."

    Katie pointed out that even though the seal is the first thing you see, the point of the sidebar is, "If you disobeyed a law of the king or a message he sent, you could have your head chopped off."

3. Tell students that this book will go in your special crate or in a place on a bookshelf. During independent work time, an individual or small groups can check it out and read parts that interest them.

Suggestions for Following Up

1. Invite students to find an informational text feature in one of their books, and then show it to their group, read it aloud, and discuss it.

2. Encourage students to use these features in their writing.

Read Aloud as a Catalyst for Thinking About Unfamiliar Themes

Webster defines catalyst as "a substance which speeds up or slows down a chemical reaction, but which itself undergoes no permanent chemical change." For a catalyst read aloud, I choose a text that will deepen and expand students' understanding of a theme, a big idea, or an issue, such as growing up in an inner city or a rural area, and war—issues that students may have little direct experience with.

The catalyst read aloud developed in my eighth-grade classes when students were studying the short story and grappling with the issue of growing up in an inner city.

My students attend Powhatan School, an independent K–8 school, nestled in the Blue Ridge Mountains of Virginia. Powhatan's students live in small towns or in the country. Signs of growing up for them mean getting a driver's license and a part-time job. Brainstorming and group discussions elicited more ideas, such as taking care of a pet or younger sibling and no longer needing a babysit-

Robb reads aloud to fifth graders.

ter. I wanted more for my students. I wanted them to know that there were additional life experiences that affected growing up—experiences that they had not lived through in small towns and rural farms. Short of telling them, which I avoid doing because the telling will mean little to them, I turned to books. Powerful books not only enable students to imagine what they haven't experienced or learned, but also enable you to expand background knowledge and close experience gaps.

PLAN A LESSON FOR A CATALYST READ ALOUD: GRADE EIGHT

PURPOSE To clarify and heighten students' understanding of an issue that's difficult for them to grasp because they lack the experience and background knowledge

TIME two or three consecutive classes; set aside 10–15 minutes each day

MATERIALS A picture book or short text that clearly illustrates the issue or problem you want students to understand. Here are the three texts I used to enlarge my eighth graders' knowledge of growing up: "Once upon a Time" from *El Bronx Remembered* by Nicholasa Mohr (HarperCollins, 1975), *Hiroshima No Pika* by Toshi Maruki (Lothrop, Lee & Shepard, 1980), and *White Wash* by Ntosake Shange (Walker, 1997).

How It Helps Students

With catalyst read alouds, you can spark students' imaginations and build their understanding of ideas and concepts that they may not be able to reclaim from their personal experiences. I decided to use Questioning the Author to help students build their understanding.

Preparing the Lesson

1. Pinpoint the theme, issue, or concept that students haven't experienced. For my eighth graders living in rural areas, I chose growing up in an inner city.

2. Choose a picture book, short story, myth, legend, or fairy tale that spotlights aspects of the issue you want students to grasp.

3. Prepare your read aloud by studying the text and planning the detail you will highlight for Questioning the Author.

Presenting the Lesson

1. Read the text out loud.

2. Pair up students or organize them into small groups.

3. Use QtA queries to engage students in discussion about the issue. This is the query I use: *What is the author trying to tell you about growing up through the plot details?*

4. Invite pairs or group members to share their ideas for a whole-class discussion.

5. Have students head a journal page with the title of the text and write what they learned from listening, discussing, and sharing. Here are a few excerpts from eighth graders' journals:

    • "War makes you grow up; it's about losing things. You see people dying, you lose your home and sometimes your family. You have to help sick people even though you'd rather play. You become an adult even if you're little." (*Hiroshima No Pika*)

    • " 'Once upon a time' is like a fairy tale only it's about three girls in the South Bronx who come upon the dead body of a gang leader. They'll never be the same—they lost part of being a kid. Seeing death can do that." (*El Bronx Remembered*)

    • "When the gang beats up Mauricio and paints Helene-Angel's face white, the happy feelings they had every day fly away. Bad things—horrid things like this make you grow up and see that life isn't perfect." (*White Wash*)

6. Use students' instructional texts to explore issues surrounding growing up.

SUGGESTIONS FOR FOLLOWING UP

1. Continue to read texts that spotlight the issue and concepts you want students to understand. Have pairs or small groups flesh out the issues in the text.
2. Ask students to write in their journals about what they have learned from the read aloud and their discussions.
3. Ask students to find examples of the issue in their independent reading and write about them in their journals.

Read Aloud to Show Students All About Journal Entries

Journaling about reading takes a starring role in my differentiated reading classroom. Students grow as thinkers when they have multiple opportunities to explore concepts, themes, issues, and genres. Reading students' writing helps me assess their understanding. I always show students how a journal entry works by inviting them to help me complete the entry with a read aloud. I record the journal response on chart paper so students have a model they can turn to as they complete specific entries later.

PLAN A READ-ALOUD LESSON TO SHOW STUDENTS HOW JOURNAL ENTRIES WORK: GRADE SEVEN

PURPOSE To show students both how to set up a journal entry and what an effective response looks like

TIME 10–15 minutes

MATERIALS Any read-aloud text; for this lesson I used "The Party" by Pam Muñoz Ryan

HOW IT HELPS STUDENTS It's important for you to show students how to set up their journals and also how each new journal entry you introduce works. Inviting students to collaborate after you think aloud and showing them a response enables them to observe the thinking behind each entry. It also gives them an opportunity to experience working with peers on a response.

Preparing the Lesson

1. Prepare the chart by writing your name and date at the top. Title it "Drawing Conclusions About Characters' Personalities" and write "'The Party' by Pam Muñoz Ryan."

2. Using a colored marker, divide the chart into two columns.

3. On the left-hand side, write the character's name; I write "Narrator." Under the name, write "Personality Traits."

4. On the right-hand side, write "Prove It! Use Story Details."

5. Add numbers on the left-had side to note the number of traits you plan to write about. Leave space between each number so you can prove your conclusions on the right-hand side. I set the chart up for two personality traits.

> Drawing Conclusions About Characters' Personalities
>
> "The Party" by Pam Muñoy Ryan
>
> Narrator   Prove It!
> Personality Traits   Use Story Details
>
> insecure   Finds reasons for not being invited: stringy hair, coat, ugly hair. Blames herself.
>
> anxious   Her stomach hurt. Worried all day about not receiving an invitation.

FIGURE 3.1: Here is the chart I created for a lesson on drawing conclusions.

Presenting the Lesson

1. Explain to students the journal entry format on the chart.

2. Print "insecure" on the left-hand side. I think aloud to prove my conclusions, and then write notes on the chart. Here's what I say: *I know the narrator is insecure when she finds reasons—like her stringy hair, her coat, her ugly looks—for not being invited. She blames herself for being in the out-group.*

3. Organize students in pairs or small groups.

4. Write "anxious" on the chart. I invite sixth graders to find support from the story for this personality trait. Here's what seventh graders say:

   • "She [the narrator] said her stomach hurt as she hoped she would get an invitation."

   • "She worried about not getting invited all day. She kept thinking about what the other girls said about the party."

   • "She wondered why she wasn't invited and tried to find reasons."

Suggestions for Following Up

1. Continue to use your read-aloud texts to model different journal entries.

2. Introduce a new journal entry by setting aside time to collaborate with students to show them what the entry looks like and the kind of responses you're hoping students will offer.

Read Aloud to Introduce Issues for a Unit of Study

Teaching content is important to language arts, science, and social studies teachers. Learning and recalling facts from a novel or an informational picture or chapter book is the first step. From my experiences, using the content to study an issue, such as segregation, or a problem, such as how wars can be avoided, asks students to apply what they've learned to bring meaning and relevance to a unit of study.

Let me show you how an issue can elevate students' thinking when you invite them to make inferences and connections. My read aloud for a fifth-grade class that was studying biography was a short selection about Sojourner Truth from *Rabble Rousers: 20 Women Who Made a Difference* by Cheryl Harness. The issue students focused on was what causes men and women to work steadfastly for change. The issue nudged students beyond the facts that Sojourner Truth wanted to help the poor, slaves, and women— which is questioning to collect facts—to using them to draw these conclusions about her. After a think-pair-share, fifth graders shared these issue-related ideas, which I noted.

- "She wanted to help the poor, slaves, and women. She never gave up, even when people called her names and wouldn't listen to her speeches."
- "She had a strong belief and was determined to change people's thinking. She never gave up."
- "She was religious, and this helped her bear up when others yelled insults or wouldn't help. She's like Martin Luther King—religious and strong."
- "She traveled all over to spread her beliefs. This shows she was dedicated to working for freedom and fairness because she had little money and walked a lot."

What these student comments reveal is that having an issue supports linking facts to inferences, connections, and conclusions.

PLAN A LESSON THAT INTRODUCES AN ISSUE: GRADE FOUR

PURPOSE To introduce students to an issue on which they will reflect throughout a unit of study

TIME 10–15 minutes over two consecutive days

MATERIALS A picture book that highlights a specific issue. Fourth graders are reading biography and studying both the issue of creating change and the personality traits of change makers.

HOW IT HELPS STUDENTS Read alouds that raise students' awareness of an issue also start them thinking, discussing, and clarifying their understanding of an issue. The more students consider an issue, the better able they will be to connect it to books they are reading during the study.

PREPARING THE LESSON Select two or three (or more) picture books that you will read aloud during your unit of study so students can hear different perspectives on the issue and deepen their understanding of it. Listed are the picture books I have fourth graders listen to: *The Story of Ruby Bridges* by Robert Coles (Scholastic, 1995), *Mirette on the High Wire* by Emily Arnold McCully (Putnam & Grosset, 1992), *Mama Went to Jail for the Vote* by Kathleen Karr (Hyperion, 2005), and *Barn Raising* by Craig Brown (HarperCollins, 2002).

PRESENTING THE LESSON

1. Pair up students and ask them to discuss, for two to three minutes, the term *change maker*. Use these prompts to stir discussion: *What kinds of changes can people make? What kinds of changes affect the world? A family or community? One or two people?*

2. Circulate and listen to students' discussions. Allow more or less time depending on what students' conversations show you.

3. Ask students to write their name and the date on a journal page and head it "Change Makers." Then have students write all they recall from their conversations, adding any ideas that pop into their minds as they write.

4. Invite volunteers to share their thoughts.

5. In one class, I read aloud all of *Mama Went to Jail for the Vote*, as the text is short. At the end, I write these prompts on chart paper: *Was Mama a change maker? If yes, explain the change she worked for. What personality traits helped Mama achieve these changes?*

6. Ask partners or groups to discuss the prompts and share their findings. Tell them

that after discussing and sharing, you'll ask them to write.

Here are some ideas fourth graders shared:

- "You don't need to be violent to make change—you can use votes."
- "You can get your message to the president by marching in a huge parade in front of the White House."
- "Mama ignored Papa, who thought women should only serve men. She didn't argue with him. She did what she knew was right."
- "You can picket like Mama with a message you want the president to see."
- "You could go to jail to show how much you believe in getting the vote."
- "Mama was determined to get the vote. Even six months in jail didn't stop her."

7. Have students head a journal page with the title and author of your read aloud, then write what they recall from the discussion and sharing. Tell students to use the prompts on chart paper to jog their memories.

8. Continue exploring the issue with other read alouds. Follow steps one to seven so students talk, share ideas, and then write.

Suggestions for Following Up

1. Have students reread their journal entries that explain both the term *change maker* and the personality traits needed to create change. Ask students to clarify their ideas and jot down new ideas that surface as the study unfolds.

2. Invite pairs or small groups to discuss why the persons in their independent reading biographies are or are not change makers, as well as discuss their character's personality traits. Partners or groups can share what they've learned with the entire class.

Weave Issues and Core Questions Into Your Units of Study

Now that you have explored how reading aloud can prepare students to study an issue, theme, or concept, you'll want to start mulling over the kinds of issues adolescents might enjoy studying and applying to their instructional reading texts (see chapters 4 and 5). It's a fact of life that young adolescents constantly wrestle with issues and questions that

A List of Informational Picture and Chapter Books for Specific Issues

You'll find as you read and reflect on many of these books that you can use them to raise students' awareness of multiple issues. An example is Weatherford's picture book, *Freedom on the Menu: The Greensboro Sit-Ins*, which can be used to discuss justice and injustice, human rights, and creating change.

Prejudice and Segregation

This Is the Dream by Diane Shore and Jessica Alexander, illustrated by James Ransome (HarperCollins, 2006)

Through My Eyes by Ruby Bridges (Scholastic, 1999)

The Story of Ruby Bridges by Robert Coles (Scholastic, 1998)

Freedom on the Menu: The Greensboro Sit-Ins by Carole Boston Weatherford, paintings by Jerome LaGarrigue (Dial, 2005)

Oh, Freedom! Kids Talk About The Civil Rights Movement With The People Who Made It Happen by Casey King and Linda Barrett Osborne (Scholastic, 1997)

Justice/Injustice

Bound for America: The Forced Migration of Africans to the New World by James Haskins & Kathleen Benson, paintings by Floyd Cooper (Lothrop, 1999)

Days of Jubilee: The End of Slavery in the United States by Patricia C. and Fredrick L. McKissack (Scholastic, 2003)

I've Seen the Promised Land: The Life of Dr. Martin Luther King, Jr. by Walter Dean Myers, illustrated by Leonard Jenkins (HarperCollins, 2004)

Keeping the Promise: A Torah's Journey by Tami Lehman-Wilzig, illustrated by Craig Orback (Kar-Ben Publishing, 2003)

Love to Langston by Tony Medina, illustrated by R. Gregory Christie (Lee and Low, 2002)

Human Rights

The Declaration of Independence: The Words That Made America by Sam Fink (Scholastic, 2002)

Gettysburg: The Legendary Battle and the Address That Inspired a Nation by Shelley Tanaka, paintings by David Craig (Harcourt, 2003)

continued on next page

Harvesting Hope: The Story of Cesar Chavez by Kathleen Krull, illustrated by Yuyi Morales (Harcourt, 2003)

The Librarian of Basra: A True Story From Iraq by Jeanette Winter (Harcourt, 2005)

Pink and Say by Patricia Polacco (Philomel, 1994)

Caring for the Environment and the Natural World

Do the Whales Still Sing? by Dianne Hofmeyr, pictures by Jude Daly (Dial, 1995)

The Journey: Stories of Migration by Cynthia Rylant (Scholastic, 2006)

Miss Lady Bird's Wildflowers: How a First Lady Changed America by Kathi Appelt, illustrated by Joy Fisher Hein (HarperCollins, 2005)

Change Makers and Visionaries

Enemies of Slavery by David A. Adler, illustrated by Donald A. Smith (Scholastic, 2004)

Martin's Big Words: The Life of Dr. Martin Luther King, Jr. by Doreen Rappaport, illustrated by Bryan Collier (Scholastic, 2004)

World by Jane Breskin Zalben (Dutton, 2006)

Wilma Unlimited: How Wilma Rudolph Became the World's Fastest Woman by Kathleen Krull, illustrated by David Diaz (Harcourt, 1996)

Mama Went to Jail for the Vote by Kathleen Karr, illustrated by Malene Laugesen (Hyperion, 2005)

relate to friends, families, and school and home rules and regulations. Weaving issues and core questions into your reading instruction sparks lively discussions and makes the reading relevant to what your students experience and struggle with every day.

Issues and core questions breathe life and energy into whole-class and small-group discussions, adding the twist—the connector—that adolescents need to bond to books, ideas, and concepts. So if you're required to teach *Romeo and Juliet* in ninth grade, you might grab your students' interest by asking them to discuss this core question, *What can mess up a teen romance?* That's a compelling enough query to help students slog through tough reading and/or viewing. It's a question that helps today's students understand that for thousands of years, others have conspired to wreck young love.

Make sure, however, that as you travel into a genre, that you ask students if they see other issues in texts that they'd like to explore. For example, in one of my classes, we were exploring the genre of historical fiction. When working with a group reading *Lyddie* by Katherine Paterson (Dutton, 1991), the issue I raised was, can education really change lives for the better? However, the core question or issue my students raised while reading was, what role does chance or

Students are eager to add to the discussion about the oceans and pollution.

fate play in our lives? Their issue was one they fleshed out with enthusiasm because, as Richie, an eighth grader, put it, "So many things happen that we can't control. I wanted to see how these [chance events] change decisions and what we and the characters do."

What follows in the chart on pages 96–98 is a menu of some issues and related core questions that you can choose from—issues and questions that you'll introduce through read alouds. These issues and questions also support meaningful discussions, thinking, and journal writing, whether every student reads a different book (see Chapter 4) or small groups read the same book (see Chapter 5). In addition to exploring these issues in books, students can also reflect on core questions that emerge from issues, which can then be used to make connections to their life experiences, their independent reading texts, and their reading in content classes. As you plan your units of study, using genre, topic, theme, reading strategies, journal writing, and assessments as threads to weave together the unit's cloth, I hope you will add an issue. Issues move students beyond the facts and encourage them to use facts to infer, connect, and conclude.

ISSUE	PROMPTS and QUESTIONS
Stereotyping	• How are other cultures stereotyped in your text? • How did you recognize the stereotyping? • What dangers do you see in stereotyping groups?
Conformity/ Nonconformity	• Why do people want to fit in? • Are there advantages to being part of the in-group? If so, what are these? • What brings people to the need to conform? • What kind of personality do you think nonconformists have? • Is it tough to not conform? Why? • How do characters or other people view conforming or nonconforming in your book?
Rebellion	• Is the rebellion toward family members, friends, or school, or is it part of a war? • What causes rebellion in your book? • Is the rebellion well-received? Explain why or why not. • How does rebellion affect the lives of others? • Does rebellion change people's lives? Explain how.
Relationships with: parents, friends, siblings, romantic partners	• What bonds relationships and brings people closer? • What messes up relationships and separates people? • Why are relationships with others important? • How does your book deal with relationships that adults frown upon? • How do power and control affect relationships?
Human rights	• What are rights all human beings should have? • Do people or governments, or both, violate human rights? Explain your position. • How can you stop the violation of human rights anywhere in the world? • Should countries take an ethical stand in favor of maintaining human rights? Explain your position.

ISSUE	PROMPTS and QUESTIONS
Justice/Injustice	• Explain what is just and/or unjust in your book. • Is it possible to repair injustices? Explain. • How does injustice affect people's lives? • Is the law always just? Explain.
The Natural World: global warming, erosion, preserving species, preserving the rain forest, and so on	• What can we do to preserve the natural world? • Why is nature important? • Is everything about nature good? Positive? Explain. • Why do we have natural disasters? • Why are trees, parks, and open land important? • Are there conflicts between nature and technology? • Why are forests important? • What can we learn about changes in nature from the oceans? From global warming? From glaciers? • Are all species on earth important to keeping balance in nature? Explain your position. • What kinds of pollution does your book deal with? • Why does pollution affect people's lives? • What can be done about air and water pollution? Food pollution?
War/ Peaceful Resolution to Conflicts	• Why do countries make war? • How does war affect people's daily lives? • How can people achieve peace? • How does war relate to human rights? To justice and injustice? • Is war part of relationships? Explain how. • How can conflicts be resolved peacefully? Does your book show this? • What increases anger and frustration among countries? Between characters/people? • Is war inevitable? Explain why or why not. • Does power and control have anything to do with war? Explain.

ISSUE	PROMPTS and QUESTIONS
Physical and Emotional Abuse	• What makes relationships abusive? • Can you get out of abusive relationships? How? • How can someone break the cycle of abuse? • Why do the abused try to protect their abusers? • What have you learned about emotional abuse?
Fears	• Can fears control lives? Explain. • How can you overcome fears? • What causes the buildup of fear in characters/persons? • Why do characters and people fear the unknown?

Pause, Reflect, and Consider Six Questions . . .

Including multiple read alouds for different purposes definitely uses extra class time. It seems that every year we're asked to do more within the same time limits, and we feel that our class time continually shrinks. I understand that feeling but have learned to shove those emotions and voices aside to do what I know can build my students' reading power and stamina.

If you and I are to reach every reader by using multiple texts for instruction, then the read aloud steps up and assumes a starring role. Here are some questions to mull over—questions that can help you not only clearly see the role of read alouds in your class, but also budget your time to balance read-aloud instruction with mini-lessons and independent work. And all the time you'll be striving to meet every student's needs.

- Am I reading aloud for fun every day?
- Am I using issues to help students think and infer about facts and details?
- Have I chosen one or two reading strategies to focus on and model in a unit of study?
- Do I show students how different journal entries work with read alouds?
- Are my read alouds helping students better understand the structure of fiction and nonfiction?
- Am I using my librarian to help me find picture books and short texts to read aloud?

Chapter 4

Whole-Class Instructional Reading and Differentiation

Differentiated Whole-Class Instruction That Matches Students and Books

et's visit two sixth-grade classrooms where we can explore two views of whole-class instructional reading. Both classes are in the same middle school in southern Virginia and meet 5 days a week for 45 minutes. In the first class, there are 28 students: 5 students read at a third-grade level, 6 read at a fourth-grade level, 12 are on grade level, 3 read near a seventh-grade level, and 2 students are English language learners and read at a second-grade level. The teacher has had ten years of experience.

In this sixth-grade class, instructional reading centers around the same text for all students. To introduce students to biography, the teacher uses two short selections from a grade-level basal anthology. Today, as we enter this class in which students are sitting in rows, the teacher is introducing them to biography. She asks them to read the first two chapters of *The Greatest: Muhammad Ali* by Walter Dean Myers. As I walk around the room, I notice that about half of the class reads the chapters. A few students look at the photographs in the biography, but don't read. Two write notes to each other, one puts her head on her desk, and several doodle on a piece of notebook paper. About 5 minutes into the 20-minute, silent instructional reading period, the teacher gathers around her the students who are not reading and proceeds to read the chapters aloud. After the silent reading period, the teacher reviews the cause/effect/infer strategy by reading aloud a passage from the basal anthology. Everyone follows in the anthology. Finally, the teacher assigns homework: independent reading for 20 minutes and a grammar worksheet on linking verbs. When class ends, the frustrated teacher sighs and says, "What else can I do? They can't read the book, so I read it to them." This is one way to manage whole-class instructional reading, but there is another way. Let's observe the second sixth-grade class.

The teacher of this class of 30 students has had seven years of teaching experience: five in a large urban school district, where she learned how to do what she and I call "differentiated whole-class instructional reading" from a mentor whom she describes as a "master teacher." This is her third year in this rural middle school. Her class is even more diverse than the other sixth-grade class we just visited: four students read at a third-grade level, five at a fourth-grade level, five at a mid-fifth-grade level, eight are on grade level, three at a seventh-grade level, and five English language learners read at a mid-second-grade level. Students sit at desks in groups of six. If you were to use a grade-level basal in this class, you would instruct 11 students. If you were to attempt to meet the needs of all students, you would need to organize and meet with six instructional groups three or four times a week—a nearly impossible task. However, this teacher meets her students' diverse instructional reading levels with a variation of whole-class instructional reading.

Each of her 30 students is reading a biography at his or her instructional level. Some pairs may read the same title, but most students are reading different books. The teacher opens class by reading aloud a short biographical poem "The Many and the Few" by J. Patrick Lewis. Then she reads and thinks aloud to model the cause/effect/infer strategy with a passage from *Wilma Unlimited* by Kathleen Krull (Harcourt, 2000). She asks students to comment and ask questions about her think aloud. On the chalkboard are directions for the next 20 minutes of silent instructional reading, which she reviews before asking students to find a comfortable space to read.

This student is reading a book at her instructional level.

- Read the next two chapters of your book.
- Use a self-stick note to jot down a tough word and the page it is on.
- If you finish your biography assignment, read your independent reading book.
- I will confer with Josh, Keisha, Carla, and David. Bring your book, journal, and a pencil.

When the teacher confers with Josh, she focuses on making inferences from the cause and effects he's identified. Keisha and Carla practice figuring out the meanings of their tough words by using context clues. With David, she focuses on pinpointing causes and effects. You're probably wondering, how does she know what to do? The teacher has taken observational notes (see pages 161–165) on each student and has looked over assessments from past units of study, as well as data she's collected from reading surveys, tests, and conferences. By getting to know each student so well, she's able to provide the exact kind of support each student needs. It's important to note that no conference lasts more than five minutes because the teacher keeps the focus on a single point.

If we hope to teach each learner in our classes, I believe we need to embrace the second model of "differentiated whole-class instructional reading." In this model, the read aloud became the teacher's common instructional text, and students had the opportunity to improve their reading skills because each one read a text at his or her instructional level. Students who needed support met with their teacher for short bursts of instruction and monitoring. Note, too, that students' homework provided opportunities to practice reading at their comfort levels.

Know Your Students' Instructional Reading levels

Review pages 38–41 in Chapter 2 to help you as you figure out each student's instructional reading level.

As You Continue to Read . . .

As you continue to read this chapter, you'll learn how to organize differentiated whole-class reading instruction. Along with my plans for a unit of study on biography, I've included detailed, week-by-week lessons for the unit; the open-ended questions I use to promote discussion; and descriptions of two assessments. But first, I'd like to share ten questions that teachers repeatedly ask me about differentiated whole-class instructional reading, and my responses to these questions. I hope these will help you construct a clearer mental model of this kind of teaching.

How Whole-Class Instructional Reading Helps You Differentiate

- It matches each student with a book at his or her instructional level.
- It allows you to hold one-on-one conferences to provide strategic and text structure support.

Ten Frequently Asked Questions About Differentiated Whole-Class Instructional Reading

1. **What's the first thing I should do?**

   The first step in making this kind of whole-class instructional reading work is to organize your teaching around a theme or topic rather than one book. Add the layer of an issue to the genre, theme, or topic and discussion is enhanced. For example, if students are studying realistic fiction, they may discuss the issue of what causes smooth and rocky relationships among family members. For the theme of survival, students might consider how people survive abusive relationships or survive alone in harsh climates. Having students read different books means that students will bring a variety of ideas and perspectives to their discussions. Besides, using multiple texts enables students to advertise favorites to one another.

2. **How do I find so many books?**

    You can check out books from your school library, public library, class library, and reading resource room if your school has one. Keep instructional books in your classroom, as this kind of reading should be done with your guidance and support. Moreover, you won't lose track of books if they stay at school. For more suggestions on gathering books, see pages 176–179 in Chapter 6.

3. **What kinds of conferences do you complete?**

    During differentiated whole-class instructional reading, I may confer with students about a reading strategy we're working on (see page 128), or I may ask them to discuss specific aspects of the structure of fiction or nonfiction. However, for students who read far below grade level before conferring about a strategy and a text structure, I may confer to monitor comprehension by asking them to retell part of a text. I may also ask students to show me how they use context clues to figure out a tough word or ask them to connect issues and themes to their texts. Those students who can work independently complete partner conferences and turn in completed forms.

4. **How do you keep conferences to five or fewer minutes?**

    The key is to focus the conference on a single topic. For example, you might confer about a student's strategy application. I might ask a student to give me one example of how an issue connects to their book. The forms I developed, on pages 123–124, will help you narrow your topic. If time is still a problem, then I suggest that you purchase a kitchen timer and set it for five minutes. You can also place your conference corner opposite your classroom clock so it is easier to keep track of time.

5. **How do I assess and grade students?**

    You can assess by grading students' journal entries and essays and by giving tests that invite students to focus on text structure and issues in their books. For example, to assess comprehension of realistic fiction, I may ask students to complete journal entries that discuss drawing conclusions about characters' personalities, or what caused change from the beginning to the end of the book, or the protagonist and his or her problems, or antagonistic forces, or the kinds of relationships that seemed real, and why. Short conferences enable me to assess individuals on their knowledge of a genre and on their ability to discuss and apply a reading strategy and connect their book to an issue. Conferences help me decide on the scaffolds each student needs to improve his or her reading skill and stamina. Other assessments I use are tiered activities that students and I develop. Students may choose from a small menu of tiered activities, and I find that most of the time they select projects that they can successfully complete. (See pages 129–137 for more on tiered activities.)

6. **When you use multiple texts, do you need to have read every book?**
   The answer is no! A few teachers, those who read a steady diet of children's trade books, may have read all or most of the books for a unit of study. When you have time, or during your free periods, you can try to skim several books before a unit starts, but don't be discouraged if this is not possible.

   You'll know whether a student has or hasn't read a book by the amount of specific details in his or her response to questions. For example, you should probe further when you get a general response such as this: "The main character is the detective, and she's really smart. She solves the whole mystery." Invite the student to name the character, give examples of why this character is smart, and explain how she solves the mystery. If the student can't do this, then perhaps either the book is too difficult or the child might not have read it. I usually ask, in as kind and as gentle a voice as possible, "Why is it tough for you to remember details?" Avoid being confrontational. If the book was too difficult, provide the student with two to three choices that you believe he or she can read.

7. **What do you do when you discover that a student hasn't completed his or her reading?**
   Finding that a student has not read his or her book should be handled with care. Our goal as teachers is to help students develop a passion for reading. Zach, a student in my eighth-grade class, arrived in class with a dislike for reading. On the first day of class, he told me that he did not do any of the required summer reading. "Will you call my mom?" he asked.

Differentiating Reading Instruction

"Absolutely not," I replied. "We'll work this out together." My reason for not contacting Zach's parents was to build trust and give this middle schooler the opportunity to solve his problem. At several lunch meetings, I asked Zach, "Why do you dislike reading?" Zach moved from shrugging his shoulders and saying, "Dunno," to telling me, "I never found a book I could and wanted to read." Now I had a place to start, but it still wasn't a simple task for me. First, I found Zach's comfort reading level, for I wanted him to read a book that was easy. Next, we discussed his interests; I discovered that Zach loved horror movies and sports. With this information, we were able to tailor his first forays into reading with Goosebumps books by R. L. Stine and sports books by Matt Christopher. By the end of November, Zach had dipped into comics and had read Jeff Smith's graphic novel *Bone: Out From Boneville* (Scholastic, 2005). Before the end of the first trimester, Zach asked me if he had to make up his summer reading. "You already have," I said. I decided to let the summer reading go because Zach had begun to enjoy reading.

8. **Does every student read the same number of instructional books?**

No. Use your good judgment when working with students on this issue so you can differentiate. Your stronger readers might choose longer books—say 500 to 600 pages—which will limit the number of books they can complete in a four-week unit. Struggling readers usually read shorter texts, and they may complete several books during a unit of study.

I suggest that you negotiate with your class the minimal number of books students complete during the study. At the beginning of a unit, I always prepare a handout for students that contains due dates for reading and for any writing that grows out of the reading (see page 109). Students tape a copy of the handout into their response journals, and I post a copy on a bulletin board.

Use these guidelines to jot reminders, on the chalkboard, of upcoming due dates and to help students learn to budget class and at-home time so they meet work deadlines. Scaffold the process and support students by breaking a long-term assignment into parts, giving each part a separate due date. For example, if all students have to create a Readers Theater script based on a section of their book, then break up the task and set due dates for each numbered part: (1) choose the section in your book and list the characters you'll include, (2) write a first draft, (3) revise your draft, (4) ask classmates to help you practice and perform your Readers Theater. Explain to students that turning parts of an assignment in on time means you will read it and suggest ways to revise. You can also identify those students who need more than a note with suggestions and offer them help during short conferences. Developing time-management skills takes practice and teacher guidance. Moreover, meeting deadlines has as much to do with students' success and progress as the amount of support you can offer them as they work toward completing long-term projects.

Review these assignment dates several times a week to help students pace themselves and retain the due dates. Include dates in your daily homework assignment. I find that although these dates and guidelines are important to me, they are not crucial to my students. Continual reminders can help students learn to manage time and complete their work. Not revisiting guidelines and due dates can derail the momentum of the study because you'll find that several students will have forgotten the dates and not completed work on time.

9. **What kinds of activities do you create for a class of students who read different books?**
You'll want to create Big Picture Plans for your unit of study for whole-class instructional reading (see pages 54–55). These plans should be so detailed that they become your teaching map for the length of the unit. The plan should list your decisions: the choice of reading and vocabulary strategies for modeling and student practice, the selection of read alouds, a variety of instructional texts from which students may choose, the kinds of journal entries students will complete, issues for discussions, the amount of instructional and independent reading required, and tiered projects that meet the varied reading and writing levels in your class, such as puppet plays, interviews, posters, and creating and performing original Readers Theater scripts (see pages 165–166).

10. **Do teachers organize groups of students to discuss instructional books?**
Absolutely! When students are halfway through, and then again when they are finished with their instructional books, I like to take some of the week's class time to meet with small groups for a 10- to 15-minute discussion. (One or two of these daily discussions won't consume too much class time.) During these discussions, you can ask group members to converse about an open-ended genre question (see page 108 and appendix

pages 275–280), or you can ask them to connect their book to the issue you've been discussing. Holding these conferences reinforces the social aspects of reading and moves interactions beyond you and the student to the group sharing their thoughts and ideas.

Now that I've responded to some common queries teachers have about differentiated whole-class instructional reading, let me walk you through a unit of study for biography. I hope that reading and reflecting on the elements of a unit of study will enable you to adapt what I do to meet your students' needs.

Planning a Biography Unit for Differentiated Whole-Class Instructional Reading

I begin planning for any unit of study by doing these three things. First, I choose appropriate read-aloud texts—the common teaching texts that will reach all students (see Chapter 3). Second, students and I develop open-ended discussion prompts that will work with any book students may be reading. Third, I decide on student assignments and due dates and create a guideline sheet for students so they understand their unit requirements. In addition, I develop weekly plans to make sure that I'm modeling reading strategies, conferring, and allowing enough time for students to complete their work. I've included examples of the different kinds of conferences I use to assess and monitor students' reading progress.

Read-Aloud Texts for a Biography Unit

I have found a series of picture books and short texts by Kathleen Krull that work well for modeling how to apply a strategy, showing how a journal entry works, and exploring the genre of biography, as well as some of the features of nonfiction. These books are readable, short, and accessible to adolescents. All are published by Harcourt.

- *Lives of the Athletes* (1997)
- *Lives of the Presidents* (1998)
- *Lives of the Writers* (1994)
- *Lives of Extraordinary Women* (2000)
- *Lives of the Artists* (1995)
- *Lives of the Musicians* (1993)
- *Wilma Unlimited: How Wilma Rudolph Became the World's Fastest Woman* (2000)

PROMPTS AND QUESTIONS FOR DISCUSSING ANY BIOGRAPHY

Sets of open-ended questions like these enable you to have each student read a biography at his or her instructional level, yet discuss key points about the genre of biography with you, a partner, a small group, or as a class. Always have students use specific details from their book to support their responses to these questions.

Biography Questions

- Discuss two to three important accomplishments this person made. Explain why you believe each one is important.
- Do you feel the person's accomplishments were positive or negative? Explain.
- Did others who lived during this time period view this person's accomplishments in a different way from the author's point of view? From your point of view? Explain.
- Can you find details that show the time period in which this person lived? What did you learn about this historical time period?
- Can you find two to three obstacles this person had to overcome? Explain how he or she overcame each one.
- What persons and/or events influenced the person's life? Explain how each person or event affected decisions, education, and/or courses of action.
- Did education change this person? Explain how.
- Can you connect with any of the relationships that this person had with family members or friends? Explain the connections.
- What do you most admire/not admire about this person's contributions? About his or her personality? Explain.
- Are this person's accomplishments still affecting people's lives today?
- What personal connections did you make between your life and the person's life?

> **MANAGEMENT TIP**
>
> You may want to write the questions from the list on large chart paper and ask students to choose one or two to discuss and/or write about in their journals. I like to write each question on a small index card and create several decks of these question cards that I can reuse. I give each group a deck and have the group members choose one or two questions. Or you may want to select questions for individuals or groups to discuss and write about.

- What failures did this person experience? How did he or she overcome these?
- What flaws and weaknesses in this person's character did you notice? Did these change? Explain how.

GUIDELINES FOR STUDENTS

Figure 4.1 shows a handout I created for my sixth-grade class. It's important to note that I don't ask students to do more work on extra books they read. I don't want them to feel as though I'm punishing them for reading additional books or magazines. I always encourage reading beyond the minimum. I find that students can read more than the minimum as long as there's plenty of time in class to read, and your basic homework is reading 25–30 minutes a night.

Note that I also adjust expectations and assignments for those students who struggle with writing about reading, and I use separate criteria for evaluating their work. During silent reading, I confer with those students who need extra support for journal work

---

Student Guidelines: Biography Unit of Study

Time: 7 weeks

Negotiated required reading: Complete two biographies at your instructional level. In your reading log, list any extra, easy-to-read books and magazines that you have read in your reading log; there will be no extra work for these.

Independent reading: Read one biography at your comfort level. After that, you have free choice for independent reading. Make sure you list what you've read in your book log.

Due date for first book: Complete half your book by January 17; complete the entire book by February 1. There will be 20 to 25 minutes for sustained silent reading of your instructional biographies each time our class meets.

Project for first book: Complete one to two journal responses (see Mrs. Robb to negotiate the number). Choose from (1) draw conclusions about a person's personality traits, and (2) describe changes in the person's personality and/or values from the beginning of the book to the end. You may use drawings and words to complete your journal work. Refer to my read-aloud text samples on chart paper that the class collaborated on.

Teacher-led book discussions: We will have two discussions: one halfway through the book, and one at the end. Work with your reading partner and use your book to explain these structural elements: the protagonist and two key problems; two antagonistic forces and how each one worked against the protagonist. Next, in your journal, jot down notes on these structural elements before sharing in a group discussion. To support your thinking, use the chart on structural elements that we created as a class.

Due date for second book: Complete half your book by February 18; complete the entire book by March 10.

Project for second book: Oral Book Talk (see guidelines)

Figure 4.1: Here are the guidelines I prepared for a sixth-grade biography unit.

and organizing their book talks. Again, remember to use your read-aloud text to model how you plan and complete journal entries, and plan and present an oral book talk.

Once I've posted the open-ended genre questions on chart paper, and before I pass out the guideline sheet to students, I take some class time to organize reading partners for the unit of study. Partners change from unit to unit, and I pair students who can support each other; therefore, partners are at or near the same instructional reading levels. *I* am the partner for struggling students, those who read three or more years below grade level. My goal is to scaffold certain tasks, like explaining the structural elements of biography, so that these students can experience success, absorb the information, and gradually become independent.

This is the ideal time to review terms such as *instructional reading level* and *comfort reading level* with students. Make sure you point out that instructional reading stretches students' thinking and challenges them, whereas comfort reading is for independent

Guidelines for Oral Book Talk

Time: 2–3 minutes; prepare notes on an index card; rehearse at home so you can speak slowly and comfortably and make eye contact with your audience.
Topic: "People Do Change"
You'll need to bring your book to class for this activity.

- State the title and the author.
- Reflect on the person's personality and think about how he or she changed from the beginning to the end of the book.
- Describe what the character was like at the beginning. Read a short passage from the beginning of the book that reveals his or her personality.
- Explain how and why the person changed. Was the change in personality traits? In values? Read a short passage from the end of the book that shows the change.
- End your presentation by recommending or not recommending this book. Give specific reasons, using the help sheet (see appendix pages 278–280).

Teacher-student conferences: For your first or second book, you will confer with Mrs. Robb about a reading strategy we're practicing (see conference form on pages 123–124). You will receive the conference form beforehand so you know the kinds of questions we'll discuss.

practice and should be easy, enjoyable, and interesting. During independent reading, students apply what they have learned during instructional reading to build stamina, vocabulary, and fluency (Anderson, Wilson & Fielding, 1988; Guthrie, Wigfield, Metsala, & Cox, 1999).

THE SCHEDULING BASICS OF A WEEK-BY-WEEK PLAN

To make the process of thinking through this entire unit visible, I've included my schedule of teaching and learning experiences and activities for each week. You'll need to adapt this schedule to your teaching situation and needs. It's fine to add activities if you have time, or to replace learning experiences with those that suit your students.

Make sure you set aside 20 to 30 minutes a day for instructional reading. Whether you have 45- or 90-minute classes, it's important to provide students with a large block of time to read in class. Remember, this is the part of your instruction that can improve students' reading and analytical thinking skills. During the period of instructional or independent reading, you can confer individually with four to six students a day, or you can use this time to work with an individual, pair, or small group on applying a strategy to the reading. I schedule instructional reading three times a week, and independent reading twice a week. This shows students how much I value both kinds of reading.

Week One

- Have students choose an instructional reading book and one independent reading book. Try to offer each student several books to choose from. What I like to do is spread books out on the floor or on tables in three groups: easier, grade level, and above grade level. Then I invite groups to choose their books.

   During this selection process, support readers who read two or more years below grade level as well as reluctant readers, who read on grade level but dislike and avoid reading. Be available to ensure that they choose books that interest them, and ones they can read. If you observe a student pick up a book up without looking at the front and back covers, suggest one or two books that he or she might enjoy. Ask all students to double-check their book choices by reading two to three pages; they should understand 90 percent of the words and be able to retell the section. Make sure that you monitor this process with students reading below grade level. Pair up the rest of the class so students can help each other find the appropriate book.

- Read aloud and think aloud about structure or about how to apply a reading strategy.
- Have students read their instructional book for 25 to 30 minutes, three times a week, and their independent reading twice a week.
- For homework, assign students' first independent reading book—their choice of a biography at their comfort level. Give a due date; you can aim for the end of the third week.

Week Two

- Read aloud and think aloud about structure, or model how to apply a reading strategy.
- Use a read aloud and think aloud to model how to write a journal entry for "Draw Conclusions About a Person's Personality Traits." I use *Wilma Unlimited* by Kathleen Krull. You'll find a sample journal entry reproducible on page 281 in the appendix.
- Have students read their instructional book for 25 to 30 minutes, three times a week, and their independent reading twice a week.
- While others read, confer individually with five to six students on their instructional books. Choose from conference forms on pages 123, 124, and 128.
- For homework, assign students' independent reading book. Remind them of the due date (the end of the third week).

Week Three

- Read aloud and think aloud about structure, or model how to apply a reading strategy.
- Ask students to use a read aloud to collaboratively compose a journal entry for "Draw Conclusions About a Person's Personality Traits." Record the entry on large chart paper so it becomes a resource and model.
- Have students read their instructional book for 25 to 30 minutes, three times a week, and their independent reading twice a week.
- While others read, confer individually with five or six students on their instructional books. Choose from conference forms on pages 123, 124, and 128.
- For homework, assign students' independent reading book and announce the due date.

Week Four

- Read aloud and think aloud about structure or about how to apply a reading strategy.
- Have students present their oral book talks over two days.
- Have students read their instructional book for 25 to 30 minutes, three times a week, and their independent reading book twice a week.
- As others read, confer individually with five to six students on their instructional books. Choose from conference forms on pages 123, 124, and 128.
- At the start of the week, ask students to complete their first journal entry, "Draw Conclusions About a Person's Personality Traits," using their first instructional biography. As a resource for students, display the collaborative journal entry you wrote as a class.
- Have students choose a second independent reading book, and remind them that it's due at the start of week seven. Some students will read more than two books. You can't evaluate all of them. Have students write all completed books in their book log (see appendix page 265).
- Ask students to continue reading their independent reading book at home.

Week Five

- Read aloud and think aloud about structure or about how to apply a reading strategy.
- Have students read their instructional book for 25 to 30 minutes, three times a week, and their independent reading book twice a week.
- As others read, confer individually with five to six students on their instructional books. Choose from conference forms on pages 123, 124, and 128.
- Introduce the second journal entry, "Changes in the Person's Personality and/or Values From Beginning to the End." Do this in a think aloud based on one of the short read-aloud texts you've completed.
- Ask students to continue reading their independent reading book at home.

Week Six

- Read aloud and think aloud about structure or about how to apply a reading strategy.
- Using a completed read-aloud text, collaborate with students to compose the second journal entry, "Changes in the Person's Personality."

- Have students read their instructional book for 25 to 30 minutes, three times a week, and their independent reading book twice a week.
- Hold teacher- or student-led small-group discussions using the prompts on pages 182–183.
- While others read, confer individually with five to six students on their instructional books. Choose from conference forms on pages 123, 124, and 128.
- Ask students to complete their independent reading book at home.

Week Seven

- Read aloud and think aloud about structure or about how to apply a reading strategy.
- Have students complete their instructional reading. Those who've finished their books can do independent reading.
- Tell students at the start of the week that they will need to complete their second journal entry, "Changes in the Person's Personality," by the end of the week, using their second instructional-level biography.
- Use two days for a second round of oral book talks. As an alternative, students can present a dramatic monologue, a Readers Theater, or an illustrated timeline of a person's life.
- Hold teacher- or student-led small-group discussions, using the prompts on page 108.
- Complete conferences on instructional books.
- Tie instructional books together by asking students, *What kinds of personality traits do people have who make significant changes that affect our lives?* Write students' responses on chart paper and discuss.

In the next section you'll read about using conferences as assessments for differentiated whole-class instructional reading. These one-on-one meetings enable you to understand each student's strengths as well as any needs that require scaffolding.

> ### Conferring Supports Interventions
>
> As you confer with individuals, you'll observe that some students need extra support with either skimming to gather details, drawing conclusions about a person, or creating a timeline. Hold frequent, 5- to 7-minute meetings with these students while the rest of the class reads or writes. Sitting side by side, model the strategy and then gradually release responsibility by turning the process over to them.

Conferences: The Backbone of Assessment and Differentiation

In a five-minute one-on-one conference, you can learn more about a student than in either a 20-minute meeting with a group of six or seven students, or a whole-class lesson. One-on-one conferences offer opportunities to observe students' body language, to prompt students with questions that elicit why they may have abandoned a book, or to show you how a strategy supported students' comprehension and helped them to build new understandings. With the information you gather from conferences, you can differentiate instruction by adjusting students' instructional reading levels and the kinds of assignments they will complete. Equally important, a conference can spotlight the scaffolds a student may require and can offer you opportunities to provide the extra teaching needed for a student to move forward with reading comprehension.

Recently, I had four eighth graders reading at a beginning fourth-grade level. My conferences with these students focused on evaluating their retellings of text. Once retellings were rich, I conferred with them on applying a strategy or connecting an issue to the text. My point is to take the time to get to know each student's strengths and needs, not only to have them reading at their instructional level, but also to refine and offer assessments that can help them progress. That's what differentiation is about—not one-size-fits-all, but matching the work to the student.

In this section, you'll explore and reflect on conference forms that evaluate students' retellings and their use of strategies and that focus on discussing fiction and nonfiction texts.

ASSESS THROUGH RETELLINGS

By the middle grades, students who have difficulty retelling benefit from additional practice and explicit modeling by the teacher. When retelling becomes a challenge for students, it's usually because the book is too difficult for them to read or they lack background knowledge on the topic, impeding their ability to make connections. Or perhaps they're being asked to retell too much. Once your students know the guidelines and your expectations, their retellings will improve with practice—as long as they can read and understand the text.

In the primary grades, retelling is a measure of not only comprehension and recall but also correct book placement. Retelling shows teachers that students have retained and understood the information or narrative thread of a text. This is important; without memory of what happened or of the information learned, students can't engage in productive discussions and use facts to think. My feeling is that by fourth grade, the retelling of one or two pages of a text can assist teachers as they place students in instructional texts. Students can also use retellings of paragraphs or a page of text to self-monitor their recall and comprehension and decide whether to reread or move on to the next paragraph.

Once students show you that they can complete rich retellings, introduce them to summarizing. Summarizing is a selective process in which students choose a few key details and organize them into a short paragraph. (See appendix page 282 for guidelines on summarizing narrative and informational texts.) However, for students in grades four and up who read far below grade level, it is best to assess them through retelling.

Take the Time to Teach Students How to Retell

Asking students to retell without a set of guidelines can make the task daunting and mysterious. The importance of teaching and modeling the retelling process became very clear to me after I observed a sixth grader struggling to retell "The Party" by Pam Muñoz Ryan (see page 259–261). Providing students with a mental model and some simple suggestions can make the difference between their experiencing success or failure. What follows are some suggestions that can help you support students as they prepare to retell.

1. Tell students that the purpose of retelling is to help you know more about their recall of narrative and expository texts.
2. Model how you retell, and make your thinking visible. Use the retelling forms on pages 119 and 120 as guidelines for what to include.
3. Ask students to read and retell a text at their independent or comfort level if you're trying to help them find an independent reading book. You can also ask students to retell a page or two from a text to see if the instructional level is on target.
4. Have students retell by thinking about the elements on each form.
5. Listen carefully and praise what worked. For those students who struggle to read and

retell, you might want to record two to three retellings over a period of time so they can hear their progress.

6. Pair up students who need retelling practice and ask them to retell specific sections of texts to each other.

7. Move students who learn to retell sections of text toward summarizing an entire text. Use the reproducible on appendix page 283 to support summarizing.

Partners retell to one another.

Sample Oral Retelling Using
"The Party" by Pam Muñoz Ryan

I've included a detailed retelling here so you can see how reflecting on what didn't work can support differentiation and enable a learner to progress. A teacher I was coaching in a junior high school asked me to observe one of her ninth-grade students retell "The Party." Ninth grader, Rosa (pseudonym), was instructionally on a sixth-grade level and had enjoyed the story; she even offered her opinion about the ending, saying that the girl took the invitation because she wanted to be part of the in-group. Her teacher felt that Rosa should be able to retell one to two chapters from a book, but Rosa's retellings lacked detail, and events were not sequenced. Recently, Rosa's teacher showed a small group how she retold a chapter. Students' reactions, the teacher told me, ranged from "I got it" to Rosa's "I can't do that." Rosa's retelling that follows certainly backs up her feelings. However, we can use such a retelling to say, "Well, she'll never get it," or we can think of ways to differentiate the retelling process to meet Rosa's needs and help her progress.

ROSA'S ORAL RETELLING: The girl wants to go to a fancy party. She doesn't get invited. She's sad. At the end she gets an invitation. I think she takes it.

Scaffolds Can Differentiate the Retelling Process

Even with modeling, you will find that students, like Rosa, can struggle with retelling. When I asked Rosa to tell me why her retelling was so short, she said, "I get nervous to do it. Then I don't remember. I know the story. I just can't do it."

There are many clues in Rosa's responses; that's why it's always helpful to kindly and gently ask a student, "Why?" First, having high-anxiety levels can interfere with recall. My feeling was that Rosa focused all her mental energy on worrying and feeling that she couldn't do it rather than on working through a process. Second, I interpreted Rosa's "I can't do it" to mean I don't know how to go about doing this. Here are suggestions I made to Rosa's teacher.

- Give specific guidelines about your expectations for the retelling. For example, for fiction, you may ask a student to name the main character, his or her problem, and describe one key event. For informational text, ask a student to state the topic and two facts he or she learned about it. For a student who struggles, as Rosa does, choose only two to three specific guidelines about what you are looking for in a retelling. At this point, I felt that the guidelines on the retelling form were too overwhelming for Rosa.
- Have Rosa reread the section she needs to retell so the text is fresh in her mind.
- Have Rosa retell two or three paragraphs.

What Other Students Do While You Listen to Retellings

It's important to offer students activities to do while you confer or ask a student to retell. I stick to reading or writing activities and offer students two choices. However, if a journal entry or a chunk of reading is due that day, then that activity becomes a priority. Here are some options I offer to students.

- Read the next section in your instructional book.
- Read your independent reading book.
- Complete a journal entry.
- Work on a piece of writing from your folder.
- Quietly confer with a partner about a book.
- Quietly do an oral retelling with a partner, following the guidelines on the assessment forms on page 119 or 120.

Retelling Checklist: Narrative Texts

Title and pages of retelling _____

Directions: Jot down notes next to each section. You may want to record the retelling on an audiocassette.

Elements Noted in Student's Retelling	Teacher's Notes

☐ Used written/mental notes

☐ Identified settings (time and place)

☐ Identified the main character

☐ Described the main character's problem(s)

☐ Included plot details

☐ Mentioned other characters

☐ Made connections

☐ Speaking patterns
  • Spoke in complete sentences.
  • Told details in sequence.

☐ Goal for next retelling

Additional notes and comments:

Retelling Checklist: Informational Texts

Title and pages of retelling _____

Directions: Jot down notes next to each section. You may want to record the retelling on an audiocassette.

Elements Noted in Student's Retelling	Teacher's Notes

☐ Used written/mental notes:

☐ Stated the topic:

☐ Provided rich facts:

☐ Stated the main idea:

☐ Made connections to self, other topics, issues:

☐ Synthesized information by using own words:

☐ Speaking patterns:
  • Spoke in complete sentences.
  • Told details in sequence.

☐ Goal for next retelling:

Additional notes and comments:

Differentiating Reading Instruction © 2008 by Laura Robb, Scholastic Professional

- Have Rosa jot down some notes before she retells.
- Keep Rosa on short texts until she experiences many successes, and then increase the amount of text for retelling.

Struggling students, and even some solid readers, can have difficulty with retelling large amounts of text. That is a tough task as students have to mentally organize details, retain them, and then retell. Always make sure that you give students guidelines that will enable them to choose the details needed for their retellings. This makes the process reasonable and provides students with the success they need to progress.

Use the suggestions in the sidebar on page 118 to help other students remain busy as you work with individuals on retelling. You will be working on retelling with only those few students who need this practice before moving on to summarizing.

ASSESS WITH BOOK CONFERENCES

During book conferences, I focus on the instructional nonfiction and fiction texts that students are reading. Conferences include discussing narrative elements and the features of informational texts. As you confer, you can ask students to make personal and world connections and to consider whether the information they read changed their thinking. The focus here is the structure of texts, assessing students' ability to use details they recall to infer, make connections, and analyze texts. Try to hold one to two book conferences during each unit of study. In a short three- to four-week unit of study, one conference with each student may be all you can manage.

These five- to six-minute book conferences are an important part of differentiating instruction and are also important assessment tools. I find that I can meet with a student at a separate table, sit next to him or her on a rug and chat, or pull up a chair and work side-by-side. During these book conferences, my goal is not only

Robb confers with Ben about his journal entries.

to determine whether a student has gained knowledge of a genre and its structure but also to see if he or she is able to connect text events to an issue. I find that I can complete three to five conferences during a 25- to 30- minute silent instructional or independent reading block. These conferences let me know whether students need extra help with understanding why characters change or with connecting information to an issue. This is the core of differentiation: discovering students' needs and providing the scaffolds that develop both understanding and the ability to analyze texts.

Follow-up Conference with Laura

March 29, 2006

Book: *Sideways Stories From Wayside School* by Louis Sachar

Topic: Help Laura move from retelling to selecting details that show why Laura felt the book was funny and why some details surprised her.

Points Discussed with Laura using her retelling.

• Her retelling halfway through the book showed fine recall of details.

Laura explained that she likes retelling and feels good doing it.

• I modeled how to pull out or choose details from the retelling to show how these can use these details to show that they surprised her and use other details to show that these made her laugh.

After I modeled, Laura said: "Mrs. Jewels surprised me because she's different from teachers I have. Mrs. Jewels gets mad if a students doesn't tell a joke they know to the class. She also thought it was okay and good to sleep in class. That even made me laugh."

• I reread what Laura said and showed her where these details were in her retelling and how she had showed me she could choose the details that matched either funny or surprised.

• Next, I asked Laura to find two more details for "funny" and surprised." She was able to do this and I told Laura that she had the details to write her paragraph.

• How will you organize your writing. Laura thought for a while. Then she said that she would do funny first and then write about surprised.

• We talked about paragraphing and Laura said that she would separate funny and surprised into 2 different paragraphs.

Additional Comments: I will work with Laura on her next write-about-reading assignment to help her select the details that go with the ideas she wants to show about the book. My goal is to show laura how thinking about the ideas and points she wants to make. then planning by jotting down notes, can help her move away from retelling.

FIGURE 4.2: The write-up of the notes I took when conferring with Laura.

Some Suggestions for Making Book Conferences Work

To keep a book conference focused, decide on the one topic you will cover and stick to your prepared questions. I find that when conferences cover more than one key topic, students experience anxiety, confusion, and eventually stop listening. Jason, a fourth grader, explained this point well: "If I have to put in my head too many things to do, I

Differentiating Reading Instruction

Student's Name _____ Date _____

Reading Conference: Fiction

Jot down notes based on the conversation between you and your student. Focus your conference, choosing from the questions and prompts below so that it's no longer than five minutes.

Title and Author _____

What drew you to this book?

What kind of fiction is this? Give me two to three examples that helped you figure this out.

Name the protagonist and one key problem he or she faced. Describe how the protagonist dealt with this problem.

What personality traits did you observe for the protagonist? Another character? Explain.

Did you connect to a character, event, or problem in the story? Did the book remind you of a movie? Another book? An issue or problem in your life? Pick one or two of these connections and explain.

Describe a significant or major change in the protagonist from the beginning to the end of the story. Then explain what caused the change and why it occurred. Was it because of a character? A conflict? An event? Inner thoughts and emotions? Having to deal with problems?

What issues is your book concerned with?

Additional comments:

Student's Name _____ Date _____

Reading Conference: Nonfiction

Jot down notes based on the conversation between you and your student. Focus your conference, choosing from the questions and prompts below so that it's no longer than five minutes.

Title and Author _____

What about this topic interests or fascinates you?

List two or three fascinating pieces of information, or two or three interesting ideas you learned.

Did the book change the way you think? If so, explain how.

Explain how this information could help or change people's lives.

Would you look for another book by this author? Another book on this topic? Explain why or why not.

Does this book deal with issues you feel are significant? Explain.

get tired, so I just stop listening." What follows are a few tips that can help you facilitate effective and productive conferences about students' reading.

- Decide which questions on the conference form you'll ask. You can also pose questions that aren't on the form. Two or three questions are adequate.
- Tell students you're going to take notes so both of you can recall what's been discussed.
- Keep reminding students to provide specific story examples to support answers. Details let you know how much students recall and whether they've read the text.

I've included a completed form with comments for each book conference reproducible. These completed forms show you students' responses to each type of conference. You use these to guide your conferences.

Comments: Great comprehension. Excellent support.

Reading Conference: Fiction
Melissa F.   March 8, 2006
The Chocolate War by Robert Cormier

Questions to discuss:
What issues is your book concerned with?

Notes based on Melissa's response:

- Human rights is a huge issue here. Brother Eugene has a nervous breakdown when Archie has new recruits unscrew the desks & chairs just to the point they'll collapse.

- Jerry doesn't have the choice to not sell the chocolates after his assignment ends. At the end he's beaten close to death in a boxing match with Emile Janya. That's a violation of basic human right to make responsible choices.

- Brother Leon abuses students – he humiliates abt. grades and the chocolate sale.

- The adults have abandoned the students – not all – but definitely Brother Leon. Brother Jacques – I'm not sure what this issue is – abuse & power & control maybe.

FIGURE 4.3A: Melissa, an eighth grader, points out issues in *The Chocolate War*.

Comments: David did a good job, especially when he reread to collect details.

Reading Conference: Nonfiction - Biography
David M.   Sept. 22, 2006
Five Brilliant Scientists by Linda Jones

Questions to discuss:

Name the protagonist and one key problem he or she faced. How did the protagonist deal with this problem.

"David chose the short biography-"George Washington Carver" to answer this question.

Notes based on what David said:
- He was smart and wanted to go to school. That's the problem.
- He went to high school..
- Studied plants and farming in Iowa.

Robt: Why was going to school a problem? I have a used Skim page 16.
David: He was African American – most schools wouldn't take him. Carver had to find schools that would let former slaves come to classes.
Carver studied & experimented with plants. He worked hard & other families let him stay with them. He invented products made from peanuts.

FIGURE 4.3B: David, a fifth grader, practices discussing the problem Carver faced.

ASSESS WITH STRATEGY CONFERENCES

A strategy conference enables you to gain insight into whether a student can explain how a strategy works and whether he or she can apply a reading or vocabulary-building strategy to an instructional text. In five to seven minutes, you can discern what your students understand about the strategies you're focusing on during a unit of study. I suggest that you meet with each student halfway through a unit to evaluate their application of a strategy. Those who "get it" can continue reading. Now you can differentiate by organizing those students who need your support into small groups to reteach them the strategy. With a student who needs even more support, work one-on-one, showing how you apply the strategy to his or her book. Then ask the student to practice in front of you until he or she can show you understanding of the strategy.

Figure 4.4 illustrates the needs of a fourth grader who has difficulty supporting his predictions. Under "Additional Notes," I've included instructional scaffolds to support her. If you're like me, jotting down your thoughts enables you to quickly know your status with a student. This saves you from rummaging through your memory to recall what you did yesterday—especially if you are supporting four to seven students.

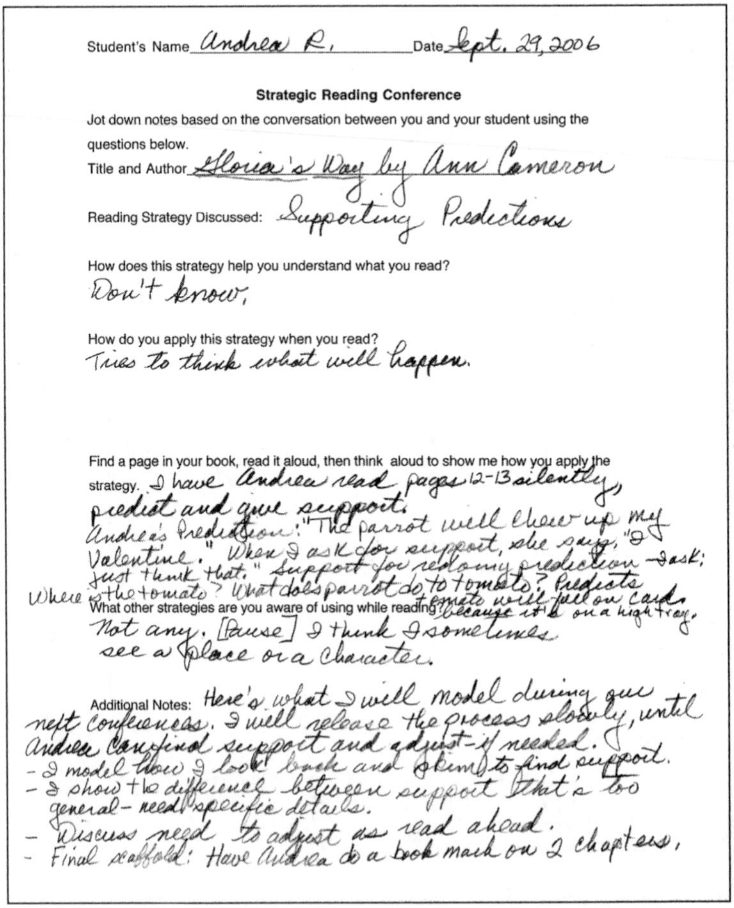

Student's Name _Andrea R._ Date _Sept. 29, 2006_

Strategic Reading Conference

Jot down notes based on the conversation between you and your student using the questions below.

Title and Author _Gloria's Way by Ann Cameron_

Reading Strategy Discussed: _Supporting Predictions_

How does this strategy help you understand what you read?
Don't know.

How do you apply this strategy when you read?
Tries to think what will happen.

Find a page in your book, read it aloud, then think aloud to show me how you apply the strategy. _I have Andrea read pages 12-13 silently, predict and give support. Andrea's prediction: "The parrot will chew up my Valentine." When I ask for support, she says, "I just think that." Support for reading prediction—I ask: Where's the tomato? What does parrot do to tomato? Predicts_

What other strategies are you aware of using while reading _tomato will fall on card because it's on a high tray._
Not any. [Pause] I think I sometimes see a place or a character.

Additional Notes: _Here's what I will model during our next conferences. I will release the process slowly, until Andrea can find support and adjust—if needed._
- I model how I look back and skim to find support.
- I show the difference between support that's too general—need specific details.
- Discuss need to adjust as read ahead.
- Final scaffold: Have Andrea do a book mark on 2 chapters.

FIGURE 4.4: Note the kinds of scaffolds this fourth grader tries.

Differentiating Reading Instruction

Some Suggestions for Making Strategy Conferences Work

I suggest you have one reading strategy conference with each student in your class during a unit of study. However, for students reading two or more years below grade level, you may want to meet with them several times so you can help them absorb and successfully apply a reading strategy for improved recall and comprehension. Here are some suggestions for putting students at ease and helping them develop a tool box of supportive strategies.

- Hold a reading strategy conference after you've introduced a strategy with a read aloud several times and students have had experience practicing the strategy with their instructional reading books.

- Ask students to discuss what they know and understand about the strategy before and after they apply it to a text. This gives students a chance to collect what they remember and to use this knowledge to refresh their memory and deepen their understanding.

- Make sure to let students know that as you read, you use the same strategies they do.

ASSESS STUDENTS WITH PEER BOOK CONFERENCES

Once students have experienced a book conference with you and feel comfortable with the process, move them to conferring with a partner. (See the peer conference form on page 130.) If you have an especially large class, conferring can be a source of great pressure. Turning the conference process over to students allows time for supporting those students who struggle, or for circulating around the room and listening to pairs' conversations. Furthermore,

Partners have a peer conference.

Student's Name _____ Date _____

Strategic Reading Conference

Jot down notes based on the conversation between you and your student. Use the questions below.

Title and Author _____

Reading strategy discussed:

How does this strategy help you understand what you read?

How do you apply this strategy when you read?

Find a page in your book, read it aloud, and then think aloud to show me how you apply the strategy.

What other strategies do you use while reading?

Additional notes:

while you can confer with only one student at a time, a class of partners can complete conferences and provide you with valuable data within 10 to 15 minutes. Ask partners to jot down notes that let you know the content of their discussion. Figure 4.5 shows how detailed the notes of these sixth graders are. It's clear that Josh needs support with understanding science fiction as a genre; notice how Michael's book on robots causes him to think deeply about issues these computerized creatures raise.

> Mike–Smart Robots by Mark Hamlin. Robots can do good, explore space + learn more about planets. Use them to find bombs and they can guard and patrol dangerous places. I'm concerned about replacing a real cat or dog with a robot pet or having robots do so much that we get bored like in Bradbury's "The Veldt."

FIGURE 4.5: Notes that sixth graders Michael (above) and Josh (below) wrote after their peer conference.

> Josh: Last book in Universe - Philbrick great adventure. what adventure like in Future. brain probes - scary - think abt time when there were books - this is an adventure book - lots of scary things happen on search for Bean. Meet Monkey Boys, travel the "Pipe" a go to Eden.

More Assessments That Work With Differentiated Whole-Class Instructional Reading

Besides holding one-on-one conferences with students to get inside their reading heads, there are other assessments that work well when every student in your class reads a different book. In addition to journal work, you can ask students to complete book talks and bookmarks, create art and Web site projects, and present dramatic monologues. I like to offer students the choice between book talks and dramatic monologues because students value choice. I find that the majority of my students choose what they can do well. Moreover, making positive choices develops students' self-esteem, confidence, self-efficacy, and responsibility (Guthrie & Wigfield, 2000). Most students make productive choices. If a student selects a project that's too difficult, meet with that student, discuss alternative possibilities, and gently guide him or her to choose the project that supports learning and success.

Peer Book Conference

Directions:

1. Jot down notes that reflect what you and your partner discussed. Use the prompts below to spur the discussions.

2. Give the completed form to your teacher.

Partner's Name _____

Title and Author of partner's book _____

Preparation checklist: book _____ pencil _____ form _____

- -

What genre is the book? Give two or three examples that support your answer.

Choose one of these prompts, place a checkmark next to it, discuss it, and jot down the high points of your conversation on the back of this form or on a separate sheet of paper.

☐ Retell your favorite part.

☐ Discuss the information you learned.

☐ Explain how the book changed your thinking about the topic, an issue, or an idea.

☐ Discuss an issue your book raised. Explain how your book dealt with it.

☐ Describe two settings and explain how each one was important to the story or text.

☐ Explain one key conflict and the outcome.

☐ Discuss a character or an event you connected to, and explain why.

☐ Discuss why you think the protagonist changed from the beginning of the book to the end.

☐ Explain how the information you read about can change the way we live, can save lives, can help the environment, and so on.

☐ Select a favorite illustration, photograph, or passage from the text and explain why it is your favorite.

☐ State a problem a character faced, and explain how it was resolved. If it wasn't resolved, explain why.

Differentiating Reading Instruction © 2008 by Laura Robb, Scholastic Professional

Journals. I never grade students' response-to-literature journals. The journal is their thinking and learning odyssey into a variety of texts. Marking up a journal, whether it's a student's or adult's, raises negative and often angry thoughts in the writer's heart and mind. If I want to use a specific journal entry for assessment, I do the following:

- Make sure students have practiced this type of entry and understand it.
- Tell students that the entry they complete will be graded.
- Have students complete an entry, in class, on a separate sheet of paper.
- Ask students to use notes about a book to complete a journal essay during several class periods.
- Permit students who need to draw to use illustrations and writing to complete an entry.

When I return the entry, I have students tape it into their journals so they have a complete record of their writing about independent and instructional reading and teacher read alouds. You can explore myriad ways to use journals to foster reflecting on texts and linking ideas and concepts in Chapter 7.

Book talks. These are an ideal way for students to advertise books to one another and for you to evaluate their ability to think independently with text. In Chapter 6, you can explore 12 book-talk guidelines for students. Equally important, when students lead book discussions, present plays, and summarize their groups' findings for the class, they develop skill and confidence in their ability to do presentations.

Dramatic monologues. My students give high ratings to dramatic monologues because a monologue combines acting and showmanship with analytical thinking. First, I give them a guideline sheet to follow as I present a dramatic monologue based on a recent read aloud (see page 132). I prepare notes and then use these to present the monologue. I'm careful to model everything I want students to do.

Students and I discuss my presentation and the inferences I made from the text. Dramatic monologues ask students to get inside a character's skin and become that person—a bonding experience they can transfer to other books. Moreover, it's crucial for students to build a mental model of what a dramatic monologue is like. This gives the guidelines meaning and ensures that students can follow them to craft their own monologues.

Robb's dramatic monologue for "The Party" by Pam Muñoz Ryan

Why is it me who's always left out? The group I thought I was a part of is all talking about Bridget's party. It's the cool, in-event to be invited to. Guess what? I wasn't invited. I know Bridget and I are different. I take school seriously and want good grades. Bridget worries about how she looks. Like when we were partners on that sixth-period project. I tried to impress Bridget with my hard work and getting a high grade. Believe me, she was totally unimpressed. All she did was look at teen magazines and tell me, "You're too serious. Smile more." I know she thinks I'm a dork and wouldn't invite me. But you know, I want to be invited. I want to be included. I have feelings. I get so down when I know my friends are whispering things they don't want me to hear. I'm always thinking they're making fun of me, my hair, my clothes.

Here's the big kicker, though. At the end of the day, Becky came up to me at the school bus line and told me that maybe Bridget would invite me 'cause Barbara had turned her down. And you know, Bridget did. She held out the invitation to me just before I was going to step on the bus. My head argued, "Take it!" and "Don't take it." I really wanted to go. I didn't want to feel left

Robb's Notes for Dramatic Monologue

First Event: Narrator desperately wants to be invited to Bridget's party. Wants to be part of in-group. Doesn't get invite & blames self. Thinks her hair is stringy—narrator also thinks Bridget feels narrator is too serious about school. Explain project they worked on.

Second Event: Near bus after school. Barbara turns in her invite to Bridget. Narrator hopes she gets it. Bridget offers invite to narrator. Show back & forth in narrator's head: take it? not take it? Audience needs to decide.

Try to capture narrator's anxiety & feelings of being an outsider.

FIGURE 4.6: Notes I used to write my monologue.

out again. I wanted a chance to show that I was fun to be around. But did I want to be Bridget's afterthought? Did I want to be invited just because someone else turned the invite down? What do you think I told Bridget?

Eighth-graders' observations

Here's what eighth graders said when I asked this question, *What did you notice about my monologue?*

- "You stayed true to the story—you didn't say what she [the narrator] decided."
- "You had your feelings and thoughts in it. Like when you said you didn't like feeling on the outside, and you said that Bridget was 'unimpressed.'"
- "It pretty much followed your notes."
- "You tried to make us hear her [the narrator's] voice speaking when you said things like: 'Here's the kicker' and 'My head argued. . . .'"

I've included the monologue plan by Hattie Schiavone, an eighth grader. Hattie's plan contains enough details to show me that she can craft a fine monologue. If a stu-dent's plan reveals the need for detailed additions, the planning stage is the place to support that child. You can work with him or her or you can pair the student up with a classmate who can scaffold the planning stage.

It is important that students considering presenting a dramatic monologue receive a guideline sheet, like the one on page 134, to be clear about my expectations.

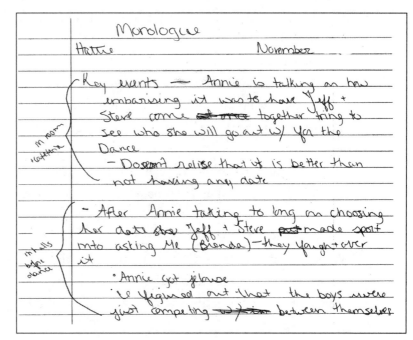

FIGURE 4.7: Hattie's plan for her monologue.

Student Guidelines for Planning and Presenting a Dramatic Monologue

A dramatic monologue is a presentation in the first person. You choose either a character from a novel or a person from a biography and then become that person. You'll present part of that character's or person's life, sharing his or her inner thoughts and emotions in an interesting and dramatic manner.

Preparing to Take Notes

- Choose a character from the book you've just completed.
- Select two key events in that person's life.
- Think about these events as if you are that person living through these events.
- Use the personal pronoun *I* when talking.
- Make inferences about these events and the people involved.

Now Take Notes

- Use a 4-by-6-inch index card—both sides, if needed, or use notebook paper.
- Put your name and the date at the top of the index card. Next, write the title and the author of your book.
- Use these headings:
  - First Event: include setting, the event, and interactions with others
  - Second Event: include setting, the event, and interactions with others
- Tie the events together with your personal feelings and thoughts about yourself, others, and the event.
- Hand in your notes to me so I can read them and offer feedback.
- Speak with me to sign up for time to practice your monologue with a partner at school.
- Practice your monologue at home.

Present Your Monologue

- Write the title and the author of your book on the chalkboard.
- When you speak, make sure your tone is conversational.
- Vary your expression so it matches the feelings and thoughts of the character or person you are portraying.
- Make eye contact with your audience.

Differentiating Reading Instruction © 2008 by Laura Robb, Scholastic Professional

Design a poster. Advertise an author and his or her book, or books. Include bulleted reasons for why this book is a terrific read.

Make a movie. Tape 8 ½-by-11-inch unlined white photocopy or construction paper together to create a movie based on part of a book. Each piece of paper represents a separate frame. Write captions under each frame. Illustrate a poem or scene from a book.

Make a labeled diagram. From an informational text, draw and label a diagram and use it to make a presentation to a group or to the class.

Design an illustrated timeline. Illustrate four to six key events in a book. Showcase major and/or minor characters or focus on several important settings.

Make a cartoon. Turn a scene from a book into a cartoon.

Create a Web site for a character or person.

- Create a name for your Web site.
- Write a review of your book. Include the title and the author. Explain why the book appealed to you. Use the questions that follow to help you review the book.

Great Moves Monologue

Hattie Schiavone   November 7, 2006

In the eyes of Brenda:

Annie is the luckiest person I know. She has a phone and TV in her room and attracts the most popular boys in our class. They being Steve and Jeff. One day after school I went over to Annie's house. All she wanted to do was talk about her latest problem. In the cafeteria when she was getting her food; Jeff and Steve dashed up to her and asked her simultaneously to the up coming dance. Of course to her this was *so* embarrassing. She talked as if I knew exactly how she felt. But you know what, I would give anything to be like her in the looks and the boys department. I am sorry to say this on her part but I hope she doesn't have a date for the dance so we can go together like most best friends do.

So about this dance date problem of Annie's, I got involved. That was all I needed, to get it rubbed in that I don't have a date every time I have a class with Jeff or Steve. Annie was taking too long to decide on who to choose for the dance. One day the impatient, but hott, Jeff leaned over to me during our class together and asked if I was Brenda, Annie's best friend. He wanted me to use my best friend powers to get her to go with him. How far is he willing to go. Then my next class I ran into Steve. Man! Steve and Jeff must be clones of each other because he wanted me to do the same thing, use my best friend powers on Annie. I did not do what was asked of me. I didn't try to persuade her.

The next day I was at my locker packing up my backpack and Jeff and Steve came running up to me. They were almost talking gibberish. I did make out that they were asking me to the dance. Yes, me! And all of the sudden I knew how Annie felt. Heat rising to my cheeks and forehead. I didn't know what to say or do. Then I glanced away from the boys and saw her there. Annie, her face filled with jealousy. I knew she was thinking took them from her. How could she think I would do that?

Then , to both of our surprise Jeff and Steve were tangled on the floor fighting, but like young puppies play fighting. That's when it hit me that they weren't picking girls up for a relationship, they were doing it for the sport of it, for male competition between them selves. Luckily I noticed this before Annie could cry her contact lenses out. I explained it to her.

Now all is well for us. We have each other, with no boys getting in our way.

FIGURE 4.8: Hattie's monologue.

Was it suspenseful?

Did you enjoy the genre, and why?

Was the end of each chapter a page-turner? Explain.

Did the topic interest you? Why?

Did you learn new information? Explain.

Did you connect to the book? How?

- Interview peers who read the book. Ask them to tell whether they liked or disliked the book, and to give reasons. Post these critiques on your Web site.
- Post photos of you and/or peers reading and discussing the book.
- Create a message board where others can ask you questions or add comments about the book.
- Add appropriate graphics.

Design a Web site for your favorite author and his or her books.

- Create a name for your Web site.
- Post a biography about your author.
- List books by this author.
- List your favorite books by this author.
- Point out a genre this author is known for. Write whether you enjoy it, and why.
- Add appropriate graphics.
- From peers, collect book reviews for books by the author to add to the blog or Web site.
- Create a message board for peers to write how they feel about this author.

Prepare a PowerPoint presentation. Create a PowerPoint presentation that explains what you've learned about a person, why a character has changed from the beginning to the end of a book, or what information you've learned about a topic. You may also transform the time-line book talk (page 201) into a PowerPoint presentation by following these suggestions:

- Choose a character from your book.
- Choose four to five important events he or she lived through.
- Plan your timeline and have your teacher approve the plan.
- Create your timeline and include the following:
  - title and author of the book, and your name
  - the name of the character

- graphics that enhance your presentation

- a brief summary of each event (You can scan original illustrations of some events into your PowerPoint presentation or use images from the Internet. Be creative and original.)

• Present your PowerPoint presentation.

Periodically, set aside time to ask students to give you ideas for alternative assessments. There are many ways to evaluate what students have learned and what they understand. In your differentiated reading program, it's also important to tap into students' computer literacy, for this is the medium our students enjoy and know.

Sometimes you want to, or be required to, give tests or have students write essays. Here are things to keep in mind when you do so.

Tests. You can tier reading tests by providing students with a text at their independent or comfort reading level. Students can use their current independent reading book or a short text you select. Tier the actual test by adjusting the kinds and the amount of questions you ask. For example, a proficient reader might be asked to write about how and why a character changes, whereas a weaker reader might be asked to focus on using the text to explain some narrative elements. The goal of tiering is to help students progress and improve; it is not to show those who struggle that they cannot do work that their peers complete.

Essays. Many schools require that students write analytical, informative, or persuasive essays during seventh and eighth grade. Expecting students who read and write at different levels to complete the same essay means that some will succeed and others will fail. Look at the essay at right that a tenth grader had to write. This negative experience only

Written Expression *(continued)*
Grades 7–12

16. **Prompt A**

Most students have an opinion one way or the other about the requirement that physical education or gym classes must be taken in school. Write a letter to the editor of your school paper stating your position either for or against required physical education classes. Include at least 3 supporting arguments for your position. You can have as long as 15 minutes to write and can use the scratch paper for a rough draft if you wish. You will not be penalized for crossing out and rewriting, but using correct spelling and punctuation is important.

> I am For GYM its good For the body.
> I am aganst GYM becuse the FHivek
> uI Sport
> Im For both Becuse its to Fizeky
> and Bood For the body.

FIGURE 4.9: This tenth grader should be learning how to plan and craft a paragraph.

reinforced this students' feelings of inadequacy.

A commitment to differentiation and tiering should prompt teachers to ask themselves, "How can I improve this student's writing skill?" Teachers can help students like the one whose writing is shown in Figure 4.9 to generate ideas and plan a short paragraph, not a fully developed essay. Once this tenth grader can use the writing process and craft a paragraph, moving to an essay with multiple paragraphs will be doable.

Pause, Reflect, and Consider Five Questions . . .

Differentiated whole-class instructional reading makes it possible for you to meet each learner's needs. If this is a first time for you, I suggest that you design and implement a four- or six-week unit of study. Evaluate your feelings and students' progress by reflecting on these questions:

- Have you thought through your unit by creating Big Picture Plans?
- Have you included a variety of learning experiences and assessments so you can differentiate for each student?
- What kinds of adjustments and accommodations will you make for struggling students?
- Are you offering choices of books at students' instructional reading levels?
- Are you using read alouds to show how you complete a journal entry, apply reading strategies, and think about issues and genre structure?

Chapter 5

Small-Group Reading Instruction and Differentiation

Supporting All Readers With Teacher-Led Reading Groups

During my first five years of teaching, I had every student in my fifth-grade class reading the same book. I revised this teaching practice the day I overheard one student say to another: "I can't read the words . . . I don't understand it. How can I discuss the character's decision?" This student's words replayed in my mind all day and evening. What could I do for him? Were there other students who were struggling?

The next day, I circulated around the classroom and asked every student the same question about the novel I was using for reading instruction—*My Side of the Mountain* by Jean Craighead George (Puffin, 1960). "Is this book easy to read, just about right, or tough to read?" The information I gathered revealed a wide range of reading levels—a much broader range than I'd been aware of. For some students, the book was too difficult; for others, too easy. I realized that this meant I had been effectively teaching fewer than half my students! The need for me to change my teaching practices to improve the reading proficiency of all students was obvious.

And so I did away with the one-book-for-all-students approach and began to organize my students into reading groups that reflected their needs as readers. I start the year with whole-class instructional reading because it enables me to establish routines and get to know each student's reading strengths. Once I know students' strengths and needs, I organize small-reading groups.

Middle school students give high ratings to small-group work because it taps into their social nature and allows them to observe, process, and value diverse ideas and thinking. Students' self-evaluations of small-group reading instruction illustrate how important exchanging ideas is to them:

- "Working in a group let me see what others thought. I didn't feel lonely like when I worked alone."
  —tenth grader
- "I like talking and hearing what my friends think about our book."
  —sixth grader
- "Talking in a group helps me learn. I get ideas from my

Group members discuss their reading.

friends. I like to share mine [ideas]." —seventh grader

- "I feel good when someone says, yeah, that's a neat idea." —ninth grader
- "It [group discussion] helps me understand the reading better." —eighth grader

Alternating whole-class instructional workshop with small-group instruction respected the social needs of my students. Now I had two ways to differentiate reading instruction—ways that supported students' progress and also provided me with a break from the detailed planning I did for small groups.

It's important to note that group work is one of the hallmarks of the differentiated classroom (Kommer, 2006), but only when groups are flexible. The groups need to change in response to students' progress, needs, and interests (see pages 144–146).

As You Continue to Read . . .

As you continue to read this chapter, you'll find suggestions that will help you and your students move smoothly through a unit of study for small reading groups. I've structured this chapter so that you first explore information that enables you to prepare for group work: suggestions for choosing books, the ins-and-outs of flexible grouping, the establishment of routines that enable students to work independently while you meet with a group, and tips for organizing and planning lessons. With this foundation, you'll be ready to think about ways to focus and differentiate reading lessons. You'll review sample lesson plans, and you'll hear the voices of students in two teacher-led groups. In addition to mulling over some assessments that are ideal for small-group instruction, you'll also consider the importance of taking observational notes as a way of helping you make decisions about reorganizing groups. Work slowly. Find a colleague who wants to study the chapter with you, and who also feels ready to implement small-group instruction. The support you can offer each other will enable you to collaborate on selecting books and planning lessons and to

How Small-Group Instruction Helps You Differentiate

- Flexible groups allow you to support students' specific needs.
- Group discussions strengthen students' inferential thinking.

share feedback that will strengthen your efforts. To build your mental model of what small-group instruction looks like, join me in my classroom as I organize two reading groups. Even though I have a 90-minute block, I try to limit reading class to 45 minutes so that I have time for writing workshop.

A Visit to My Class During Small-Group Instruction

I've organized my class into two strategic reading groups. In the first group, students read *Nothing but the Truth* by Avi (Avon, 1993) and they work on using dialogue, events, inner thoughts, and the elements in a documentary novel to draw conclusions about the personality traits of characters. In the second group, students read *Under a War Torn Sky* by Laura Elliott (Hyperion, 2001) and they work on connecting the issue of human rights to the book and then using the issue to draw conclusions about character's personalities.

After students have completed their warm-up and I have finished a five-minute read aloud, I review the guidelines I've written on the chalkboard that specify the groups I'll meet with, plus the independent work assignments.

Nothing but the Truth Group
Rebecca, Nick, Mike, Meg,
Elle, Dylan, Spencer

Under a War Torn Sky Group
Katheryne, Riley, Jeannette, Rosalynn,
William, Hannah, David, Ben

Needs Help: Post your name if you need to see me in my time between groups.
Independent Work Choices:
- Sustained silent reading of instructional book
- Journal entry due Friday—three days to complete it
- Independent reading of free-choice text

I work with each group for 15 minutes and have set up my group area directly opposite the clock in my class. From this vantage point, I can also watch the class as I work with a group. Each group comes to the half-round table with their book, journal, and a pencil.
Nothing but the Truth **group:** First, I call for a quick and brief retelling of the pages

already read. Next, I turn to today's focus of modeling drawing conclusions about the decisions characters make. Students have observed me modeling with a read aloud, but I still take the time to model using a passage from the pages we will discuss. Then, I ask students to try to do the same with a section of their reading. Students work with a partner. If a group has an odd number of members, students work in a group of three. A discussion follows each sharing.

Check help board: Emily's name is under the "Needs Help" heading. She's having trouble using what she knows about the characters, conflicts, and relationships to state the theme of a text. I pair her with Kate, who can walk Emily through the thinking process. Josh's name is also there. He thinks he took his journal out of class yesterday by mistake and wants to check his locker.

Under a War Torn Sky **group:** Again, the group opens with a quick retelling of the main events. The focus for this group is on the issue of human rights. Students will find and share with the group examples of human rights violations in their book. First, we review what human rights are, and then move to the book. I organize the group into four pairs, and give each pair a specific section to review and present to the group. While they work, I notice that three students, sharing an oversized pillow, are chatting and giggling instead of completing independent reading. I gently remind the three to return to reading. Meanwhile, partners in the group share with each other the connections they made between story details and human rights. At our next meeting, we'll discuss the points partners made.

Wrap-up: As students hand out writing workshop folders, I tell them what I noticed. I always share two to three positives to reinforce the kind of preparation and behavior that makes group work productive. Today I point out that every student came to group prepared and that the chatting stopped as soon as I mentioned it.

Robb's observations: The reading-group period had an energy and pace that I worked hard to achieve. Before students entered the class, I had written on the chalkboard what they would be doing. I had also written in a planning notebook the focus and pages to be covered for each group (see pages 156–158 for more on planning). For me, this kind of planning is crucial because if I switch gears quickly, there's no time to mull over what I need to do with a group.

Getting Started With Small-Group Instruction

As you prepare your first unit of study for small groups, there are several things to consider and many decisions to make. You'll need to decide what book each group will read, how many groups you will have, and which students will be in each group. You'll also need to establish routines with students so they can work on their own. As you'll read throughout this section, planning is key.

MAKING BOOK SELECTIONS

The process of selecting books for reading groups is similar to the way I choose texts for differentiated whole-class instructional reading. I like to select a genre plus an issue or theme. Again, as with whole-class instructional reading, the shared genre, issue, or theme provides common discussion ground for students in all groups. This shared focus helps keep students from feeling sorted into ability groups. It also enables me to tie the unit together by having each group explain to the class what they have learned about the genre, issue, or theme. As groups offer diverse perspectives on an issue or theme, they transform the learning from a focus that uses just one book to a study of multiple perspectives that uses two or three different books.

To meet the instructional needs of the diverse groups of students we teach, I try to organize three different groups—although sometimes two is enough. I limit myself to three reading groups because I believe that trying to manage more than that in a departmentalized schedule doesn't permit enough time for meeting with groups each week. I also find that if students have enough background knowledge and motivation to read a book, they can be in a group that is reading a book slightly above their instructional level—as long as I am there to support them. As we explored in Chapter 3, your read alouds are an important way to scaffold students and support those who are stretching to a higher reading level because read alouds enlarge students' knowledge of the genre, issue, or theme.

FORMING GROUPS

Small, flexible strategic reading groups enable you to provide students with the instruction they need to become skilled readers and analytical thinkers (Fountas & Pinnell,

2001; Kucer, 2005; Robb, 2000). You may want to organize groups for different purposes, for example, to work on deepening students' knowledge of applying a specific reading strategy, to help students link an issue to the text, or to study text structure. Because students learn to use reading strategies, absorb new vocabulary, and develop their analytical thinking at different rates during the year, flexible grouping allows us to shift students to different groups as they absorb a reading strategy or show that they need additional practice applying a

Partners prepare their presentation during small-group work.

strategy. By having a flexible approach to grouping, you can continually regroup students as their needs change (Fountas & Pinnell, 2001; Hiebert, 1983; Jongsma, 1991; Opitz, 1998; Robb, 2000; Roller, 1996). For example, Ben, an eighth grader, is a slow reader who prefers shorter texts. He asks to be in the group reading Laura Elliot's *Under a War Torn Sky* (Hyperion, 2001). When I mention that the book has 284 pages, Ben starts telling me how much he knows about World War II, so despite this being a long book, he wants to read it. Ben's knowledge combined with large doses of enthusiasm for this historical period convince me to place him with this group. This decision turns out to be transforming for Ben. "I know I can read long books," he tells me after completing it. "You just have to want to real bad." It's important to listen to our students so that we let them tackle difficult books they may care about and want to read. During the same unit of study, two groups practiced cause/effect/make an inference, and the third group—the one reading *Under a War Torn Sky* practiced identifying the important ideas in the book, and they connected the issue of human rights to the story. Part of differentiating reading instruction asks you to pinpoint the strategies students will practice, and these will differ group by group. To manage these different groups, you will need to establish class routines before plunging into small-group instruction.

My Reasons for Book Choices That Differentiate

Here are summaries of the decision-making process I used for each sixth-grade group's book selection. My notes are usually just words and phrases, but I expanded them here so you can better observe my process.

Shiloh group: six students

This group's reading rate is slow; one student reads at grade level; the rest read about a year below grade level. They don't enjoy reading. They don't engage with texts and usually complete the minimum amount of independent reading. They see and feel "nothing" when they read. I think this book will spark feelings quickly because it's action packed and appeals to readers' emotions about mistreating animals. It explores what motivates people to abuse pets. I'll review the making inferences strategy with them as well as work on the strategies of making connections and visualizing. If there's enough time, we'll explore the issue of relationships between children and adults, and children and pets.

Old Yeller group: ten students

These are all solid, grade-level readers. Four students are what I'd call reluctant readers: they read and recall information, but they don't like to read during class time and at home. They don't engage with books. The strategies I'll work on with this group are visualization and posing questions. I'll also review making inferences. My hope is that these strategies will bond students to this book by giving them practice with making mental images and finding unstated meanings about events, conflicts, and characters' personalities. We'll also discuss family relationships and relationships with self and pets.

The Yearling group: five students

These students can read any text well, have great recall of details, and can think inferentially. The challenge with this book is its length. For each group discussion during the six-week unit, students will need to read many more pages than other groups.

In this book, we'll get deeply into relationships with adults, other children, and animals. Students can compare/contrast characters, discuss character decision-making and motivation, and think about how and why characters change. We'll talk about the metaphor of life as a journey or an odyssey, and discuss what Jody, the main character, learns and becomes on his journey.

ESTABLISHING ROUTINES LEADS TO SUCCESS

In Chapter 2, I discussed the importance of taking the first three or four weeks of school to establish workshop routines. You might be thinking, but my framework isn't workshop, so why do I have to do this? From my experiences coaching teachers to include small-group work as one part of differentiating reading instruction, I have found that plunging right into group work without establishing routines is the greatest cause of frustration as well as the feeling that small-group instruction doesn't work. So set aside enough time to establish routines and build students' mental model of the components of small-group instruction.

Since I always open the school year with differentiated whole-class instructional reading, my students are familiar with the routines on pages 33–39. What follows are the additional routines you need to introduce and have students practice so group work runs smoothly. I begin discussing and practicing these routines about two weeks prior to the end of a whole-class instructional reading unit of study. This ensures that students will understand their responsibilities right from the beginning.

- **Discuss changes in student choice.** I think it's best for you to make book selections for each group, for two reasons. First, budget limitations may prevent you from ordering extra titles. Second, I find that asking groups to come to a consensus on book choice is an impossible task. Help students understand that they will always have choices for both independent reading and whole-class instructional reading. When you're forthcoming with this information, students accept your decisions because they understand them.

- **Introduce the journal entries.** With your read aloud, always introduce a model of the journal entry that students will be writing and take the time to complete a collaborative entry. Post a journal entry model as a resource. Group work runs smoothly when students understand your expectations.

- **Discuss independent work times.** Be clear about the kinds of work you will ask students to complete on their own. If you want them to use a computer program, then show them how it works. The path to success with independent work is for students to have experienced the activity and to understand it well enough to work on their own.

- **Explain "Needs Help."** Assure students that in between meeting with groups, you will take a few minutes to respond to pressing questions. To avoid having students immediately look to you to solve their work problems, post and review a "Needs Help" chart like the one at right.
- **Invite students to create behavior guidelines.** To ensure that group and independent work are productive, I negotiate with students the behavior guidelines they'll follow while working on their own. When you work with a group, always sit where you have a view of the rest of the class.

Now that you have a mental model of group work and the kinds of routines you need to practice with students, you need to understand how to organize students into your first round of reading groups. Sample behavior guidelines are shown in the box at right.

> ### Needs Help
>
> If you need help, here's what you should do:
> - Reread directions and try again.
> - Ask your reading partner.
> - Ask a classmate.
>
> If you still need help:
> - Put your name on the board under "Needs Help."
> - Work on another task until the teacher can help you.

> ### Behavior Guidelines for Teacher-Led Reading Groups
>
> - Work quietly or silently.
> - Check the chalkboard for independent choices.
> - Follow the "Needs Help" guidelines if necessary.

PREPLANNING REMINDERS FOR TEACHER-LED READING GROUPS

While I'm establishing routines for small-group reading during the last two weeks of whole-class instructional reading, I also need to determine students' instructional reading levels and create a "Big Picture Plan" for the unit.

Determine students' instructional reading levels. Start by reviewing the assessments you used at the start of the year to determine instructional reading levels (see pages 38–41 in Chapter 2). You'll also need to adjust students' levels by evaluating their progress during the first six weeks. The careful observations about students' retellings and their ability to apply reading strategies in response to your read alouds will support your decisions. If a student has the background knowledge to meet the demands of a challenging book, coupled with a strong desire to read the book, then bump that student up. If you're unsure, then start that student in an easier text and build his or her strategic reading strength.

Create Big Picture Plans (see pages 54–56 for sample plans). Here are some key decisions you'll make as you design a plan for a unit of study.

Key Decisions for Planning a Unit of Study	
Decide what genre and issue you will focus on, and estimate the number of weeks you will need to complete the unit.	I decided on realistic fiction for sixth graders and planned a six-week unit. The issue was relationships with family and with pets.
Choose the books for your small groups.	For this sixth-grade unit, I planned to have three groups, so I selected three realistic novels that focus on young adults' relationships with animals and families. Each book met the instructional needs of students in each group: *Shiloh* by Phyllis Reynolds Naylor (Atheneum, 1992), *Old Yeller* by Fred Gipson (Harper, 1956), and *The Yearling* by Marjorie Kinnan Rawlings (Scribner, 1966). (See the box on page 145 for summaries of my reasons for selecting these books.)
Choose your read-aloud texts.	I chose *No More Dead Dogs* by Gordon Korman (Hyperion, 2000) because it gives students a humorous perspective on animal stories.
Choose the reading strategies that you'll teach.	For my first round of small-group reading instruction, I wanted to foster my students' ability to bond and engage with books, so, for two of the groups, I decided to focus on making connections and on visualizing. *The Yearling* group will discuss character development and the historical period. (See the box on page 145 for my decision-making process.)
	Continued on next page

Select the reading strategy you will review with groups that need extra practice.	I decided to review making inferences with all groups.
Plan one or two journal entries. These can relate to reading strategies, to issues, or to the structure of realistic fiction.	I decided that the *Shiloh* group and the *Old Yeller* group would focus on journaling about the reading strategies they were practicing. *The Yearling* group would work on relationships, making decisions, and solving problems.
Create a list of tiered assessments.	Besides two reading tests that would assess students' application of strategies practiced at their instructional levels, I wanted students to complete one or two journal entries. Students would also choose two other activities from these options: composing diary entries from a character's perspective, writing and performing a Readers Theater script, illustrating two to three events from their book, or presenting a dramatic monologue.

Two Tips That Make Teacher-Led Reading Groups Run Smoothly

Once students understand routines, and you've organized three groups and chosen a book for each one, you're ready to plan group meetings and prepare a guidelines sheet for students. Here are two tips that make groups run smoothly.

First, create a weekly small-group meeting grid. I keep mine in my planning notebook because, with frequent middle school schedule changes, I'm always adjusting it. Having a record of meetings ensures that each group receives the same number of lessons. My weekly grid for three groups is shown on page 151. Note that each group had 15 minutes of silent reading, and the third group, which I planned to meet with during the next class, had 30 minutes to complete instructional and independent reading.

Second, design a guidelines sheet for each group (see Figure 5.1). It's important to include the number of pages students will read and the due dates for discussion. Also, list due dates for a choice of assessments that students can do during sustained silent reading.

Weekly Small-Group Meeting Grid

45-minute classes: Alternate reading groups with writing workshop. Meet with each group for 15 minutes. Use the rest of the time for a read aloud, mini-lessons, independent reading, journal writing, or projects.

Monday	Tuesday	Wednesday	Thursday	Friday
1 and 2	Writing	3 and 1	Writing	2 and 3
30–35 min.	45 min.	30–35 min.	45 min.	30–35 min.

90-minute block: Writing workshop occurs after reading groups meet.

Monday	Wednesday	Friday
1 and 2	3 and 1	2 and 3
30–35 min.	30–35 min.	30–35 min.

Simply transfer these from your Big Picture Plans to a handout for students like the one that follows. Have them paste the handout in their journals. Note that I give students the assignments for the entire unit. This builds responsibility. When students ask me, "Can I read ahead?" I always say, "That's fine. Just make sure you reread a section so it's fresh in your mind when the group meets."

PREPARING GROUPS TO READ THEIR BOOKS

You'll need 25 to 35 minutes to prepare students for small-group reading and discussions. Begin by having students open to a clean journal page

Required reading assignments: Refer to the assignment sheet for your book.

Required assessments for a realistic fiction unit of study:
- Journal entry due_____
- First reading test on _____
- Final reading test on_____

Assessment choices: Complete two and follow the planning sheet.

Due dates: Your assessment choices are due December 15, the week prior to the end of this study. If you are performing, please schedule a time with Mrs. Robb. If you complete a project sooner, please hand it in. Hand in your plan or first draft to Mrs. Robb so she can confer with you to provide feedback that will support your revisions.
- Readers Theater script and performance (You may work with two or three other students on a script.)
- Dramatic monologue on a character you choose
- Two illustrations of events in your book
- Four diary entries written by a character in your book
- Letters written by two characters to each other. (Two exchanges or four letters.)

FIGURE 5.1: Students receive a guidelines sheet with due dates and tiered assessments.

and write their name, the date, and this heading: What I Know About Realistic Fiction. Then, ask students to discuss with a partner everything they know about the genre. Next, have students list in their journals what they know and what they recall from the paired conversations. Working as a whole group again, ask students to share their journal notes, and write students' thoughts on chart paper. You will soon know whether you need to boost students' knowledge of the genre with extra read alouds. If students' sharing shows they know a great deal about the genre, then have them pair-share-write about the issue you're including in your unit.

Next, prepare students to read their individual books by asking them to study the cover illustration, think about the title, read the first two pages, and then predict what they think the book will be about. (If you are doing a unit on informational texts, ask students to study the photographs or illustrations in the first half of the book.)

Moving Forward: Tips to Use Throughout Your Small-Group Unit of Study

There are tasks that you will complete each week and each time you meet with groups. This repetition provides the structure necessary for students to learn and to work well independently. Each time groups meet make sure you do the following:

- Review behavior and the "Needs Help" chart.
- Explain the independent work choices.
- Read the names of group members who will meet with you.

Also, continue to read aloud for the fun of it, to introduce strategies and text structures, to model how you prepare journal entries, and to connect issues to the story. Always use your read aloud to introduce and model a new reading strategy a week before students practice it in their groups. This could mean that you will be think-

> ### Scaffold: What to Do When Students Write Nothing
>
> Meet with students who write nothing in their journal to discover why this occurred. If students don't write because of a lack of background knowledge, help them build it through your read alouds. You may want to use picture books so you can read two to four books in the genre being studied. If students struggle with the writing, support them by asking them to tell you what they know as you write for them. Write for students until they gain the confidence to complete the writing independently.

ing aloud and modeling one to three strategies each week. However, it's fine for all students to hear these think alouds; everyone benefits from review and repeated visits to a strategy.

Take the time to plan and focus your lessons. Each week, in my planning notebook, I plan the lessons for the three books I'm using. The tips that follow can help you keep your lessons to 15 minutes. You can also find sample lessons from my planning notebook on pages 155–158. These lessons provide a framework you can use to plan your own lessons.

Tips for Focusing and Differentiating Instruction in Your Group Lessons

"I intend to spend 15 minutes, but discussions go off in so many directions that I'm spending 30 minutes with one group. The rest of the students are talking, off task, and getting little out of the class. Maybe group work isn't for me." I often hear comments like these as I work with teachers around the country. Believe me, I can empathize; it takes discipline to remain within time limits. You can complete a small-group lesson within 15 minutes as long as you focus the discussion on one strategy, the issue, or the theme.

I recently sat in on a teacher-led discussion in a fourth-grade class. The group's book was *The King's Equal* by Katherine Paterson (HarperCollins, 1992). The teacher opened the lesson by introducing Questioning the Author (see page 273 for queries to use), explaining that students would be practicing this strategy with parts of Paterson's text. Immediately after this focused introduction, one student brought up the weekend camp out that he and his dad went on near the Shenandoah River. The other five group members began to share their weekend adventures; students never had time to apply QtA to the book.

At the end of 25 minutes, the teacher assigned the next set of pages to be read and dismissed the group. "I didn't want to stop the sharing; they were so enthusiastic," she told me during our debriefing later that day. And students *were* motivated to tell their stories. However, while this conversation may have been helpful if students were exploring topics for stories they planned to write, it was inappropriate for reading instruction. Here are some ways to keep the focus of your lessons within reasonable time limits:

- Practice applying one of the strategies in your unit of study.
- Share and discuss a completed journal entry.
- Connect an issue to the text.

- Practice figuring out tough words, using context clues.
- Discuss genre structure and features of fiction and nonfiction.
- Explore themes or main ideas.
- Use open-ended questions students composed to discuss a section.
- Use Questioning the Author queries (see appendix page 273) to enlarge inferential thinking.

Careful and thoughtful weekly planning is vital for helping you remain focused during a lesson. Keep in mind, too, that your opening remarks, such as "today we'll be practicing cause and effect, and then making inferences"; or "today, we'll look at how the issue of civil rights affected each character"; or "today we'll be Questioning the Author to discover what the author wants us to think and understand," let students know the agenda and keep you and them on task. During each small-group lesson, listen and watch carefully so you can assess students' and groups' needs and provide scaffolds for individual or group support.

Differentiated Lessons That Respond to the Needs of Three Diverse Groups

My Big Picture Plans support my plans for small-group meetings because I focus on one or two reading strategies, issues, the structure of realistic fiction, and vocabulary and context clues. I'm always cognizant, however, of the mix of students I have each year, and I monitor their changing needs as the school year progresses. So, for students who have no toolbox of reading strategies, I may have to depart from my Big Picture Plans and work on predict/support/adjust, or making personal connections, before launching into how and why a character changes during a book. This is the meaning of differentiating instruction—not locking yourself into a prepared pattern, but responding to the needs of your students. With one group, I might emphasize how and why a character changes, whereas with a second group, I might focus on making personal connections to the story. With a third group, I might concentrate on building vocabulary using context clues. Remember, I group students around strategic needs as well as instructional reading levels. It's also helpful to give lessons a consistent framework or structure as this lets students know what to expect, and it makes your planning easier. The structure I use is described in the box at right.

SAMPLE LESSON PLANS

It may be helpful for you to see a sample student guidelines sheet and to read and mull over the first four group lessons from my realistic fiction unit. The lessons are for the book *Miracle's Boys* by Jacqueline Woodson (Penguin/Putnam, 2000). As I noted above, each group lesson opens with a quick retelling of the chapters students have read. I start the retelling, and then students take turns completing it. Retelling should take no more than three minutes.

Lesson 1 on page 156 shows how I model drawing conclusions about a character and asks students to discuss issues about relationships. Lessons 2 and 3 ask students to draw conclusions and continue to discuss relationship issues. The reason I can do this in these second and third lessons is that students have observed me drawing conclusions about a character in several read alouds. In Lesson 4, I engage students in using context clues to figure out vocabulary. (See appendix page 272 for this lesson.)

These are the bare-bones notes I write

How to Structure Lessons for Small Groups

Following a consistent pattern during group lessons is advantageous to students. I structure lessons as follows:

1. Open by having students do a retelling of the pages they have read. This is a short refresher course in recalling plot details. Let students skim through the pages as they do this.

2. Model how you apply a specific reading strategy, and/or invite students to think aloud and share their process.

3. Review the strategy you modeled and/or students practiced.

If you have time:

1. Ask students discussion questions about issues, text structure, and what the author wants you to know.

2. Practice using context clues to figure out word meanings as needed.

Realistic Fiction Big Picture Plans

You'll find "Big Picture Plans" for the three books in this unit on page 55: *Miracle's Boys* by Jacqueline Woodson (Lexile, 660, Guided Reading Level Z), *Crash* by Jerry Spinelli (Lexile, 560, Guided Reading Level V), and *The Great Gilly Hopkins* by Katherine Paterson (Lexile, 800, Guided Reading Level S).

Student Reading Assignments for *Miracle's Boys* by Jacqueline Woodson

Assignment #	Pages	Due Dates
1.	1–15	
2.	16–36	
3.	37–47	
4.	48–60	
5.	61–71	
6.	72–88	
7.	Assessment: Journal Entry	
8.	89–107	
9.	108–118	
10.	119–131	
11.	Assessment: Readers Theater	

FIGURE 5.2: Each group receives its reading assignments for the entire unit.

to jog my memory. In fact, I do a lot of abbreviating to make this process move quickly. Jotting down notes, week by week, keeps your focus when switching groups, and supports your efforts to complete a lesson in 15 minutes. I find it important to include any page numbers if you plan to refer to them during each lesson.

Lesson 1 *Miracle's Boys*, Pages 1–15

- Post independent work on chalkboard: all groups read the next set of assigned pages in their books. Have students choose a realistic fiction book for an independent reading.
- Students take turns retelling the main events.
- Sample think aloud for drawing conclusions: use pages 1 to 3 to draw conclusions about Lafayette.
- Relationship issues to discuss: use pages 1 to 15 for support.

Ask: How does Lafayette remember his relationship with the old Charlie? Why does Lafayette feel that his relationship with Newcharlie has changed? What caused these changes? Why is Newcharlie angry at Lafayette? How does anger affect a relationship?

Lesson 2 *Miracle's Boys,* Pages 16–36

- Post independent work on chalkboard: All groups start a journal entry on drawing conclusions. Work on journal entry—due end of week. All read next pages in their books and do independent reading.
- Students take turns retelling the main events.
- Have students think aloud for drawing conclusions: Ask students what they recall about drawing conclusions.

  Next, ask students to skim and retell paragraph two on page 24 to their partner.

Then pairs talk for one to two minutes and figure out what they learn about Newcharlie's personality.

Discuss process used for drawing conclusions.

- Discuss relationships and ask, What makes them work? What messes them up?

Lesson 3 *Miracle's Boys,* Pages 37–47

- Post independent work on chalkboard: see Lesson 2.
- Have students take turns retelling the main events. Then have students share what they recall about drawing conclusions. Review the strategy if necessary.
- Next, invite partners to reread the sections below and help each other draw conclusions about the character. Then have pairs share.

Accept any conclusions about personality that students support.

- Page 38, paragraphs 1 and 2. Lafayette's personality.
- Page 39, paragraph 2 to page 40. Newcharlie's personality.
- Page 43, last paragraph to the top of page 45. Ty'ree's personality.
- Page 46, paragraph 4 to end of page 47. Lafayette's and Ty'ree's personalities.

Lesson 4 *Miracle's Boys,* Pages 48–71

- Post independent work on chalkboard: see Lesson 2.
- Invite students to take turns retelling the main events. Review the process of drawing conclusions, if necessary, then move to vocabulary.
- Think aloud for vocabulary and context clues: Have students turn to page 64 and find *huddled* in the middle of the page. Model how you use context clues.

Have pairs use context to figure out the meanings of these words: *limousine*, last line on page 65; *scuffed*, fifth line down from the top of page 66; *yanking*, last line on page 68; *sagging*, fourth line from the bottom of page 69. Pairs share their process.

- Review drawing conclusions: Do this if time, otherwise, do at start of lesson 5.

Skim page 66, first paragraph to its end on page 67. Ask: What can you conclude about Ty'ree from these details?

Now it's time for you to hear two small-group discussions so you can picture their focus and rhythm. Notice that I keep to my plans, which I've designed to improve student thinking and the application of strategies and issues.

Teacher-Led Discussion Groups in Action: Grade Seven and Grade Five

So you can hear and process the interaction between group members and the teacher, I've included parts of two discussions that I transcribed from an audiocassette along with my comments about the discussions.

Grade Seven *Miracle's Boys* by Jacqueline Woodson (Penguin/Putnam, 2000).

Each of the seven boys in this group was reading two years below grade level. All the boys needed practice with inferring by using text details. This is a transcription from an audiocassette recording I made of part of Lesson 3 (see page 157), in which pairs present their conclusions about different characters to the group. Listen to pairs share. One student presents his findings. The other adds his thoughts after the presentation. At the next meeting, partners switch roles.

FIRST PAIR, page 38: We think that Lafayette starts seeing himself as good-looking after his aunt tells him he's handsome now that he's grown.

ROBB: Anything to add?

FIRST PAIR: Yeah. I think that when he looks in the mirror to check out his face. It shows that he wants to look good—maybe even feel good after his mom died. How you feel can make you look sad or mean or good.

ROBB: I noticed how you used feelings to help you infer and draw conclusions about Lafayette at this point. [*I nod toward second pair.*]

SECOND PAIR, page 39: We know Charlie is angry that his mom died when he tells Lafayette that he would've saved her if he was home. Charlie is mean when he says to Lafayette, "How come you [Lafayette] didn't save her?" It's like he's blaming his brother.

ROBB: Anything to add? Anyone in the group want to add something?

STUDENT 2: I think Charlie being in Rahway has made him mean with no feelings. He's stiff when his aunt hugs him. The author says his eyes are hard with no feelings.

ROBB: With both answers you've given us a clear picture of what Charlie is like now.

GROUP OF THREE, page 43: Ty'ree's smart. He was gonna go to MIT. He got lots of awards at graduation and built rockets. But he's responsible and will take care of his brothers and get a job instead of going to MIT. He feels sad, though. He looks through his high school yearbook, and the author says it's like he left something behind.

ROBB: Anything to add?

STUDENT 3: I think that Ty'ree gives up his dream to help his family. That's good and that's bad. It's good for his brothers and will keep them together. It's bad for Ty'ree 'cause he's so smart and has to do jobs that are dumb.

ROBB: You both used lots of details to support your thinking. I like the evaluation of Ty'ree's decision. There are good and bad parts to it.

So, at this point, what is Woodson telling us about losing a mother and a father?

STUDENT 4: It changes your life.

ROBB: How?

ROBB: [*No one answers. I try another prompt.*] Why does Ty'ree get a job instead of going to college?

STUDENT 5: He wants to keep the three together. He wants a family.

STUDENT 3: It changes your family. It hurts.

STUDENT 2: You maybe wouldn't want to live with someone like your aunt or a strange family.

STUDENT 3: Lafayette doesn't feel it like Charlie and Ty'ree. It's that he's young, maybe. I'm not sure things hit him as hard.

STUDENT 1: Maybe the author's also saying that it's so hard that you can only show meanness like Charlie or push your dreams away like Ty'ree.

ROBB'S COMMENTS: I am delighted with the way group members help one another with the thinking. Notice that I didn't jump in with an answer, but asked the question,

"How?" then rephrased the question. Try to let students figure things out. And, if they don't get it, let it go. What you're aiming for is to get students thinking and probing. It's about them, not about you and me.

Grade Five *The Defenders* **by Ann McGovern** (Scholastic, 1970).

The five students in this group are all solid readers. Transcribed here is the group's retelling of the chapter's key points that opens each meeting.

STUDENT 1: Thompson wants the Seminoles to sign a treaty again. They would lose their land in Florida if the treaty is signed.

STUDENT 2: Osceola was a Seminole. He was at the meeting. People looked to him as their leader. All the chiefs there wouldn't sign.

STUDENT 3: Thompson got mad. He told the chiefs that Americans wouldn't look at them as chiefs. Osceola got real mad. He put a knife through the treaty on the table.

STUDENT 4: Thompson grabs Osceola and put him in jail. He would go free when he signed the treaty.

STUDENT 5: I think he got sick in prison.

ROBB: Can you explain this with more detail? [long pause]

STUDENT 5: Only read the first chapter.

ROBB: Read chapter two now, then we'll talk after class.

STUDENT 1: He wouldn't sign a treaty because it said that if a Seminole had Negro blood, he couldn't go west. Osceola and his people hid black Seminoles and other blacks.

STUDENT 2: Osceola said he'd sign the treaty to get out of jail and help his people. He would never give up the land or give over people to slave catchers.

ROBB'S COMMENTS: All but one student had fine recall of these opening chapters. When I spoke to the unprepared student, I asked, "Why didn't you complete the reading in class yesterday?" (My goal is to avoid making assumptions and see what the student says.) "I was working on my story instead," was the reply. After discussing with him that the group needed and valued his input, I told the student that I felt pleased that he was enjoying his writing, but I also wanted him to complete his reading. I asked him to read the pages, and sent him to another part of the room. "If you finish (he did) before the group meeting ends, then join us," I said. I don't allow a student who chose to not do the work to hear the discussion because I feel that this encourages him or her to try to repeat the behavior. I also check with students to make sure that they complete the reading in class before they turn to other activities.

After my first round of small-group lessons, I give myself a breather by returning to whole-class instructional reading for five to six weeks. Soon, however, I'm thinking about my second round of small-group instruction. As you read on, you'll gather some insights into the importance of flexible grouping and learn how I use observational notes to help me make grouping decisions. Then you'll explore the framework and guidelines I use to make new grouping decisions after I complete my first round of small-group instruction.

Making and Using Observational Notes

Finding the time to jot down what you've observed about students' work during reading group meetings can be daunting and overwhelming. I've experienced this myself. It's best to start small and observe one student during a reading-group lesson. Here's what I do. At the conclusion of one reading group, in the two or three minutes it takes the second group to get settled in, I jot down my observations on a self-stick note, while my memory is fresh. If there's a time crunch because I need to help a student, I try to take notes during my planning period or while students work independently. There are days when I'm unable to take notes until students have left for the day.

Once you've become comfortable and at ease observing one student during group-reading lessons, try to add two, then three, and then four. You may want to focus on those students who need scaffolded or supportive instruction.

It's important to tell students what you are doing and explain how it can help you improve their reading skill. Students are just like us; they feel the same way we do when an administrator observes and writes furiously the entire time. The first reaction is that the notes are all negative. I tell my students that they can read the notes and that we will discuss them during a conference.

When you take notes, try not to editorialize and make judgmental statements such as, "Adam disturbs his group on purpose so they won't read; he wants them to be like him." Write what you see and hear, but be as objective as you can. The above notes can be rewritten as, "Adam talks to group members during independent reading. He holds his book open but doesn't read."

To show you how objective observational notes can support grouping decisions, I've included summaries of two sets of notes. The first set of notes is from several observations of Ana during group work as well as during a follow-up conference. The second set of notes is based on two group observations of Tony, plus the follow-up conference I had with him. You can also review my decision-making process for both students. These brief meetings are another building block of differentiation because they can clarify my observations and give me new insights that help me plan scaffolds and interventions. Study the transcriptions from my notes that follow and see if you agree with my interpretations and instructional decisions.

SUMMARY OF OBSERVATIONAL NOTES FOR ANA, GRADE FOUR

Here are the notes I took while Ana and her group were practicing making inferences with *If You Decide to Go to the Moon* by Faith McNulty, illustrated by Steven Kellogg, (Scholastic, 2006).

- Doesn't participate when asked to infer. Did that each time.
- When working with a group partner on inferring, partner does all the thinking and talking.
- Participates in retellings of sections; she volunteers to do this.
- Journal work based on read alouds shows Ana's having a tough time inferring. She retells.
- Unprepared once, but always prepared after that.

Robb's Follow-Up Conference With Ana:

[*Robb reads notes and waits for response.*]

ANA: I'm good at retelling. [long pause]

ROBB: You sure are. What about making inferences?

ANA: I do it for characters.

ROBB: Yes, you do, and you do it well! Can you help me understand why you aren't inferring with informational books?

ANA: Ummm. I just can't.

ROBB: Let's work together on a passage from this book. I know you can infer.

ANA: Shrugs her shoulders and mumbles, "Okay."

ROBB: I'll show you how I infer today. Then we can practice together tomorrow.

[Here is the section of text I model from McNulty's book *If You Decide to Go to the Moon*:]

Space is dark and empty . . .

There is no air in space; no clouds; no rain;

ROBB: I can infer that space is different from Earth. We have clouds, rain, and sun, and in space, it's dark, sunless, and dry. I can infer that people can't live in space wearing everyday clothes. There would be no air to breathe. The pictures show me how dark space is. What I did, Ana, was take details about space and relate them to what I know about Earth. Bringing what you know to a text helps you infer.

ANA: It seems easy when you do it.

ROBB: With some practice, you'll be able to infer with informational books, too.

ROBB'S COMMENTS AND INSTRUCTIONAL DECISIONS: Note that I was careful to point out to Ana what she could do well—retell sections of the McNulty text and make inferences about characters in narrative texts. I also checked Ana's journal to see how she was inferring with the read-aloud text, and to see if she was able to work better with a partner or by herself. I decided to model right away so Ana could see how I used what I know about Earth to infer and connect to space. I also let her know that we would meet again so I could model and eventually release the process of inferring to Ana. I decided to keep Ana in this text. She loves Kellogg's illustrations and her independent reading is all fiction. Stretching Ana with informational text will be beneficial.

SUMMARY OF OBSERVATIONAL NOTES FOR TONY, GRADE EIGHT

Here are the notes about Tony that I took right after I led the reading group that had just started *The Great Gilly Hopkins* by Katherine Paterson (Crowell, 1978).

- Did not participate in today's retelling.
- When Tony worked with partner on cause/effect/infer, his partner did all the talking.
- Tony was a great contributor during our first group when he read *Hatchet* by Gary

Paulsen (Bradbury, 1988).

- He has not made any contributions during the first two meetings. He pushes his chair back as if to separate from the group.

Robb's Follow-Up Conference With Tony:

[*Robb reads notes and waits for response.*]

TONY: [*Shrugs his shoulders. Says nothing.*]

ROBB: Can you tell me why you didn't participate?

TONY: I read the pages. I don't remember them.

ROBB: Can you tell me why you don't remember?

TONY: I dunno. I read the words. They don't stick.

ROBB: How do you feel about this book? [*The Great Gilly Hopkins*]

TONY: Don't like girl books.

ROBB: I'm pleased that you were honest with me, Tony. Would you like to join the group reading *Crash* (Jerry Spinelli)? That means you'll have to read the first four chapters by Friday to be on track with the group.

TONY: I'll try it. Josh says it's cool and funny and mostly about boys.

ROBB: Here's an extra copy you can take home. Let me know how the reading's going tomorrow.

TONY: Sure. [pause] Thanks.

Suggestions for Making Grouping Decisions After a First Round of Group Lessons

Before organizing new groups, I carefully consider each student's progress. I review and evaluate their progress on journal entries. I read the observational notes I've made. I look at assessments, such as Readers Theater scripts and tests. I also reflect on my interactions and observations during strategic group meetings. Grouping decisions depend on a student's ability to

- apply practiced strategies independently
- use text support to answer analytical and inferential questions
- use context clues to figure out the meaning of new words
- write about their reading in journals
- complete tests that assess the strategies and analytical thinking we have been practicing
- participate regularly in group discussions
- work well together, with no overt personality issues

ROBB'S COMMENTS AND INSTRUCTIONAL DECISIONS: Though I felt that Tony was capable of a more challenging book, I moved him into the group reading *Crash*, a book below Tony's instructional level, because of his personal feelings about a book with a girl as a main character. Motivation to read is very important, and Tony was not bonding to this book. Because I know that Tony reads on his own and works hard to improve, I could make an instructional decision that would enable Tony to be a productive member of a group and enjoy the reading.

I understand that taking observational notes adds another layer to all that you already have to do; however, the more you engage in the process, the easier it becomes. The information you gather about students during reading groups better equips you to make decisions about grouping, about intervening for one-on-one support, and about differentiating strategy instruction. Now, along with the other data, your observational notes provide an effective resource for planning your next reading groups.

Assessments for Small-Group Reading Instruction

In the Big Picture Plans on pages 54–56, I've noted some possible assessments that are ideal for small groups reading the same book. One that students particularly enjoy is Readers Theater because they love to perform. To ensure that students write scripts worthy of performance, share the guidelines that follow.

READERS THEATER SCRIPTS

During small-group lessons, I show students how to create their own Readers Theater scripts. Students may work with a partner or a small group to create the scripts. I find that having more than four students working together can result in one or two doing the work for everyone. If your groups are large, have pairs compose different scripts. Students will need time to rehearse before presenting their dramatizations. After each presentation, the "audience" can discuss the issues they observed and the personality traits of characters. The guidelines on page 166 outline the steps students need to follow.

Guidelines for Writing a Readers Theater Script

1. Choose a part of your book that is rich in dialogue.

2. When setting up your script, use the words the characters speak in the text.

3. Include transitional paragraphs and background details. You may have one or more narrators. Shorten paragraphs without dialogue but make sure that the audience understands the plot.

4. Create enough narrators so everyone in your group has a speaking part.

5. As you read the script, use the appropriate tone of voice, facial expressions, and body language to express the feelings and personalities of the characters. There are no props or sets.

6. Set your script up as follows.

   • List the characters.

   • List the number of narrators.

   • Do not write your script in your journal. Write it on separate paper. You may use the computer and printer.

   • Follow this format:

Narrator 1:	Summarize words of author here.
First Character:	Use words from book.
Second Character:	Use words from book.
Narrator 2:	Summarize words of author here.

In addition to Readers Theater, my students enjoy conducting interviews. Here are some guidelines for this assessment.

TALK SHOW INTERVIEWS

Students need to plan these out and rehearse them.

- Two students collaborate on interviews using the same instructional book; one student is the interviewer; the other, a character.
- Pairs work together to craft questions and think through answers. Answers should use facts and inferences from the text.
- Pairs present to the class. The "audience" discusses what they learned about the character and his/her relationships.

Notice that I have students work together in groups during class to compose the script. My school has laptop computers, so I reserve two of these—one for each group—and keep them in my room for a week. Before the days of laptops, two groups worked in my classroom, and I sent other groups to use the computers in nearby classrooms, with each teacher's permission. In my classes, this is always a group experience: the group writes and performs the script. I want to be there during the planning and composing process to answer questions and offer extra support to those who request it.

After each performance, the "audience" of students asks the characters questions. The characters' responses can use any details or inferences from the text. Students give Readers Theater high ratings as they enjoy both performing and the follow-up questions. I also rate it highly because it includes writing, develops reading fluency, and requires that students interpret a character's feelings and personality traits.

These two students are taking notes for a project.

OTHER ASSESSMENTS FOR SMALL-GROUP INSTRUCTION

Because the preparation for group work is intensive, you may want to limit the number of additional assessments you offer students. Journal writing occurs during your read aloud; you can also have students practice a journal entry that relates to a reading strategy they are practicing. (See sample entries on appendix page 281.) For example, if a journaling activity focuses on figuring out a character's personality traits, give students a copy of the reproducible with lists of adjectives that scaffold this task. You'll find this resource on appendix page 283. You can also print these traits on chart paper and have students review them.

Pause, Reflect, and Consider Six Questions . . .

Adolescent learners have boundless energy: mental, emotional, and physical. Before you turn the page and delve into the chapter on independent reading, think about these questions. I return to them at least twice a month, before I plan a new unit of study for small groups. These questions drive me to evaluate my planning and instructional practice, and they help me ensure that I am differentiating instruction to meet every student's needs.

- Am I matching books to students' instructional levels?
- Am I scaffolding students by giving them clear guidelines for projects?
- Am I providing choices for projects and then tiering them so students can successfully complete them and learn from them?
- Do I change and differentiate the instructional activities to meet the high energy of adolescents as well as their diverse learning styles and needs?
- Do I model the kinds of thinking and journal writing I want students to complete?
- Am I differentiating instruction by teaching each group the strategies group members need?

Chapter 6

Independent Reading and Differentiation

Developing Students' Reading Stamina and Personal Reading Lives

*D*uring the lunch break at a conference I presented at Johnson Williams Middle School in Clarke County, Virginia, three middle school teachers talked to me about their independent reading program. In the morning I had emphasized the importance of students reading at school and at home at their comfort level, for at least 60 minutes a day (see appendix page 262). I had also explained why giving students choices in the reading is an important part of differentiating reading instruction, because students choose books on topics they care about and use materials that they can read with ease and enjoyment. This daily practice improves students' fluency and reading rate, and it enlarges their vocabulary and prior knowledge.

One of the three teachers explained the problem they had with independent reading: "Our school district requires 25 minutes of independent reading a night for homework. But all students have to complete written work on their reading, including a retelling of the pages read and predictions with support based on that night's reading."

Another teacher added, "The students say they hate reading. They write very little and tell us that reading isn't fun anymore."

The third teacher asked, "What do you think about this kind of homework?"

"Well," I replied, "I like the 25 minutes a night of independent reading. My question to you as well as to the administrators who designed this assignment is this: Can all of you show me the journals you keep each night on your independent reading?"

"No one keeps a journal," chorused the three teachers.

"Then why ask students to do something that's not authentic—something no adults in your district or any other district do?" Then I added, "Independent practice reading should be enjoyable and not a punishment. Writing every night makes the reading a negative experience, and you're seeing this in students' reactions."

"How do we [teachers] know if students are completing their reading?" asked a teacher. This is a question I repeatedly hear when I discuss the power and importance of independent practice reading. Teachers can monitor some of students' independent reading through one-on-one conferences, via bookmarks and book talks, and by having them list their completed books in a book log and then discussing the log in their groups every six to seven weeks. But asking students to complete written assignments on every book they've read doesn't work. It punishes both the proficient and struggling reader, deterring reading instead of encouraging it, because students either read less to avoid doing extra work or don't list in their logs all the books they've read. It also creates extra work for middle school teachers who have to read an excessive amount of nightly entries. Actually, most of this homework often goes unread, sending the message to students that this is just busy work, having no purpose other than to check up on them.

And yes, some students will not read every night. But my question is, "Do we teachers abandon an independent reading program because a few students might not read?"

My response to this is a resounding and emphatic, "No!" Independent reading can inch students toward proficiency. In fact, it can be a transforming experience, as it was for Michael, one of my students. In September and October, Michael reluctantly read one book. But in December, Michael discovered Roald Dahl, and wrote this in his journal: "In December, I completed one book on the first and finished another book on the 11th and then one on the 15th, and then one on the 20th. I started reading books by

This student is absorbed in an independent reading book.

Roald Dahl. His books were easy to read and got my attention." Note that Michael uses the word "easy" to describe the reading. This is because he's reading books at his comfort level and loving it. He's racking up miles on his reading odometer and building stamina the whole time. The amount of time students spend reading independently matters. In fact, research shows that the amount of time that students spend reading is the best predictor of reading achievement (Anderson, Wilson, Fielding, 1988; Krashen, 1993).

As You Continue to Read . . .

As you continue to read this chapter, you'll explore suggestions for enlarging your classroom library, for how to use book talks and students' book logs effectively, and for organizing and managing student-led book discussions. You'll

How Independent Reading Helps You Differentiate

- Providing students with books at their comfort levels ensures that they will build reading stamina.
- Having a choice in reading materials is motivating.

also find open-ended questions for fiction and nonfiction. You can use these to help students prepare for book discussions in which each student has read a different book. I'll also show you how to teach students to create their own open-ended questions.

What the Research Says About Independent Reading

Research shows the importance of independent practice reading in developing fluency, vocabulary, background knowledge, and reading rate. At that same conference I mentioned at the beginning of the chapter, Dr. Joan Kindig, assistant professor at the University of Virginia discussed how independent reading affects learners' vocabulary development. Students with the best vocabulary are readers, Dr. Kindig pointed out (Anderson & Freebody, 1983). Moreover, good readers read about 1 million words a year (Nagy & Anderson, 1984). Students who learn 3,000 new words a year from reading and from class instruction are in the normal vocabulary growth range. Each time learners encounter a word in print, they learn 10 percent more about that word. Dr. Kindig also explained that students' vocabulary knowledge is not comprised of word definitions; rather it is a series of connected concepts that have been stored after each encounter with a word (Beck et al., 2002; Spencer & Guillaume, 2006). So the traditional vocabulary assignments in which students look up a word in the dictionary or copy a list of words and their definitions from the chalkboard are ineffective. They do not help students absorb a word to the point at which they can think with it and use it in discussion and writing; wide-range reading does (Graves, 2006; Michaels, 2001).

When a student has a large and wide range of known words related to a topic, these words become part of the student's background knowledge for that topic. For example, the comprehension of texts about slavery will differ widely between a student who has five words related to slavery and a student who has 40 to 50 words. So, learning and enlarging vocabulary strengthens students' background knowledge and enables them to comprehend more challenging texts. Vocabulary power is closely connected to daily independent reading, both in and out of school and should be a part of every language arts curriculum (Armbruster et al., 2001; Buehl, 2001; Nagy & Anderson, 1984; Snow et al., 1998).

Tap Into Students' Diverse Literacies to Motivate Reading for School

Independent reading at school and at home has great value for adolescents, yet students in this age group read less during the middle and high school years than they did in elementary school (Hall, 2006; Lenters, 2006; Reis & Fogarty, 2006). Many reasons account for this diminished independent reading: sports activities, music and dance lessons, work, and the need to watch younger siblings. Kimberly Lenters, in an article in the *Journal of Adolescent & Adult Literacy*, describes a large group of adolescent learners as "resistant readers" (2006). What Lenters's research revealed is that resistant readers often have rich, personal reading lives outside of school, but their choices of graphic novels, comic books, and magazines don't measure up to teachers' expectations or school districts' requirements. In 2000, Donna Alvermann and her colleagues completed a study of reading behaviors among adolescents in after-school media clubs. These researchers discovered that there were groups of learners who resisted school reading and writing but who engaged in complicated reading and writing activities around computer games. Recognizing students' abilities in areas outside of school, and then building on these strengths in school is what differentiating independent reading is all about.

An example of this kind of resistant reader is a ninth grader I'll call Richie. Richie devours magazines about NASCAR racing, cars, and building motors, and he researches these topics on the Internet. In fact, Richie knows more about those subjects than I ever will. Richie's school views him as a reading and behavior problem because he refused to read two required books: *Jane Eyre* by Charlotte Brontë and a translation of Homer's *Odyssey*. Until I asked Richie about his personal reading life, no one had any idea about his extensive knowledge of cars and motors, or the complex vocabulary he had acquired. Richie complained about the books on the ninth-grade reading list. "I read one," he told me—*The Old Man and the Sea*—because it was the shortest one."

Even when I told his teachers about Richie's interests, they were unimpressed. "He needs to do his schoolwork," was their reply. It's my belief that middle and high school teachers need to rethink required reading for this and future generations. In many schools, this means abandoning the traditional middle and high school canon, which many students can't read and have no interest in or any background knowledge about, so they cannot engage with the text (Gee, 2000; Hall, 2006). Lenters's statement—"Resistant readers risk becoming struggling readers"—is one teachers should reflect upon and heed. Bob Dylan's song "The Times They Are a Changin'" applies to the 21st century—times are changing in social values, technological advances, family structures, and the kinds of reading students do when they can choose their own texts. We teachers need to provide students with scaffolds by tapping into students' interests and strengths. We need to build their reading stamina by offering them genres that interest them and topics they care about. Accepting that independent reading for middle and high school students might involve comics and graphic novels, video games, or other topics they care about is a first step (Damico & Riddle, 2006).

Therefore, to engage readers, teachers should allow students a choice of texts in school, and respect students' out-of-school literacies. When students like Richie become disengaged and disinterested, they may also become candidates for dropping out of high school and joining the ranks of workers in low-level jobs. Equally important, Richie may pass on his negative attitudes toward reading to his children, and so the cycle broadens and continues.

One way to scaffold reading for students like Richie, who can read, is to offer alternative texts that are relevant to students' lives—texts they can and will read. For Richie, it might be an informational book about cars and motors, or a novel with a male protagonist. For students who struggle and read far below grade level, scaffolds that differentiate should include some one-on-one teaching of reading and vocabulary strategies, along with text choices on topics that these students care about and are written at their instructional levels.

CHOICE AND TIME TO READ AT SCHOOL CULTIVATE STUDENTS' PERSONAL READING LIVES

One way to combat the waning interest in reading during adolescence is to offer students time at school to read texts they select (Allington, 2002; Guthrie, 2004; Ivey & Broaddus, 2001; Lenters, 2006; Reis & Fogarty, 2006; Robb, 2000, 2006). Choice means that in addition to books written for adolescents, we fill our classroom libraries with graphic novels, magazines, comic books, and books by adult authors who might interest students, such as Michael Crichton, John Grisham, James Patterson, and Anthony Horowitz. Choice means that we permit students to read on the Internet and read about computer games. Choice means that we celebrate the rereading of favorite books instead of thinking that students are trying to wiggle out of work. Rhett, an eighth grader, writes: "As I reread my book log, I noticed *Mr. Popper's Penguins* by Richard and Florence Atwater (Time Warner, 1966). I truly love that book. That's why I am going to reread it again— it's my fifth reread." Rhett plans to also reread *California Blue* by David Klass (Scholastic, 2000), a book he discovered in my class. He explains that this book "hasn't appeared on my book log yet, but it's going to, numerous times."

Katherine, an eighth grader, who represents the feelings of all of my sixth and eighth graders, wrote this about having time to read at school: "I love having time to read at school. I have so much to do after school—soccer practice, ballet three times a week, babysitting my young brother, house chores, and homework—I can't find time to read my books until the weekend." This feeling is universal among students I've surveyed. Students want to choose their independent reading. You and I get to choose; we need to offer the same to our students. The only restriction I place on students' choices for independent reading at school is that texts are neither pornographic nor filled with inappropriate violence.

You can help students find reading materials they connect with and want to read by asking them to complete an interest inventory. Knowing your students' interests provides topics for conversations during conferences

A rich classroom library makes it easy for students to find books of interest to them at their reading level.

and offers you the information needed to suggest reading materials. Knowing your students' interests sends the message to them that you value what they care about and feel is important. Knowing your students' interests enables you to motivate them to read, thus improving their self-confidence. The connections you form with students—connections based on their interests and their reading levels—enable you to support each child you teach by differentiating the reading materials you add to your class library. On appendix pages 267 and 268, I've included two interest inventories, one for grades four to six, and one for grades seven and up.

BUILDING A CLASSROOM LIBRARY

Educators all agree that access to books is crucial to the development of literacy skills in the very young (Neuman et al., 2001; Neumann, 2006; Robb, 2006; Wells, 1986). The same is true for students in grades four and up. My goal for all language arts and English teachers is to build class libraries with 400 to 700 books on a wide variety of topics and genres at different readability levels—libraries that can motivate students to choose texts they want to read (Allington, 2001; Krashen, 1993; Reutzel et al., 1991; Shefelbine, 2000). But, you don't have to spend school money on magazines, comics, and computer games. Instead, each year invite students to bring in magazines, comics, graphic novels, and video games to share. Take some time to review the materials before you put them in your library.

We teachers need to find creative ways to fund our classroom libraries. As I travel around the country, I find that dollars for both classroom and school libraries have been cut in high-poverty urban and rural areas as well as in middle class suburbs (Guice et al., 1996). It's important to note that youngsters in high-poverty areas have 50 percent fewer books than children in wealthier communities. And it's often the children who live in high-poverty areas who need those well-stocked class libraries to help develop their reading, thinking, and writing abilities.

Once you've made the decision to build your classroom library, give yourself the gift of time—it can take up to five years to acquire 500 books. Also, it's important to understand that each year some books will be lost, and some, especially paperbacks, will wear out from use. These are good problems, for they show that students are reading. I accept

Funding Your Classroom Library

Here are a few suggestions for funding your classroom library. Think creatively, and you'll discover ideas that will work for your school.

- Use book club offerings and earn bonus points for free books when your students place monthly orders. (Visit scholastic.com or call 1-800-SCHOLASTIC.)
- Have a small book allowance for searching local yard, library, and church sales to find books and magazines.
- Encourage your school librarian to contact Scholastic and organize a book fair. Book sales earn points toward free books. Share these "free" titles among teachers.
- Invite your PTA (or PTO) to run a fund-raiser for purchasing books.
- Collect magazines and comics from friends and family members. A friend of mine put an ad in her apartment building elevator for books, magazines, and comics and left a large carton in the elevator to receive donations. In two days, the carton overflowed with reading materials from tenants in the building. After two weeks, my teacher friend had a class library for her seventh graders.
- Bring in copies of your local newspaper.
- Investigate Scholastic's Classroom Libraries for grades K–9. Each library contains 100 books and a teaching booklet with tips for organizing space and effectively using the books in your classroom.

that I'll have to replace some titles yearly, and that's fine with me! Sometimes the school has replacement funds; other times, I replace beloved texts.

Motivate All Readers With Book Displays

When students walk into your room, they should see book displays that extend this invitation: browse, talk about books with a peer, check our reading materials. Make sure students can easily reach the materials in your library. Change displays every four to six weeks. You can ask student volunteers to help you, either early in the morning as buses are arriving or during lunch. Here are some book and reading displays that work for me and teachers I coach.

- On each shelf, display some books with front covers facing out. Change featured books twice a month and take a few minutes to point out the new books.

- Create a place for magazines, comics, and newspapers. Consider spreading them out on a table or on an empty student desk. I like to have the students who bring these to class take a few minutes to chat about them.

- Place books on your desk, on the windowsills, on top of bookcases, and under the chalkboard.

- Every six weeks, feature an author, such as Katherine Paterson or Russell Freedman, or a genre, such as science fiction or biography. Gather books by that author or in that genre and display them on a table or on your desk. Use the Internet to find a biography about the author and add it to the display. Take a few minutes to show each book and talk about the author or genre. Features can stir students' interest in an author or genre that may be unfamiliar to them.

- Create an area where you display new reading materials.

WHY CLASSROOM LIBRARIES ARE MOTIVATING

Instead of having to send students to a school library (if your school has one) for one period a week, by having a classroom library, you can make books and other reading materials available and accessible to students all the time. I find that students browse through the library during class. But equally important, they drop in at lunch and in the morning, before classes start, to look at books and other reading materials. My eighth graders coined the phrase "having books at your fingertips." This is the kind of access that is meaningful to kids.

Classroom libraries cultivate browsing—leafing through reading materials in a leisurely way. And browsing is one way that students can find the text they want to read and can read on their own. According to John Guthrie and Allan Wigfield (2000), it's students' desire, along with a belief that they can learn to read well, that creates their

Students browse to find an independent reading book.

motivation to learn, to improve as readers, and to accomplish a task. Motivation can maintain students' involvement in reading for pleasure, which in turn fosters independent reading. When students have access to books they can read and enjoy, they experience success, hence reinforcing the motivation to continue to read. If students have a steady school diet of books that are too difficult for them to understand, then their motivation, understandably so, diminishes (Shallert & Reed, 1997). Besides motivation, my hope is that classroom libraries will contribute to a rich independent reading life in which readers can develop engagement or a deep connection to a text. We teachers observe engagement at school when students choose to read, even though they can select other activities (Guthrie, 2004).

Make your checkout system easy for students. I keep a notebook on a windowsill in my room. When borrowing a book, students write the book's title, their name, and the date they checked out the book. When returning a book, they simply put a line through their name. I always encourage students to return the book to the same shelf or display rack, but of course, many don't, and I have to do this. Sometimes, in the morning, a student volunteer will help return books to their proper place. Celebrate books being out of place, for it means your students are checking out materials.

Assessing Students Who Read Different Texts for Independent Reading

As you read on, you'll explore ways to assess students' independent reading—ways that encourage students to reflect on their reading, such as discussing their books with a partner or a small group, without a teacher orchestrating the conversations. You'll also explore ways for students to showcase and advertise their independent reading to peers, such as reviewing, sharing, and evaluating their book logs with group members, or giving book talks for the entire class.

I'll also share ways in which students can work in a group and harness their reading stamina to teach poems and short stories to peers. Teaching one another is a sure path to independence in reading and in thinking. According to the research completed by Project CRISS, Creating Independence Through Student-owned Strategies, when students teach others, they retain 90 percent of the material. Teaching is also a great way for students to become experts on a text. The preparation process invites students to probe a text deeply so they can create questions that encourage classmates to infer, make connections, learn about characters and settings from cause/effect relationships, and explore themes.

In the box at right, I've listed the kinds of assessments you can gather from students' independent reading, and the pages where I present and discuss these activities. Keep in mind, though, that you won't be assessing every book students read.

> ### Assessment for Independent Reading
>
> You can use any of the conference forms for whole-class instructional reading on pages 123–124 and 128 to confer with students on their independent reading. In addition, you can gain insight into free-choice reading by using the following:
>
> - Students' write-ups of their reading log discussions (pages 191–195)
> - Oral book talks (pages 198–201)
> - Written book reviews (appendix, page 284)
> - Students' discussion agendas (pages 185–186)
> - Students' agenda notes (pages 190–191)

STUDENT-LED DISCUSSION GROUPS

Use students' independent reading materials to organize student-led discussion groups so that each student can contribute to the discussion. Consider how you want to group students. For me, four to a group is the limit; otherwise, the discussion can run beyond 20 minutes. Some groups might have three to four members, and some groups might have two students discussing their books. You can organize students around fiction and nonfiction, or around a genre such as mystery, fantasy, realistic fiction, or historical fiction, biography, informational text, short stories, drama, science fiction, fairy tales and folktales, myths and legends, or graphic novels (see appendix pages 275–277 for genre-related questions).

Since each group member will be discussing a different text, you'll want to provide students with open-ended questions for fiction and nonfiction (see pages 182–183 for sets of open-ended questions). These student-led discussions can be from 10 to 20 minutes long, depending on whether group members converse about one, two, or three open-ended questions. For example, you can reserve 10 to 15 minutes if students are discussing half of a book they have read—whether at the halfway point or at the end. Or you can set aside 20 minutes for pairs or groups of four to discuss an entire text. Choose the approach that's best for your students and your schedule. However, before you invite groups to discuss their books, use your read-aloud text to model the difference between factual and open-ended questions, and offer students prompts they can use with any text.

Open-Ended Questions for Students Reading Different Texts

Notice that these questions are not book-specific but will work with any fiction or nonfiction text. If students are reading at their comfort levels, then they are ready to move beyond factual questions to queries that invite multiple responses. The only restriction I place on students is that their thinking must be supported with details from the text. Students can cite specific details or use text details to infer. Creating an agenda of questions with quick notes that paraphrase text details enables students to move to valid and diverse interpretations and engage in richer discussions. Students can use the following questions, the Questioning the Author queries on page 273, or the genre questions on appendix pages 275–277.

OPEN-ENDED QUESTIONS AND PROMPTS FOR FICTION

- What does the author want me to think about the protagonist's problems and how she or he copes with the problems?
- What messages, themes, or big ideas is the author sending me with this story?
- How does setting affect the protagonist? Discuss two settings and show the affects on the main character.
- What characters did you connect to? Explain the connection—problems, siblings, friends, family, school, and so on.
- Are there words the protagonist or another important character spoke and/or actions the character took that helped you draw conclusions about his or her personality? Find and discuss two important sections.
- Explain what the protagonist learned about him- or herself and his or her family and friends. Name the events, people, conflicts, or decisions that enabled the protagonist to gain self-knowledge.
- Choose several minor characters and show how they affected the main character.
- Can you pinpoint other problems the protagonist couldn't solve? What were they? Explain why you think these problems weren't resolved.
- Discuss how the title connects to the story.
- Describe a conflict between two characters. Explain how the characters resolved the conflict, and what you learned about each character's personality.
- Discuss the messages you think the author is sending you about family, friends, feelings, nature, life experiences, or a historical period. Use details from the story to back up your ideas.
- Identify two different relationships in the text and explain what the author wants you to understand about these relationships.

OPEN-ENDED QUESTIONS AND PROMPTS FOR NONFICTION

- What new information did you learn? Give two examples that swayed your thinking, and explain how they added to your knowledge about the topic or changed the way you think about the topic.
- What about this book grabbed your attention? Was it the topic? Photographs? Special features? Author? Discuss these elements and explain why each fascinates you.
- Pinpoint two to three facts in the text that you believe could be part of a museum

continued on next page

Differentiating Reading Instruction

exhibition. Explain why you would display these and what you hope museum visitors will learn.

- Take a visual walk through your book. Choose two to four of these elements: chart, diagram, sidebar, letter, diary entry, newspaper quotation, or photograph and caption. Discuss the importance of each element you selected, and explain how it connects to the topic.
- Did reading this text inspire you to take civil action by writing a letter, or to work for a cause that may improve the world? Discuss facts that raised your awareness of the topic or issue, and the action or actions you might take.
- Discuss three or four new and unusual words you learned from this text. Explain how each word connects to the topic and how it helped you better understand your reading.

Invite Students to Create Their Own Discussion Questions

Once students understand the difference between a factual and an open-ended question, you can invite pairs who chose the same independent reading book to pose questions on a strip of paper, and then use these questions for their discussion.

Use a read-aloud text to model for students the difference between these two kinds of questions. Here are factual questions from "The Party" that I write on the chalkboard:

- Who is the author? Who is giving the party?

Here are the open-ended questions that I offer:

- Why does the narrator want to be invited?
- How and why does the narrator blame herself for not being invited?

Scaffolding Students With Questions That Move Discussions Forward

- Can you give some supporting details from your book?
- Did you agree/disagree with the character? Explain.
- Can you make a connection to what another group member shared?
- Are there other themes in your book?
- Can you explain why this information matters to people?
- What do you think the author wants you to understand about this information? This person? This character? Setting? Conflict?

Explain to students that their answers need to have validity—meaning that the answers must be supported with details and inferences from the text. I tell students that having two valid responses is enough. Here is a list of questions that Madeline, an eighth grader, wrote for chapters 14 to 18 of Robert Cormier's *The Chocolate War* (Pantheon, 1974).

Either when students discuss your read-aloud text or when you lead small-group discussions, call attention to the prompts you use to maintain the momentum of a discussion. In the box on pages 182–183, you'll find the questions I model with, using a read-aloud text, to show students how to keep discussions alive and energetic.

Management Tips for Student-Led Discussions With Different Texts

Together with your class, establish a deadline date for an independent reading book to ensure that every student is ready to plan and discuss. If you want, you can make this an end-of-the-month learning experience. Ask students to choose any independent reading book from their book logs (see page 265) that they completed about two to three days before month's

> Why does Brother Leon say Jerry's name everyday when he knows what the answer will be?
>
> Why did Bro. Leon issue a false report?
>
> 15. Why does Emile want the picture?
>
> Do you think on page 78 Archie seems scared of Emile? Why?
>
> 16. why does the author talk about the chalk and what does it symbolize? 84
>
> 17. Why did Jerry say no?
>
> 18. What does being buried alive symbolize? The Vigils—being stuck. What does it mean to "sleep your life away"?
>
> 19. What is not cool about what Jerry's doing?

FIGURE 6.1: Questions that Madeline poses.

end. Provide groups with a list of questions that can keep their discussions alive and meaningful. You can have students tape a typed list of the questions into their journal or you can write the questions on large chart paper for the entire class. When students use these questions that encourage deeper probing, their discussions about different texts become richer and are more likely to contain insights into themes, big ideas, and characters.

One final recommendation to keep in mind: it's best to initiate student-led discussion groups not only after you've completed a round of teacher-led reading groups, but also after you've modeled with your read-aloud how you prepare an agenda that includes choosing and responding to questions about a text. (See pages 186 for my modeling and think alouds.)

Student-Led Discussion Groups Need a Leader

Either choose one member from each group to lead the discussion by using the open-ended questions on pages 182–183, or have students volunteer for this job. Then, each time a group meets, have a different student assume the leadership role.

Scaffolding Discussions With Agendas and Notes

I find that the most successful discussions result when students take the time to plan what they will share. Choosing their questions and jotting down notes about the answers prior to their formal discussion ensures that the conversations about texts have depth. I use a part of two consecutive periods to prepare students for discussion groups on independent reading.

First period: Set aside about 10 to 15 minutes for students to create agendas that include the title and author of the book, the questions they will use, and the notes that answer the questions.

Second period: Reserve, during the next class, 15 to 20 minutes for students to complete their agendas and submit them to you. Or you can circulate around the room, read the questions, and okay them. Once agendas have been approved, encourage students to use their books to find details and inferences that answer each question. Students should answer each question by taking notes. Make sure you model the process (see page 186) so students can develop a mental model of your expectations. Students are now ready to discuss their books.

Here are the questions and notes based on "The Party" by Pam Muñoz Ryan that I use to model the process. I put the two questions on chart paper and think aloud to explain the process so students have a resource to return to as they complete their agendas and notes.

Robb's agenda: two questions:

1. **What does the author want me to think about the protagonist's problem and how she deals with the problem?** Notes: narrator blames self for not getting invited; Bridget makes fun of nar. working hard on their project; nar. feels isolated; my camp experiences.

2. **What messages, themes, or big ideas is the author trying to send through this story?** Notes: question group's values; not about blaming self as nar. did; cliques, in-groups hurt others; wonder about what friendship really is.

ROBB'S THINK ALOUD FOR THE FIRST QUESTION:

> *The narrator believes that there must a reason for her not being invited. She thinks that her feet were too big, that her face had pimples, that she must have said something wrong to Bridget. Was the narrator too studious? I think the author wants me to see how being isolated, by being the only girl not invited, can make your mind wonder what's wrong with you. Feeling left out can make you blame yourself because you are alone and out of the group totally. I think the author had the narrator look at her pimples and big feet to show how cruel teens can be to one another. I remember kids at camp not playing with me when I was 14 because I had pigtails. It took a long time for me to get over the hurt and understand that, with or without pigtails, I was the same person.*

ROBB'S THINK ALOUD FOR THE SECOND QUESTION:

> *The author makes me question the "in-group's values." Bridget invited girls she thought would make herself look better. I see how hurtful cliques are when the narrator agonizes all day about not being invited and thinks her friends are always talking about her and the party details. Just because the narrator is unpopular doesn't mean that it's the narrator's responsibility for not being invited. She doesn't need to assign blame. Finally, the author makes me think about the meaning of true friendship. By Bridget's actions and words, I know that she's not the narrator's friend.*

ROBB'S WRAP-UP THINK ALOUD:

> *Notice that the questions come from the list of queries that could apply to any text. But my notes are detailed and specific. My notes also go beyond the facts of the story, and I used details to infer, draw conclusions, and make connections.*

*I wrote out all of my thoughts so you could see how I explored unstated mean-
ings by using details from the story. Your notes can be words, phrases, and even
pictures, but I want you to think about the details to help you discover what
the author wants you to understand, know, and think. You'll also make some
connections as you share and answer questions a group member poses. Before
ending your discussions, reread your notes and add any new understandings
you learned from the conversation.*

Student-Led Reading Partnerships and Groups in Action

Inviting students to plan and participate in discussions on their independent reading has
five powerful benefits. It does the following:

- Asks students to engage in an authentic discussion experience that's similar to the
  way adults converse about books in book clubs.
- Allows you to harness the power of peer recommendations of beloved books, the
  most effective advertisement for books and reading.
- Encourages students to deepen their understandings about a text through discussion
  and responses to queries from peers.
- Moves students to analyzing and evaluating texts by using open-ended questions
  that have two or more possible ways of viewing an idea.
- Enables you to partner or group students who have selected the same text for
  independent reading.

The sample student-led discussions that follow show a derailed discussion among
fifth graders using the same book. Reading the same book does not ensure that a meaningful discussion will take place. As you will observe when you read the eighth-graders'
discussion about different texts, preparation makes a huge difference.

Grade five partners in action: Here is a conversation between two fifth graders who
both chose to read *The Sign of the Beaver* by Elizabeth George Speare (Dell, 1983). The
pair discussed without any planning. Each student opened by saying something about
the book, but the discussion quickly turned to personal matters and veered away from
the objective. This occurs more frequently when students "wing it" and don't take the
time to reflect on their reading. The pair were told to discuss chapters 14 and 15.

STUDENT ONE: Do you know anything about this Robinson Crusoe?

STUDENT TWO: Yeah, it's the book that Attean's learning to read with. I think he [Robinson Crusoe] was alone on an island and had someone to help.

Paired discussion based on preparation notes.

STUDENT ONE: I learned that Attean helps Matt. He [Attean] shows him [Matt] how to use onions in stew, what plants took away the pain from bug bites, and plants that Matt should never eat.

STUDENT TWO: Yeah. Matt teaches Attean to speak English. You going to soccer practice this afternoon?

STUDENT ONE: Yeah. Our team has won every game. We play you on Friday.

STUDENT TWO: It'll be close. We won most of our games.

STUDENT ONE: Can you come with me and my dad for pizza after practice?

From this point on, the discussion is about soccer, the position each boy plays, and the outing to the movies they are planning for Saturday. Notice, too, that in this paired discussion, they just state facts. Neither student uses information to infer, connect, or draw conclusions. With questions to guide planning and thinking, you can transform these informal discussions into using information to think about and analyze texts. The preplanning of the two eighth graders in the next discussion clearly reveals where their discussions will go.

Grade eight partners in action: I've included part of two agendas of eighth graders and their discussion based on these agendas, which I transcribed from my notes to illustrate the power of preparing for a discussion. The questions and notes keep students on topic for the discussion and help them maintain the discussion's momentum.

Hannah's agenda for *Heroes, Gods, and Monsters of the Greek Myths* by Bernard Evslin (Bantam, 1975)

Prompt: Identify one or two personality traits of Apollo, Athena, and Artemis, and find support for your choices in the text.

Dylan's agenda for *The Shakespeare Stealer* by Gary Blackwood (Penguin, 2001)

Question: What values does Widge have?

Part of the Discussion Between Hannah and Dylan. Hannah discusses her notes, and Dylan his. They turn their conversation to the values of Widge and compare them with the values of Athena and Apollo.

HANNAH: The values you talked about—loyalty and compassion—hmm, let me see if I can connect those to a god or a goddess.

DYLAN: I don't think compassion will work with what you said about Apollo.

HANNAH: Yeah. And Athene didn't have compassion for Arachne—lots of anger there.

FIGURE 6.2: Here are Hannah's notes for the personality traits of Apollo and Artemis.

But I think Athene was loyal to Athens, her city. She helped her people.

DYLAN: Maybe you could say Apollo was loyal to music.

HANNAH: I guess.

Believe me, students don't always make the connections that Dylan and Hannah made. It's the planning and thinking these students completed before sharing that gives

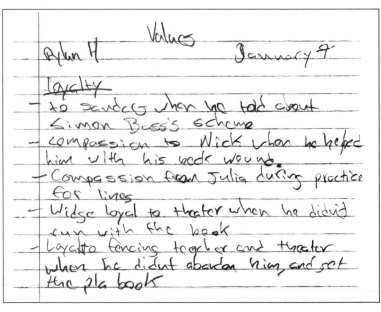

FIGURE 6.3: Here are Dylan's notes on loyalty.

these discussions power. Because pairs often exchange books, these discussions are ways to attract students to other genres and topics.

Assessing Students' Agenda Notes

Reviewing students' agendas before they have a partner or group discussion enables me to provide positive feedback and to identify those students who need more scaffolding. Some students write one-word responses to questions; others jot down notes for just one instead of two or three questions. When students struggle with digging details out of a book, it's usually because they have been frustrated reading books far above their instructional levels. These students will benefit from your support as they complete their first few agendas. Understand that they might have had years of negative experiences that may have eroded their self-confidence and their belief that their ideas have merit. Supporting these students before they experience yet another failure can make a difference in their learning attitudes and willingness to try. You can also listen to conversations students have. I find, however, that once the year starts blazing forward, I can't listen to all pairs and groups, so reviewing agendas works well for me.

Differentiating Reading Instruction

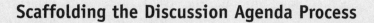

Another way to encourage reflecting on independent reading is to have students review, discuss, and self-evaluate their book logs.

MINING STUDENTS' BOOK LOGS

Every six to seven weeks I ask my students to read their book logs and discuss some aspect of their reading lists with their group. If your students sit in rows, organize them into groups for this activity. My students sit at desks that are arranged in groups of four or six. This sharing is a celebration of students' choices and a top-notch way for students to advertise a book.

Help Students Complete Book Logs

Once or twice a week, ask students to update their book logs. This takes only a few minutes, and it will ensure that students' book logs are current.

Each year, the first time I introduce the book log discussion, students roll their eyes and pass around looks that shout: "Boring!" However, once they've experienced the discussion, students recognize the value of reflecting on book logs. If you set aside time for students to maintain book logs by entering completed or abandoned books, it will become self-evident, through use, why this recordkeeping is helpful to their personal reading lives. The list jogs students' memories. When Liz Snow, an eighth grader, completed her last book log review, she noted: "I couldn't believe that I read fifty-five books. Without listing them, I wouldn't remember them all. I've marked favorites to reread this summer." Like Liz and Rhett (see page 175), many students reread favorite books. "It's like seeing a movie three times," Liz tells me. "Every time I see it, I find different things to notice, and I take in more of the dialogue." Then there are

Snippets of Students' Book Log Discussions

Grade Eight

- "I chucked this book because every time I started to read, I got sleepy. I like action-packed books and not books that go on about stuff."
- "I found a new author—Richard Peck—and plan to read all of his books."

Grade Six

- "I loved *Bridge to Terabithia* and read it in September. I don't know why I didn't look for more of Paterson's books. But now [in December] I'm checking out three so I can read them over the holiday."
- "I read only comics and leafed through magazines until November. Then my friend did a book talk on the Chicken Soup book about sports heroes. I read it. It was great. I'm looking for other Chicken Soup books to read."

Grade Four

- "I'm hooked on the Boxcar series. That's all I read. My mom wants me to try other kinds of books, but I'll finish all of these, and then I'll look [for other books]."
- "I like to read all I can find of one author. I just read six books by Patricia Polacco. Now my best friend and I are reading the Magic School Bus books."

For assessment: Have students summarize the content of a book log discussion.

Differentiating Reading Instruction

some students, like Nina, a fifth grader, who reread books that have been a challenge for them. Rereading builds their comprehension of plot details and helps them visualize settings and characters. As Nina told me: "I just had to read *Because of Winn Dixie* (Kate DeCamillo, Candlewick, 2001), and I really enjoyed it the third time. It was fun and easier by then, and I could see the places and characters."

Suggestions for Involving Students in Book Log Discussions

Having book log discussions is the ideal way for students to advertise to their peers the books and other reading materials they loved or disliked. Often after one of these conversations, students will seek out a title that a peer discussed. I set aside 10 to 15 minutes every seven to nine weeks for students to review, reflect on, and discuss their book logs. As students discuss, I circulate and listen to their comments; I jot down snippets like those in the box below to share with the rest of the class.

On page 193 are some suggestions for engaging students in book log discussions. Each discussion topic has questions that you can write on chart paper or on the chalkboard.

Reviewing and Discussing Book Logs to Foster Self-Evaluation

In February or early March, and again near the end of the year, I ask students to discuss their book logs, and then write what they've learned about their reading in journals. I use these reflections to measure and monitor how students view their progress.

In figures 6.4 and 6.5, I've included the book log reflections of Meg and Ben, two eighth graders, after they had reviewed their book logs from September to March 8. Ben, whom I'd describe as a reluctant reader, mainly because of his slow reading rate, had noticed that his reading speed had increased. He had also expanded the variety of topics and genres he read. Reading at his recreational level enabled Ben to read two books a month, and in March, he thought he could read three. Notice the positive "I can do it" tone of Ben's write-up (figure 6.4). Ben arrived in eighth grade with a negative attitude toward reading. On his survey, Ben wrote that the words he associated with reading were "annoying, boring." Contributing to this change in Ben included having choice, his acceptance of where he was with his independent reading, his giving and hearing book talks (see pages 198–201), and his experiencing positive conferences with me and his peers.

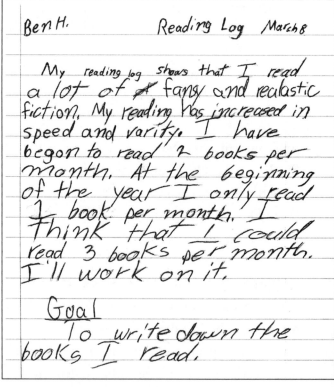

Ben H.   Reading Log   March 8

My reading log shows that I read a lot of fangy and realistic fiction. My reading has increased in speed and varity. I have begon to read 2 books per month. At the beginning of the year I only read 1 book per month. I think that I could read 3 books per month. I'll work on it.

Goal
To write down the books I read.

FIGURE 6.4: Ben discusses his book log.

Meg, an avid reader, had noticed that the number of books she had read each month varied. When monitoring students' progress, it's important for teachers not to react negatively. Perhaps the duration of time learners have to read at home and at school changes. It would be a mistake to tell Meg that because she had read nine books at the beginning of March, she would then have to continue that pattern. Choice extends to the kind of reading as well as to the amount. Again, you see a student writing about the joys of rereading books she loved. By celebrating rereading, you can help adolescent learners cultivate a personal reading life.

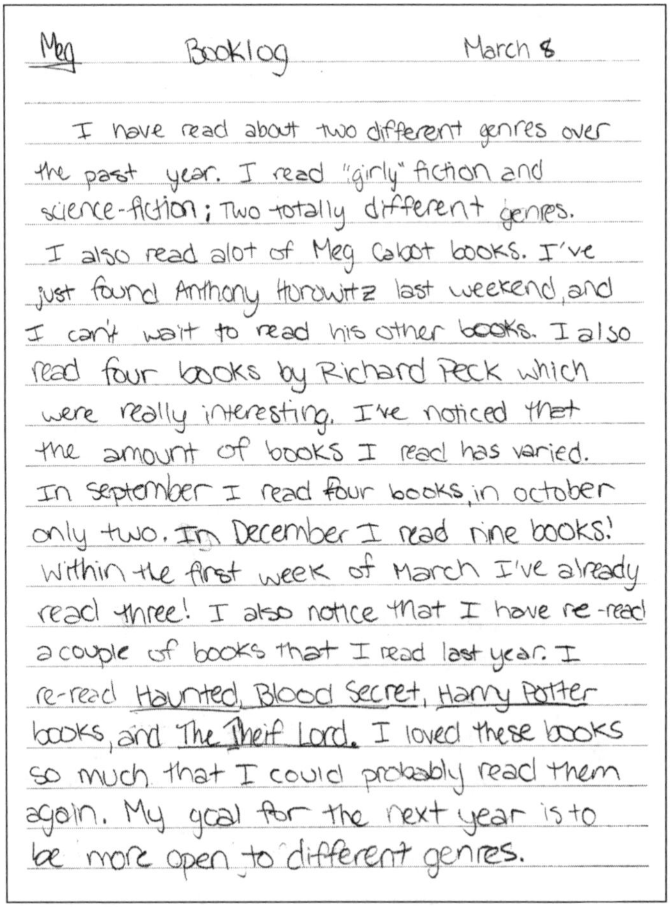

Meg	Booklog	March 8

I have read about two different genres over the past year. I read "girly" fiction and science-fiction; Two totally different genres. I also read alot of Meg Cabot books. I've just found Anthony Horowitz last weekend, and I can't wait to read his other books. I also read four books by Richard Peck which were really interesting. I've noticed that the amount of books I read has varied. In september I read four books, in october only two. In December I read nine books! Within the first week of March I've already read three! I also notice that I have re-read a couple of books that I read last year. I re-read Haunted, Blood Secret, Harry Potter books, and The Theif Lord. I loved these books so much that I could probably read them again. My goal for the next year is to be more open to different genres.

FIGURE 6.5: Meg explains that the number of books she reads each month varies.

Student Presentations: Independent Thinking with Comfort-Level Books

Asking students to present book talks or to work with a group to prepare and teach a lesson provides you with insights into their ability to think and plan on their own. When students experience success with these tasks, they not only learn a lot about process and information, but they also gain self-confidence and efficacy—the belief that they can accomplish goals and tasks (Schunk & Zimmerman, 1997; Shallert & Reed, 1997). However, students' success ultimately depends on whether they can read the texts they're using for independent work. Reading for individual and group presentations needs to be at students' comfort levels (see appendix page 262) so they can experience success and contribute to their learning as well as the learning of peers.

Abandoning a Book

If a reader dislikes an independent reading text, he or she should have the right to abandon it. I ask students to read the first two or three chapters of a book before returning the text to the class library. By that time, readers know whether they like or dislike it. Adults are always free to abandon texts; in my opinion, students should have the same privilege.

I ask students to jot down in their book logs, below the date, why they decided not to complete a book. Reasons such as "slow, no action, can't connect, too hard, boring" are typical. Forcing students to complete a text they dislike only fosters negative attitudes toward reading—something you and I want to avoid. Jaime, an eighth grader, explained her feelings about having the right to abandon a book in her May reflection on independent reading. Notice how she uses strategies like rereading, adjusting her reading rate, and using context clues to figure out tough words using context clues. Having reading choice propelled Jaime into developing a personal reading life, and she read more in eighth grade than in sixth and seventh grades.

Jaime

My reading this year has drastically increased. I've probably read more books this year than I read in my 6th and 7th grade at Daniel Morgan. I wasn't ready for it, but I'm slowly catching on.

I've learned to find clues in sentences if there is a word I don't comprehend. I see many words that I don't understand in books, but I'm learning more and more vocabulary as I read.

Also, I don't feel pressured to read a book I don't like. As long as I give the book a chance, by reading a few chapters, first.

Furthermore, I've learned to take my time when reading and to reread if I don't understand.

FIGURE 6.6: Jaime's reflection shows the importance of choice.

Student Book Talks: Top-Notch Advertisements for Independent Reading Books. Having book talks is a great way to advertise independent reading books. This section features guidelines for 11 book talks: one on issues, nine on genres, and one that uses a timeline. (See ten additional book talk guidelines in *Teaching Reading: A Differentiated Approach* by Laura Robb, Scholastic, 2008.) Since students read a variety of texts, offer them a book talk format that works for the texts they choose. The guidelines that follow discourage students from retelling the book's plot, giving away the ending, or recounting all of the information learned.

Before asking students to complete book talks, make sure you model the book talk process by jotting down notes on chart paper and presenting a model book talk. See page 199 for the notes and model book talk I used to present "The Party" by Pam Muñoz Ryan.

The suggestions that follow support book talking in your class and students' sharing of their reading with peers.

- To give students time to prepare, offer students book talk guidelines (see pages 198–201) two or three days before the talks take place.
- Ask students to use the book talk guidelines to prepare notes on a 4-by-6-inch index card; notes help students think about the points they'll make.
- Have students limit book talks to two or three minutes.
- Have students speak slowly, clearly, and make eye contact with the audience.

Students should rehearse their book talks at home so they only occasionally need to refer to their notes.

In addition, ask your students to create listening standards for the audience; here are the standards a group of sixth graders developed. I post these on chart paper and review them each time I schedule book talks.

- Be a good listener.
- Save your questions for the end of the book talk.
- Avoid laughing, making faces, reading, writing, doodling, or giggling. Such behaviors will make the book talker uncomfortable and lose concentration.
- Know that there will be time for one or two questions from the audience per talk.

When I listen to book talks, I jot down notes on a 3-by-5-inch self-stick note or in a composition book, to address how well the students are following the guidelines in the book talk. If you want to assign a grade, here's the criteria I use: allot 60 to 65 percent for the content and 35 to 40 percent for presentation. Base the presentation grade on the guidelines above. Adapt these suggestions to the grade you teach and to the needs of your students. To show you the kinds of notes I jot down during book talks, I've included copies of two assessments I had written on self-stick notes (see figures 6.7 and 6.8). One is for grade six, and the other is for grade eight. Note that I jot down several positives before using a question to ask about a missing element.

> Travis - "Issue" Bk. Talk
> Nothing But the Truth by Avi
> - Issue: lies vs. truth with Phillip Malloy + high school administrators + news reporters.
> - Taught: how believing the lie can ruin lives - e.g. Malloy & Eng. teacher, Ms Narwin
> - Made Travis think of implications of self-delusion!   A

FIGURES 6.7 and 6.8: Book talk assessments.

Book Talk Guidelines That Work for Diverse Reading Levels

The 11 book talk guidelines that follow enable students to reflect on either the genre of their book or an important issue a book raised. For students who are visual and prefer to use art as a springboard for sharing, book talk 11 invites them to create an illustrated timeline of key events to use as the basis of a book talk.

> Katy - "Folk Tale" Bk. Talk
> The Brave Little Parrot by Rafe Martin
> - Did a great job explaining genre - even pointed out that this is a "jataka" tale from India.
> - forces of good & evil + what the Parrot had to do all well done
> - Can you explain the lesson or point of the tale?   B+

Book Talk 1: Think About the Issue

- State the title and author.

- Explain the issue in your book.

- Explain two things that your book taught you about this issue.

- Discuss whether the book changed your opinion about this issue, and explain how.

Book Talk 2: Fairy Tales and Folktales

- State the title, author, and genre.

- Identify the hero or heroine and the major task he or she had to accomplish.

Teach All Students: Share Your Sample Book Talk Notes and Presentation

Take the time to build your students' mental model of preparing for and presenting book talks. What follows are my book talk guidelines, my notes, and a transcription of the oral presentation. If students need extra modeling, repeat this process before moving them to independence. Here are my notes for "The Party," in which I explored the genre of realistic fiction.

Robb's notes for "The Party" by Pam Muñoz Ryan: three realistic elements: the setting, school is realistic; the narrator's problem—not getting invited to Bridget's party; narrator's friends whispering about the party at school; connection to narrator—being left out of the in-group; feeling lonely.

Robb's model book talk:

> *"The Party" by Pam Muñoz Ryan is a realistic short story about a girl who is not accepted socially by her peers. The narrator is the only student who doesn't receive an invitation to Bridget's party. This kind of situation is realistic as it happens at our school, and I know kids who have been left out. When you're left out, you feel like it's your fault. The narrator felt this way and blamed her pimples and big feet. The narrator feels that others are talking about her and the party when they whisper in groups. This is realistic as I feel the same way—so do my friends. I can connect to the narrator because there have been times when I have been left out and felt just as bad. I also connect to the ending—finally getting that invitation. I think the narrator takes it because she wanted to go so badly.*

Students' observations and comments: here's what eighth graders noted.

- "It was more than your notes. You connected ideas to realistic stuff."
- "You followed your notes."
- "You hardly looked at your notes; you looked at us and talked slowly."
- "You followed the guidelines. It's like when we take notes for discussions. Writing ideas down helps with remembering."
- "You gave the outcome and reasons."

- Explain the forces of good and the forces of evil. Who won the struggle and why did that side win?

- Explain the moral or lesson you learned from this text.

Book Talk 3: Science Fiction Adventures

- State the title, author, and genre.

- Explain the science and/or technology in our world that the author has carried into the future. Show how the author has changed this present-day science/technology.

- What warning(s) about our world and lifestyle is the author sending? Do you agree or disagree? Explain your reasons.

Book Talk 4: Make Mine Mystery

- State the title, author, and genre.

- Explain the crime.

- Identify the detective in your book and discuss two qualities he or she has that support sleuthing out clues.

- Discuss two clues that led you to solve the mystery.

Book Talk 5: Shivery Suspense

- State the title, author, and genre.

- Read two examples of suspense from the book and explain why you felt each one was suspenseful.

- Would you recommend this book to others? Explain why or why not.

Book Talk 6: Historical Fiction

- State the title, author, and genre.

- Identify the historical period and discuss three things you learned about this period. These can relate to family, religion, friendship, jobs, schooling, and so on.

- Discuss two ways in which life during the time of your book was the same as or different from your life today.

Book Talk 7: Fabulous Fantasy

- State the title, author, and genre.

- Describe the fantasy world of your book.

- Identify the main character and explain the reasons for the tasks undertaken and journey he or she makes.

- Explain how society changed and whether the changes were positive.

Book Talk 8: Biography

- State the title, author, and genre.
- Name the person your book is about.
- Tell what this person did to change the world. Was this contribution positive or negative? Explain.
- In what ways did an event, decision, or other person influence this person?

Book Talk 9: Informational Books

- State the title, author, and genre.
- What drew you to reading about this topic?
- Discuss two new or fascinating facts that you learned.
- Did the book influence the way you think about this topic, or your understanding of it? Explain how.

Book Talk 10: Realistic Fiction

- State the title, author, and genre.
- Identify three elements, such as setting, problems, or conflicts, and explain how each one is realistic.
- Choose an event or a character with which you connected and explain the connection.

Book Talk 11: Timeline

- Choose a character from your book.
- Choose four to five important events he or she lived through.
- Plan your timeline and have your teacher approve the plan.
- Create your timeline and include the following: your name, the title and author of the book, the name of the character, and a brief summary of each event. You can illustrate some events. Be creative and original.
- Use your timeline to present your book talk.

Book talks are not just for advertising great reads. They also give you a chance to offer students choices so they can select a book talk format that they can complete. Make sure you ask students to develop some book talk guidelines themselves. That's how many of these originated.

Pause, Reflect, and Consider Ten Questions . . .

As you plan your curriculum, class schedule, and the kind of homework assignments you'll give, it's appropriate to consider setting aside time for students to complete independent reading during the school day. Current research points to benefits that go beyond fluency and reading rate to building vocabulary and background knowledge. Independent reading quite naturally allows you to differentiate instruction because students can choose books that interest them and that are on their comfort levels. Consider your students' interests and reading levels when you collect books for your classroom library. Books at diverse reading levels and books on a variety of genres, including graphic novels, comics, magazines, and newspapers, can provide your students with the choices they need to enjoy practice reading and develop personal reading lives.

Before you move on to Chapter 7, which discusses writing to improve reading, reflect on these questions. In fact, I suggest that you mull over these questions annually, before school starts.

- Do my students have easy access to books through a classroom or school library?
- Is there time during the school day for students to read at their comfort levels, for at least 20 minutes, two times a week?
- Do I ask students to list completed texts on a book log? Is there time to do this during class?
- Have I organized independent reading activities to meet students' diverse abilities?
- Is most of my homework in language arts or in English independent reading at students' comfort levels?
- Have I created inviting displays that not only stimulate students' desire to browse but also motivate them to check out texts?
- Do I understand that differentiation includes choice of text and varied readability levels?
- Can I accept that the amount students read will vary from month to month?
- Do I assess students in ways that honor their different learning styles and abilities?
- Am I a reader who shares materials I love with my students?

Chapter 7

Writing and Differentiation

Using Writing to Support Comprehension for Every Student

C lay, a fifth grader, showed me how writing both during and after reading improves comprehension and can be used to evaluate students' reading progress and needs. During his fifth-grade year, Clay worked with me for 45 minutes three times a week on self-monitoring and building comprehension while reading, as well as applying inferential reading strategies to texts. "I gotta write more when I'm reading," Clay said, during a session in mid-October. "That's how I'll know if I'm getting the stuff in the book." And so, Clay read a few paragraphs, paused, discussed the content with me, and then wrote what he recalled in his journal. Gradually, stopping every few paragraphs transformed into stopping to think, discuss, and write after a few pages or at the end of a chapter. Sometimes Clay used words to clarify meaning, to make inferences, and to self-evaluate his application of strategies. Other times Clay used drawings and detailed captions or cartoons. He approached the writing with gusto and astutely observed, "It [the writing and drawing] makes me stop and think. It helps me see what I get and don't get." Clay's words, "stop and think" and "see what I get and don't get" replayed in my mind again and again. The writing and drawing helped Clay self-monitor. He needed more than a one-on-one discussion with his internal voice when reading independently. "Most of the times I'd stop to see what I remembered, but I didn't think much. The writing helped me think."

Clay's words and the progress he made that year by reading and discussing, then writing and drawing, to self-evaluate his understanding led me to rethink the relationship between the recall of details and reading comprehension, and talk and writing. To support reading, talk and writing became integral parts of my reading instruction. Talk and writing supported students' ability to infer and analyze texts. Reading students' writing became an important assessment, as it supported instructional decisions that in turn helped me differentiate reading instruction. The primary purpose of this chapter is to show you how to use students' writing about reading to help you identify students who need additional support with reading. Then you can plan and differentiate the scaffolds you offer them.

As You Continue to Read . . .

As you continue to read this chapter, you'll investigate a menu of ways for students to respond to literature. In addition to journaling during the teacher's instructional read aloud, students also respond during small-group instruction. You'll explore ways to manage students' sharing their journal responses with classmates. You'll find suggestions for helping students self-evaluate their reading progress by reviewing and reflecting on journal entries, and suggestions for

How Writing Helps You Differentiate

- Reading students' writing helps you evaluate their understanding.

analyzing students' journals so you can plan the instructional support they need. To monitor students' application of reading strategies and their ability to connect issues to texts during reading, you'll read about another way to link writing to reading—bookmarks. The chapter closes with suggestions for using students' journal writing to plan written assignments, such as analytical essays that your school district requires, and assessments that you negotiate with students, such as creating original illustrations or a Web site. What's changed for me is that the writing is no longer an assigned weekly or biweekly journal entry. Instead writing occurs throughout reading class to monitor students' recall and comprehension before, during, and after reading as well as to provide multiple opportunities for clarifying thinking.

Changing the Journaling Landscape

It's three weeks into the school year. Sixth graders file into the classroom. Journals are on each desk, and on the chalkboard is the first journal entry heading students will need after they complete a short warm-up on antagonistic forces. "Ugh," Katie says as she slides into her chair, "not more journal writing."

"Yeah," echoes through the room as heads nod. This scenario repeats itself in my eighth-grade classroom. Why so much resistance to journaling? you might be wondering. The same question bombarded my mind each time class began and several students voiced their displeasure about thinking on paper. Students knew that these journals would *not* be graded, but resistance reared its head again and again. I had a hunch that students were not used to continually moving from brief pair-shares, or chatting with a partner for a few minutes, to writing, or on occasion, skipping the pair-share and moving directly to writing. For my students, journaling had happened once or twice a week in previous English classes. I used to ask students to respond to literature after reading a chunk of text or the entire text. However, my use of journals had shifted. Now, I invited students to explore ideas during my daily read alouds and during reading groups. Why the shift? I wanted students to develop the habit of constructing meaning *during* reading that would eventually transfer to their independent reading and reading in other subjects. So I invited students to write using Questioning the Author (QtA) to discover what the author meant; I also posed questions during my read alouds and during small-group lessons that related the text to the issue that I was integrating into the unit of study. I based this decision to journal frequently about reading on the premise that writing is an act of discovering what we think and understand (Murray, 1984; Self, 1987; Zinsser, 1988).

By the first days of October, complaints had dramatically diminished, and I decided that this would be a good time to explore students' feelings and reactions to thinking on paper. I had waited several weeks because I was hoping students had moved beyond their initial negative feelings and could now give me more balanced feedback. I met with small groups in each grade, debriefed about their journaling experiences, and noted what students said, using these questions: *Explain how you feel about frequent journaling. How can I improve this journaling process?* I found their comments to be candid, and I used them to fine-tune the journaling response process.

These debriefing meetings enabled me to differentiate my expectations and change my teaching style to respond to students' suggestions. I wanted all levels of readers to improve writing to explore ideas while reading. I hoped that students would internalize this continued practice and that building comprehension by interacting with the author

Some Comments From Eighth Graders

- "Finding the words to go beyond retelling to thinking took a long time."

- "Once I really started thinking, I needed more than a minute or two to write."

- "I thought this was a waste in the beginning. But when I reread my writing, I saw I was understanding more. This happened first in group. It was harder when you read aloud."

Some Comments From Sixth Graders

- "I hate doing this. I still do."

- "I'm writing more. I try to write what pops into my head."

- "It's easier for me. I guess because we do it so much."

- "I like when we talked first."

- "I'm glad we can draw. Drawing seems easier for me sometimes."

and text while reading would spill over into their independent reading and reading for other classes (Rosenblatt, 1978).

For me, writing is an important aspect of differentiating reading instruction, as it can develop, in all readers, from those who struggle to those who read well, the heightened level of interaction—talking to the text and author—that bonds learners to books. Moreover, students will write at their comfort level about their interactions with a text. Therefore, some will probe ideas, infer, connect, and write a great deal whereas others will write brief retellings and stick to literal meanings. These variations help you pinpoint students who require your support or peer support. Interactive reading can also motivate students to read independently and move from writing on paper to composing mental responses that can improve their vocabulary, and their ability to infer, analyze, and connect, and also build their background knowledge.

RESPONDING TO STUDENTS' FEEDBACK ABOUT JOURNALING

I took students' comments seriously and mulled over their candid feedback because my goal was to continue these journaling forays into texts and have the experience be positive. With students' feedback, I made several adjustments.

All students agreed that they needed more "think time" to write. To provide this, I adjusted my read-aloud lessons by diminishing the number of breaks and asking students to write twice: once during the read aloud and once again at the end. Sometimes students responded to a query I posed before I started the read aloud, and then wrote after I completed it. Students helped me recognize the power of having them periodically reread a series of entries and then add new ideas to their first response. I decided to have students do this more often.

Students' comments showed me that integrating talking, thinking, and writing into lessons each day, along with using a read-aloud text to model a written response, gradually made the task easier. However, you may find through observation or conferences that writing so often about reading during class frustrates some students. During a brief conference with Paul, a sixth grader, I discovered that he hated responding because of one difficulty—his handwriting couldn't keep pace with the speed of his ideas. In the spirit of differentiating, I invited Paul to use a class computer to enter his responses and tape a print out of them into his journal. This simple adjustment transformed Paul's attitude. If you don't have a computer in your classroom, consider taking down dictation for students like Paul. The point is that journal writing, teacher observations, student-teacher conferences, and debriefings can inform instructional adjustments and teach you how to support students' learning.

Over time, I also learned that when students pair-share-write during a read aloud, and during and after group discussions, they improve and enlarge comprehension of big ideas and issues (Hernandez et al. 2006; Ivey & Fisher, 2006; Robb, 2006). Elizabeth, an eighth grader, noted in her March self-evaluation, "The more I write about reading, the easier it [writing] becomes. The words just pour out." Daily practice leads to students being able to fill journal pages with ideas and hunches. They are more apt to take a chance on their initial thoughts, knowing that over time they can make adjustments. I always clearly explain to students that journal writing while reading—journal writing that builds comprehension—will not be graded.

DIFFERENTIATE YOUR JOURNAL WRITING EXPECTATIONS

I differentiate journal writing by inviting students to use different kinds of journal responses. For example, when working with reading groups, each group completes journal responses that meet their instructional needs. In my eighth-grade class, one group of students completes journal entries on narrative structure; another group writes about informational text features. The third group practices a specific reading strategy. The goal is to have students complete a journal entry that will move them forward with comprehension and thinking, so you may have two to three different journal responses occurring in one class. My students' journals contain three types of responses:

1. Writing to build comprehension while reading. This occurs during teacher read alouds and while students work with you in small groups, rereading sections of text to deepen their understanding of what an author wants them to think and know.

2. Writing that reflects an understanding of text structure in fiction, such as character development and setting, and text features in nonfiction, such as sidebars and diagrams.

3. Writing that shows students' application of reading strategies we have practiced to their instructional texts.

I like to link the reading strategies, the narrative elements, and the nonfiction features, which small groups or individual students are practicing, to journal entries because I know that frequent writing can clarify and improve students' understanding and application of these. The box on page 210 contains two examples of how I set up these kinds of journal entries. After reflecting on each one, you will be able to transform the strategies and the struc-

Robb helps a student with journal writing.

tural elements that your students are learning and practicing into journal entries. I always place my models on large chart paper for students to use as a resource. I ask students to head their journal page with their name, the date, the title and author of their book, and the title of the journal response (e.g., Synthesizing With Informational Texts).

The power in journaling lies in asking students to reread entries, and then rethink what they've written, adding new ideas and/or revising initial thoughts. When you place journal writing on center stage in your classes, it's important for students to have their journals available for writing each time class meets. You can also use students' journal writing to negotiate with them the kinds of writing projects that tap into and build on the journal work they've completed (see pages 214–217).

MANAGEMENT TIPS FOR STUDENT RESPONSE JOURNALS

In my reading-writing workshops, students' journals remain available in class so they can self-evaluate their work and note their progress. I recommend that you don't send students' journals home because many of them are not returned to class, and this becomes frustrat-

Two Journal Entries for Reading Strategies

1: Find Unstated Meanings With Cause/Effect

Name _____ Date _____

Title and Author _____

Directions: Divide your page into two columns. In the left-hand column of your journal page, write two causes and the effects of each one. Leave several lines between each cause and its effect. On the right-hand side, note the inferences or unstated meanings you discovered from these cause/effect relationships.

Two Causes and Their Effects   Explain the Inferences Made From Each

_____   _____

_____   _____

_____   _____

_____   _____

_____   _____

_____   _____

2: Synthesize With Informational Texts

Name _____ Date _____

Title and Author _____

Directions: Divide your paper into two columns. When you synthesize, you use what you already know about the topic along with details in a text to find the big ideas the author wants you to understand. On the left-hand side, list three to four pieces of important information you learned. Think about them. Now, on the right-hand side, write one or two big ideas.

Important Facts   Big Ideas

_____   _____

_____   _____

_____   _____

_____   _____

_____   _____

_____   _____

_____   _____

Two Journal Entries About Narrative Elements

1: Character's Personality From the Beginning to the End

Name _____ Date _____

Title and Author _____

Directions: Divide your paper into three columns. In the first column, write two personality traits you noticed about the main character at the beginning. In the second column, note the changes in these personality traits at the end (for example: cowardly to brave; rebellious to cooperative). In the third column, note the event, person, conflict, setting, and/or problem that caused the change.

Main Character _____

Personality at the Beginning	Personality at the End	Causes of Change
_____	_____	_____
_____	_____	_____
_____	_____	_____
_____	_____	_____
_____	_____	_____

2: Main Character as Problem Solver

Name _____ Date _____

Title and Author _____

Directions: Divide your paper into three columns. In the first column, write the name of the main character. In the second column, note two important problems he or she faced. In the third column, explain the decisions made and the actions taken by the main character to solve each problem.

Main Character	Two Key Problems	Actions Taken to Solve Problems
_____	_____	_____
_____	_____	_____
_____	_____	_____
_____	_____	_____
_____	_____	_____

Two Journal Entries for Nonfiction Features

1: Interpret Photographs

Name _____ Date _____

Title and Author _____

Directions: Divide your paper into two columns. Choose three photographs from your text. On the left-hand side, write the page number each photo is on. Study each photograph and its caption. On the right-hand side, note what you learned about the topic.

Photograph and Page Number   What You Learned

_____   _____

_____   _____

_____   _____

_____   _____

2: Become Diagram Savvy

Name _____ Date _____

Title and Author _____

Directions: Divide your paper into two columns. Choose a diagram from your text. On the left-hand side, draw and label the diagram. On the right-hand side, explain it. Then connect the information in the diagram to the topic.

Draw and Label the Diagram   Explain the Diagram

_____   _____

_____   _____

_____   _____

_____   _____

Connect the information in the diagram to the topic:

_____

_____

_____

ing for me and for students. Store journals by class and stack each class set in a crate or on a bookshelf. Tape an index card with the number of the class period on the outside of the crate, or on the edge of the bookshelf. The goal is to help students find and give out journals quickly at the start of class (ask three to four students to do this so students receive their journals in less than one minute) and return them at the end of class. Journals remain on desks, open and poised to receive ideas during the entire reading block.

Once students have completed a specific journal entry in class, two or three times, I can ask them to do the same kind of entry for a graded homework assignment, and then a test, so I can observe how students, on their own, complete entries practiced in class. If I want students to complete a journal entry such as "Draw Conclusions About a Character" (see appendix, page 270) for homework or for a test, I ask them to write it on a separate sheet of paper. Once I've read and returned their homework or test, students staple or tape their work into their journals. This way students' journals contain a yearlong record of their thinking, and I can invite them to look through sections of their journals to either self-evaluate their progress or use several entries as notes for a writing project (see pages 236–240). Furthermore, if a student shows me that independently completing an entry is difficult, then I schedule several brief meetings with him or her to scaffold or support the thinking and writing (see pages 217–218).

Journal writing engages this student.

When students write without restrictive guidelines, you can use their journals to evaluate improvement in both the content and the amount of writing. In the box on page 214, I've included some journaling dos and don'ts.

Some Journaling Dos

To enable students to write responses that show you where they are and what they need from you to make progress, you should:

- encourage students to use phrases when writing, as well as lists of ideas.
- keep your questions open-ended, such as, *How did the main character change? Explain what caused these changes.*
- use Questioning the Author. QtA opens the conversation between a student and an author and enriches the reading because the reader may better understand why the author includes certain details.
- on large chart paper, model for students what a detailed journal response looks like.
- encourage students to talk to themselves if you are eliminating the pair-share. Explain that having a conversation in their mind is similar to talking to a partner.
- ask students to keep all of their responses in a journal, including the ones assigned for homework and tests.
- determine your time limits for writing by observing whether most students are still thinking and writing.

Some Journaling Don'ts

To be sure you aren't restricting the type and amount of journal writing each student can do, avoid:

- assigning a specific number of sentences that you want students to write.
- asking leading questions with answers embedded in the query. An example of a leading question is: *Why wasn't the main character courageous?* The question lets students know that the character wasn't brave. A better question to ask is: *What conclusions can you draw about the main character's personality traits? Explain using text details.*
- posing questions with yes or no answers.
- shortening the time students are allowed to think and talk before they write.
- insisting on complete sentences. This may lead students to focus more on usage than on content.
- writing responses on separate sheets of paper. Students may lose or misplace them.

Journal Sharing

Because the volume of students' writing is considerable, and some of us English teachers may have 100 or more students, I quickly devised a way to monitor journals without consuming hour after hour of reading and responding: I ask students to share their journal work by reading it aloud. The sharing enables me to hear what students have written and understood. But equally important, it provides others with diverse response models. Eventually, even those students who are reluctant to share participate once they realize that the experience is positive and that there are many ways to interpret a text. However, you may still need to dip into the journals of those students who continue to avoid sharing so you can gain insights into their thinking about texts—insights that you can then use to make instructional decisions.

Every four to six weeks, I read a few pages from the journals of students who don't volunteer to share. For students who share frequently, I dip into their work every six to eight weeks. My responses are always positive, so as not to discourage students. Anna, a sixth grader, retells a chapter instead of making personal connections to the character or events. Here's what I write: *Your retelling is rich and shows me how much you recall. Let's work together tomorrow to use your retelling to make personal connections.* During a small-group meeting, I observe that Douglas writes, "I don't know," when I ask students to Question the Author. Here's what I write on a self-stick note for Douglas: *I appreciate your honesty. Let's talk so I can better understand why you are writing, "I don't know."* I've learned to always ask students to explain their reasons and feelings before I make assumptions. Sometimes a student's response is as easy to deal with, as was Douglas's answer: "I didn't read the pages and tried to get by." Other times, a student's response lets me know that I must scaffold the thinking process until he or she can work with a peer and then independently.

I never correct or mark students' entries, for this is their thinking journey, and I respect where they are and know that they will clarify ideas, and even change their positions, with practice and repeated teacher modeling. What I do note are the kinds of thinking I need to continue modeling while reading aloud, such as linking text details to a theme or topic, or to a strategy such as drawing conclusions about an event, or to Questioning the Author when I ask: *What message is the author sending you by including these facts?* I also note repeated errors in usage and spelling that I can transform into mini-lessons.

Make sure your students understand that they're to read aloud what they've written. I've noticed that some students will write very little, but their sharing indicates they've thought a great deal. However, other students who write little may need help to bridge the gap between what they think and what they write. If some students struggle with the physical act of writing, or if they are slow writers, invite them to use your class computer. And for students who write little because they're unsure of the value of their ideas, meet with them to build their self-confidence and to reemphasize that they can adjust and change their ideas as they clarify their thinking. Both keeping a daily record of who has shared an entry and jotting down any observations enable you to remember what you noticed (see the form on page 218). You can use this data to plan upcoming lessons and scaffolds for students who need one-on-one support.

Managing Journal Sharing

During a 90-minute block I may ask three to seven students to share their journal writing after I have read aloud. During small-group lessons, to make sure I'm not always calling on the same students, I keep a daily record of who has read an entry. The list makes clear those students who do and don't volunteer. My responsibility, after the first six weeks of school, is to meet with each non-volunteer to discover why he or she has not shared a journal response, using what students tell me to try to enlarge their self-confidence and encourage them to share. For example, Tim, a fifth grader, explained to me that he doesn't share "because they [classmates] laughed at his ideas last year." To build Tim's self-confidence and willingness to risk trying out an idea, I read Tim's responses, helped him with some revisions, and told him that he could share during the next class. It's important to find ways to give students who lack confidence and self-esteem a boost by checking their response before inviting them to share. After several successes, most students are ready to trust their ideas and risk sharing them.

Since students' writing grows out of applying a reading strategy or connecting an issue, theme, narrative element, or nonfiction feature to the read aloud or their instructional book, I always know how to focus my listening to journal sharing. For example, if I'm modeling predict and support, I'm listening to make sure that the prediction is logi-

Differentiating Reading Instruction

cal and emerges from the information students have read. I'm also listening to make sure students provide specific text details for support. Even Questioning the Author has a focus—on what the author wants us to understand about a character, or a character's decisions or problem-solving abilities, or the big ideas from facts the author includes. What follows are a few sample notes I make as I listen to students share. Notice that they are brief and that you can identify from the comment what the lesson's focus was. I've written out my comments and in the brackets, I've included the shorthand I use. You will develop your own shorthand for certain words and phrases.

- Made personal connections [made p c]
- Connected to war in Iraq [con. to iraq & war]
- Showed why the character changed [why char. changed]
- Linked issue to event [links issue]
- Visualized the setting that caused change [made vis. of set. cause, change]
- Made logical predictions [pred. log.]
- Used QtA to find 2 big ideas [QtA—got 2 big ideas]

Though I always try to be positive, there will be times when you will have to jot down things students did that show they need help. For example, I might note that a student retells instead of responding to the prompt or question, or that another student writes nothing but a few words. Instead of trusting my memory, I have notes I can reread—notes that help me decide who I need to work with and what kinds of differentiated instruction or scaffolds each student will benefit from. Note, too, that all students, even your grade-level and above-grade-level readers will require extra support—scaffolds are not only for readers who struggle. Lana (a pseudonym), one of my best eighth-grade readers, wrestled with figuring out the themes in Ray Bradbury's "The Fog Horn" in *The Vintage Bradbury* (Vintage Books, 1990). Her first response was, "It's [the short story] dumb. Who cares about a monster and a lighthouse?" After meeting with me three times and using Questioning the Author to discuss the story, Lana wrote in her journal some insights that went far beyond her initial reaction, insights that resulted from scaffolding. She wrote, "Now I get it. There's things, like the monster, no one can control. Like things in our lives we can't control, like my mom and dad breaking up. You just gotta go on, like the narrator—he went back to the new lighthouse even after the mon-

Sharing Journal Entries

Class List of Names   **Dates & Observations**

_____   _____

_____   _____

_____   _____

_____   _____

_____   _____

_____   _____

_____   _____

_____   _____

_____   _____

Differentiating Reading Instruction © 2008 by Laura Robb, Scholastic Professional

ster destroyed the old one. I think the words to remember are that 'it's learned you can't love anything too much in the world.'"

At the end of six weeks, by which time students will have had multiple opportunities to share, review your completed forms so you can compare the data you've noted with other observations of students' work and discussions. After six weeks, review collected data bimonthly to

> ## Using Writing to Plan Lessons and Interventions
>
> On pages 44–46, you'll find a list of what to look for in all types of student writing (not just journaling), along with suggested scaffolds and interventions.

enable you to develop a clearer picture of students' strengths and needs. You can use the list below as a guide to the kinds of notes you will take on the form as you listen to students. It's also important to circulate among groups as they are responding so you can observe how much they are writing.

Below is a list that summarizes what you can learn from this record-keeping form.

- Students who volunteer to share and those who always remain silent.
- Students who write little to nothing and those who write a great deal.
- Students whose responses reveal difficulty with visualizing, responding to questions about issues, and responding to queries based on Questioning the Author (see appendix page 273 for QtA queries).
- Students who have difficulty with inferential thinking and making connections between ideas in the same text.
- Students who find it easier to talk through their ideas than write about them.
- Students who are writing more after two to three months than they did during the first weeks of school.

This information enables you to differentiate the kinds of support you offer individuals, pairs, or small groups who struggle with the same issue. It's beneficial to wait until students have practiced these kinds of responses for several weeks before intervening, giving both those reluctant to share time to gain the confidence to volunteer and those writing little at the start an opportunity to reverse this tendency.

In the two sections that follow, you'll see a range of students' journaling, and then how I interpret what students write in order to plan lessons and interventions.

JOURNALING ABOUT TEACHER READ ALOUDS: GRADE FIVE

Here is the journaling process I use during read aloud with fifth graders in Kathleen Hobbs's class at Powhatan School in Boyce, Virginia. First, I prepare fifth graders to listen to the text by showing them the cover of the book and reading the title and subtitle: *Wilma Unlimited: How Wilma Rudolph Became the World's Fastest Woman* by Kathleen Krull (Harcourt, 2000). Then students think-pair-share and write what they think they know about Wilma Rudolph; several share what they've noted with the class.

During two 20-minute consecutive classes, I use Questioning the Author. I stop six times in the 32-page picture-book biography. My goal is to help students experience pausing to think while reading, to open the conversation between them and the author.

Isabel Beck and Margaret McKeown, authors of *Improving Comprehension With Questioning the Author* (2006), recommend that students state their responses by mentioning the author. So if I ask, "What does the author want me to understand here?" students would respond with, "The author wants me to understand that . . ." Though Beck and McKeown agree that students don't have to address the author in every response, they make this excellent point for frequently including the author in responses:

> ". . . it's useful to mention the author frequently to remind students that some-
> one wrote the text in their books and that they are engaged in figuring out
> what that person is trying to tell them. Students need to be reminded that
> they are trying to understand the author's ideas" (page 58).

Before reading aloud, decide where you plan to stop to question the author. You might even want to note your queries on a self-stick note, the first few times, until the process of looking for the author's ideas and not restating facts becomes second nature. Here are the queries I ask students for *Wilma Unlimited*:

- *How does the author make you feel when you learn that Wilma contracted polio before she was 5?*
- *Why does the author tell you that Wilma decided to fight back when she couldn't go to school and that she practiced her exercises even if they hurt?*
- *Why does the author have Wilma show that she can walk in church?*
- *What does the author want you to think when she tells you that Wilma won a full*

scholarship to college and that she was the first in her family to go to college?

- *What does the author want you to think when she tells you that in her first Olympics, Wilma twisted her ankle just after she came to Rome, but even with a swollen ankle, Wilma won a gold medal?*
- *What big ideas is the author sending you through Wilma's life?*

I practice QtA with the fifth grade by reading aloud several other picture-book biographies. Before I ask students to write in their journals when I pause and question, they must first think-pair-share. My purpose for having students work with partners is to help them become comfortable using the QtA strategy and to see the power in thinking about a text while reading. Having the support of a partner also helps students develop their understanding. However, in order to get inside a student's head and gain insights into how he or she thinks inferentially when using QtA, I need to ask each student to write responses without the scaffold of think-pair-share (see pages 58–59). I do this using the biography *Rosa* by Nikki Giovanni (Henry Holt, 2005).

I prepare students to listen to me read by sharing the cover picture and the title, and then asking them to tell me all they know about Rosa Parks by writing their ideas in their journals. Next, I read the biography aloud in one period because to accurately determine if students can apply QtA independently, I don't want them to have to recall details from a previous day's read aloud. Here are the five queries I use with *Rosa* by Nikki Giovanni:

- *What does the author want you to know about Rosa when she tells you that Rosa was the best seamstress?*
- *What does the author mean when she says that Rosa felt tired?*
- *Why does the author tell you that Rosa thought of other African Americans to help her say, "No"?*
- *What does the author want you to think when she tells you about the boycott against riding buses to work?*
- *Why does the author tell you about the boy getting lynched?*

Following are the journal responses for *Wilma Unlimited* and *Rosa Parks*, by two fifth graders, Tommy and Haley, as well as information about how I used their responses to support instructional decisions for them and classmates.

Analyzing Students' Journal Responses to the Read Alouds

Keep in mind that students compose these responses quickly; they are kin to fast-writes and first-draft writing. Focus on the ideas, not on sentence structure and usage. Students and I meet to discuss the content of their responses. I don't tell them how to organize a series of answers because I'm curious to see what students do. Some number their responses, others draw a box around each reaction, and some indent for a paragraph for each query posed.

Tommy's written responses to *Wilma Unlimited* and *Rosa* show his ability to use details in the text to understand the author's points and big ideas. Brief conferences helped Tommy learn to separate his answers to queries with paragraphing (see figure 7.2). Tommy includes a

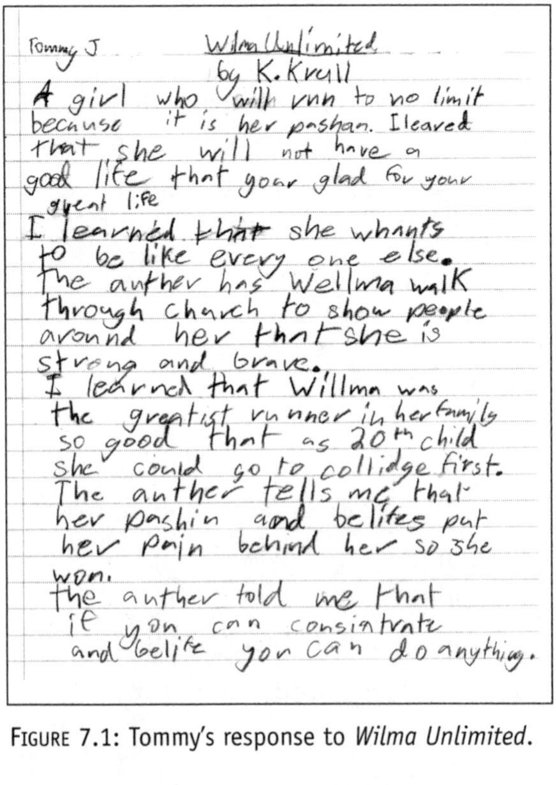

> Tommy J
> Wilma Unlimited
> by K. Krull
> A girl who will run to no limit because it is her pashan. I leaved that she will not have a god life that your glad for your gveat life
> I learned that she whants to be like every one else. The auther has Wellma walk through church to show people around her that she is strong and brave.
> I learnd that Willma was the greatist runner in her famly so good that as 20th child she could go to collidge first. The auther tells me that her pashin and belifes put her pain behind her so she won.
> the auther told me that if you can consintrate and belife you can do anything.

FIGURE 7.1: Tommy's response to *Wilma Unlimited*.

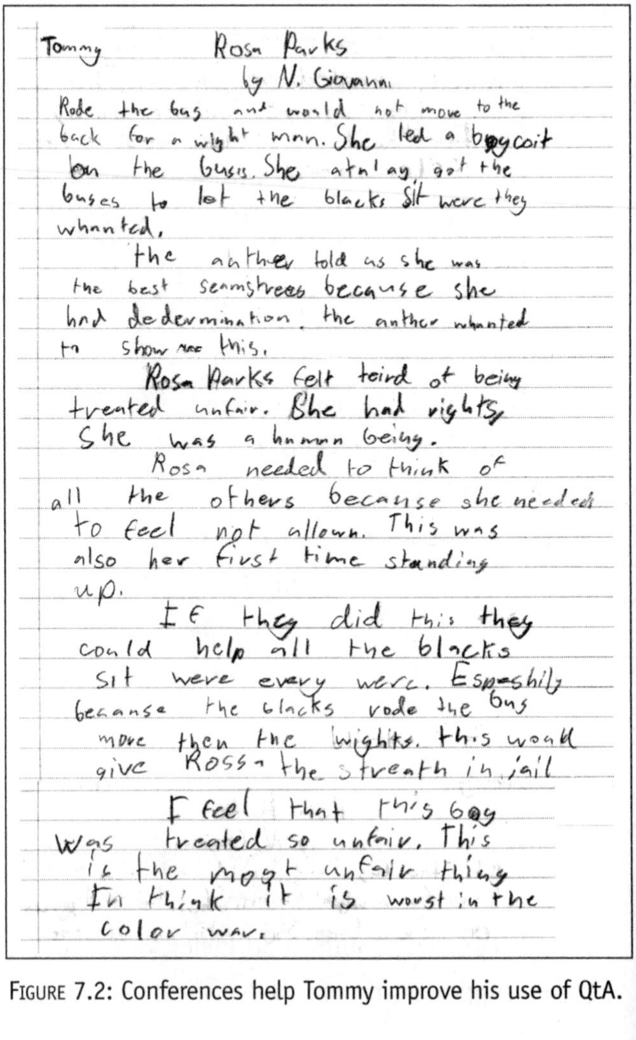

> Tommy
> Rosa Parks
> by N. Giovanni
> Rode the bus and would not move to the back for a wight mnn. She led a boycoit on the buses. She atnlay got the buses to let the blacks sit were they whanted.
> the anther told us she was the best seamstreess because she had dedermination. the anther whanted to show me this.
> Rosa Parks felt toird of being treated unfair. She had rights. She was a human being.
> Rosa needed to think of all the others because she needed to feel not allown. This was also her first time standing up.
> If they did this they could help all the blacks sit were every werc. Espeshily because the blacks rode the bus more then the wights. this would give Rossa the streath in jail
> I feel that this bay was treated so unfair. This is the most unfair thing In think it is worst in the color war.

FIGURE 7.2: Conferences help Tommy improve his use of QtA.

reference to the author once; his other responses don't mention the author. A goal will be to help Tommy understand the importance of interacting with the author in his responses. Tony's responses to *Rosa*, completed on his own, help me conclude that he can use details to figure out what the author meant—what the details tell him. Both Kathleen Hobbs and I feel confident that Tommy will do well using QtA with an independent reading book at his comfort level.

Now let's study Haley's two journal responses (see figures 7.3 and 7.4). Undoubtedly, her entry for *Wilma Unlimited* is stronger because Haley was able to think-pair-share. In her *Rosa* journal entry, Haley does not address the author and she leaves out two responses. I am pleased with Haley's use of the term *boycotting*; it shows that she understands its meaning. Haley's response to *Rosa* (see figure 7.4) shows that she needs more individual support with Questioning the Author. During a conference, Haley tells me that she didn't answer the two questions about Rosa being tired and Rosa helping other African Americans because she wasn't sure. "My mind wandered some when you read," she said.

> Haley
> **Wilma Unlimited**
> by: K. Krull
> I think it is about a woman running with no limits.
>
> The Author makes me feel sad that she might not live. I'm lucky their is a polio vaccient.
>
> The Author showed me Wilma is strong to fight back her polio and the schools just to learn.
>
> The Author makes Wilma walk in church because that is her favorite place. He knows her faith is strong.
>
> I learned that Wilma is determind to get what she wants. She is very determind to do her best.
>
> The Author tells us that Wilma is brave and determind. Wilma never gives up.
>
> The Author told us that even though Wilma had some difficulties she pulled it through. She was determind to do her best.

FIGURE 7.3: Think-pair-share helps Haley respond.

> Haley
> **Rosa Parks**
> She needed others to say no because it would take corage to say no.
>
> "No Riders today" would help Rosa Parks by boccoting the buses and lifting Rosa's hope.
>
> I think it's cruel for a 14 year old boy to be hanged.

FIGURE 7.4: Haley's response shows she still needs support.

When Kathleen Hobbs and I discussed Haley's conference, Kathleen observed that sometimes Haley had difficulty settling into sustained silent reading. We discovered that Haley's choice of reading books was far beyond her comfort level and contributed to her inattention during sustained silent reading. This was easily repaired as Kathleen worked with Haley to choose books that were not a struggle but were easy and enjoyable reads. I placed Haley in a group that would continue to practice QtA with a teacher. In one planning period, Kathleen and I quick-read the remaining student responses and used their journal entries to differentiate reading instruction in the same way we had done for Tommy and Haley.

Differentiating in Response to Students' Journaling About Read Alouds

From our evaluation of students' journals, Kathleen Hobbs and I were able to divide the class into two groups.

Group 1

- Students in this group would receive additional practice with using Questioning the Author independently while Kathleen or I read aloud. Then we planned to have this group read short texts at their comfort level and use QtA to respond in their journals. Kathleen's and my goal was to help students internalize this strategy and include the word "author" in several of their written responses. We decided to build their response stamina by starting with short texts that wouldn't overwhelm them.

Group 2

- Students in this group would apply QtA to an independent reading book that could be fantasy, realistic fiction, or historical fiction. I jotted two queries on large chart paper that students would use during their independent reading:
- *What details does the author include that show you what kind of person the character is?*
- *How do these details make you feel about the protagonist?*

    Then I asked students to put a self-stick note at the end of a chapter that was halfway through their book, and a second self-stick note at the end of their book. Though we asked students to stop halfway through their book and write answers to their queries on self-stick notes, and to do this again at the end of the book, all read right through and completed only one response at the end. Fifth graders told us that they didn't want to stop halfway through; they wanted to continue reading. I was delighted with their enthusiasm but hoped that with continued practice, they would see the merit of reflecting about a book before the end.

It's interesting to note that even though Kathleen and I used students' written work to differentiate reading tasks, two students in the second group needed more support than their journal writing had indicated to us. Tommy was one of those two students. In figure 7.5, you can read Tommy's written response using the two QtA queries. Both Kathleen and I expected a richer response from Tommy. In a conference, I asked Tommy questions and jotted down some of his responses. During our talk, it was evident that he knew so much more about Percy than his writing showed. Using the notes I took during our short conference, Tommy rewrote his response (see figure 7.6). Supporting Tommy simply meant helping him say out loud to me what he knew about Percy's personality. Our job

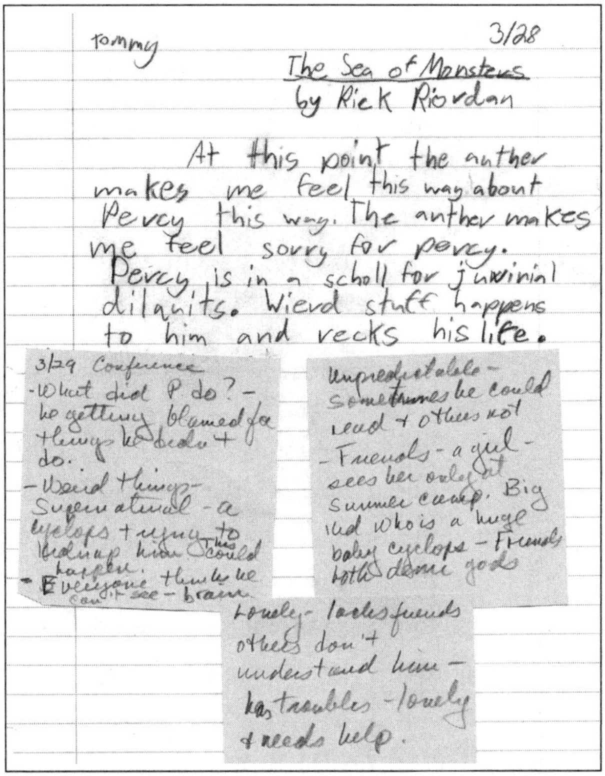
Tommy 3/28
The Sea of Monsters
by Rick Riordan
At this point the anther makes me feel this way about Percy this way. The anther makes me feel sorry for percy. Percy is in a scholl for juwinial dilaquits. Wierd stuff happens to him and recks his life.

3/29 Conference
-What did P do? - he getting blamed for things he didn't do.
-Weird things - Supernatural - a cyclops + trying to kidnap him. This could happen.
• Everyone thinks he can't see - brain

Unpredictable - sometimes he could read + others not
-Friends - a girl - sees her only at summer camp. Big kid who is a huge baby cyclops - Friends both demi gods

Lonely - lacks friends others don't understand him - has troubles - lonely + needs help.

FIGURE 7.5: Tommy's response before our conference.

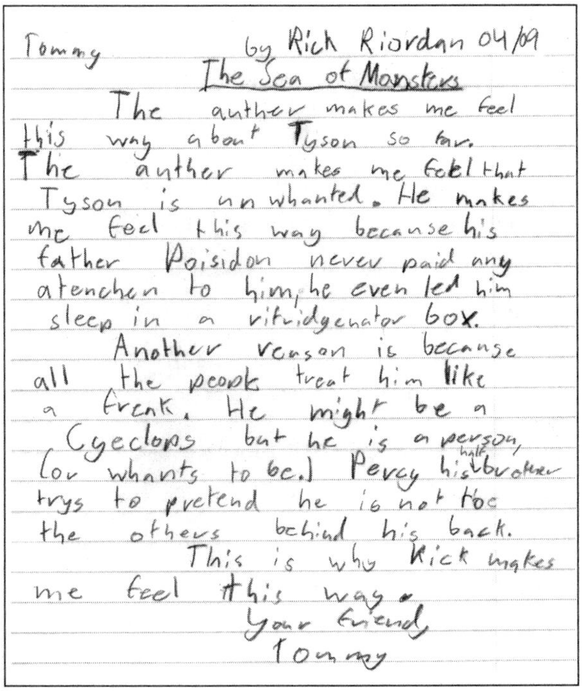
Tommy by Rick Riordan 04/09
The Sea of Monsters
The anther makes me feel this way about Tyson so far. The anther makes me feel that Tyson is unwhanted. He makes me feel this way because his father Poisidon never paid any atenchen to him, he even led him sleep in a vitridgenator box.
Another reason is because all the peopk treat him like a frenk. He might be a Cyeclops but he is a person, (or whants to be.) Percy his half brother trys to pretend he is not too the others behind his back.
This is why Rick makes me feel this way.
Your friend,
Tommy

FIGURE 7.6: Tommy's rewrite after our conference.

was to confer with Tommy, as well as other students, to move them from holding conversations with their teacher to using QtA to converse with themselves before writing.

Listening to students share, reading some of their journal entries, and observing them in class are a combination of assessments that can help you provide students with the instruction and practice necessary to improve as readers. Before I left Kathleen's class to coach another teacher at my school, I asked fifth graders to debrief their recent experiences with both a think-pair-share about QtA and building comprehension while reading. Here are some responses that I collected on chart paper:

- "It was easier when you [Mrs. Robb] read and asked questions."
- "I liked it. I got more out of the book we listened to."
- "I need more practice to do it with my own reading."
- "I learned to listen better in read alouds."
- "I like the read alouds more."

Now, let's move into my eighth-grade class and observe how reading student writing can inform your planning decisions for teaching and organizing reading groups.

Differentiating in Response to Students' Journaling About Small-Group Lessons

The caveat for interpreting texts that I give students in my classes is that they must weave support from the text into their responses. With your read alouds, you can help students learn to do this by pausing and explicitly pointing to the support in your answer. If you want students to move from talk to writing, then write your response that weaves interpretation and support on the board or on chart paper. As students respond orally and in writing, during and after the discussion, it's helpful to observe their behaviors and their written work. Observe students to determine whether or not they are able to do the following:

- weave in details from the text to support their position
- use context clues to figure out the meanings of unfamiliar words
- connect the issue that relates to the unit of study to the book they are reading
- apply an inferential reading strategy to the text

  If they can't, you may need to provide them with more scaffolds.

Erin, an eighth grader, is in a group reading *Under a War Torn Sky* by Laura Elliot (Hyperion, 2001). Her first entry during group discussions shows a need to give more story details to support her ideas (see figure 7.7). Erin and I meet, and I show her what culling details from the text looks like. Fourteen days and four short conferences later, Erin completes answers 1 and 2 of her entry during our group discussion and 3 and 4 after our discussion (see figure 7.8). Notice that the level of text support has increased. Because Erin read her first response aloud for the group, I was able to pinpoint the kind of intervention she needed—and give it to her. It's important for you to read the early responses of students who don't share so you can intervene and provide the scaffolds each student needs.

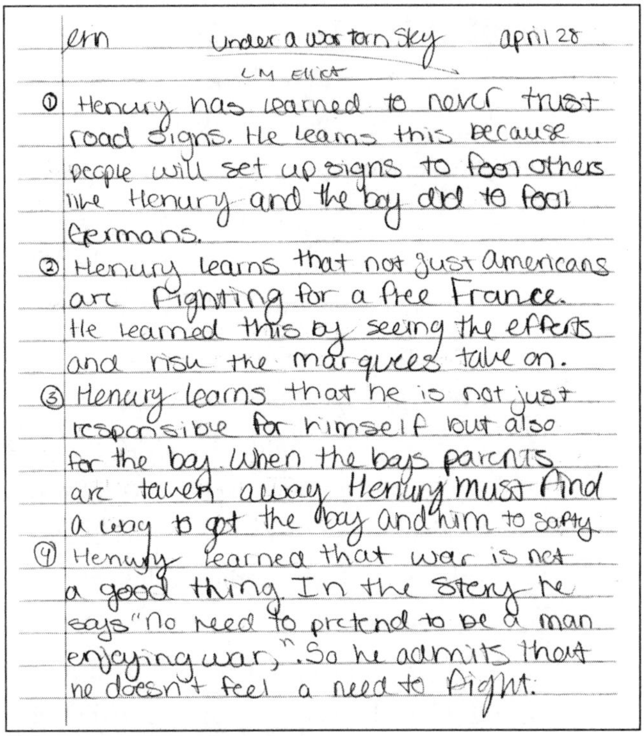
Erin Under a War Torn Sky april 28
LM Elliot
① Henury has learned to never trust road signs. He learns this because people will set up signs to fool others like Henury and the boy did to fool Germans.
② Henury learns that not just americans are fighting for a free France. He learned this by seeing the efforts and risk the marquees take on.
③ Henury learns that he is not just responsible for himself but also for the boy. When the boys parents are taken away Henury must find a way to get the boy and him to safty.
④ Henury learned that war is not a good thing. In the story he says "No need to pretend to be a man enjoying war,". So he admits that he doesn't feel a need to fight.

FIGURE 7.7: Erin's journal responses now contain more details.

Each time you change the focus of your group reading lessons—perhaps emphasizing vocabulary and context clues or connecting an issue to a text—monitor students' responses so that you can catch those students who would benefit from short conferences to improve skills. In addition, you can model the strategic areas that confuse students while you read aloud (see Chapter 3). Giving students multiple opportunities to observe how you use a strategy along with scaffolds can enable students to progress and eventually learn to apply the strategy independently.

Besides reading and listening to students' journal responses, you can invite them to review their own responses to gain insights into their thinking about texts. When students reread and reflect on sections of their journals, they can see their progress and are better able to set goals on their own or with your guidance during a short conference that focuses on their self-evaluations.

STUDENTS' SELF-EVALUATIONS OF JOURNALS

Inviting students to read specific journal pages to self-evaluate their understanding of a reading strategy, such as making inferences or determining importance, can spotlight progress, strengths, and needs to students and to you. Since Questioning the Author was a strategy I used repeatedly with read alouds and during small-group lessons in eighth grade, I invited students to periodically debrief after a think-pair-share. Two weeks before school ended, I asked students to write about the strategy in their journals. Each time students self-evaluated QtA, I asked these same three questions:

- *Does QtA help you understand the text while reading? Explain your answer.*
- *Is this strategy helpful to use throughout a longer text? Explain your answer.*
- *Do you stop to think and use QtA while reading on your own? Explain why or why not.*

In November and February, I had asked my eighth-grade students to think-pair-share about Questioning the Author, and I noted their responses on chart paper. In October, all 28 students had said that QtA was okay with read alouds but that they weren't using it independently. By February, 12 students pointed out that sometimes they used QtA with their independent reading. Here are some comments that helped me adjust my read alouds as well as decide to invite students to use bookmarks to practice QtA (see pages 233–234).

- "I use QtA when I'm in science and the textbook is tough. I reread, too."
- "I stop once or twice now when reading free-choice books. It's usually to figure out what I know about the protagonist at that point."
- "I feel my reading level has jumped five spaces now that I'm Questioning the Author when I read."

The consensus of the 14 students who were not using QtA in independent reading or for reading in other classes can be summarized in these two statements that this group repeated:

- "I don't like to stop. I want to stay in the plot and finish."
- "I feel funny stopping on my own and asking the author questions. Stopping doesn't help me understand more."

Using students' feedback, I adjusted my modeling of QtA and became more explicit in explaining why this strategy deepened my comprehension and tested my recall. The level of student sharing also changed after the February debriefing. In addition to asking students to build their understanding and savor a text while I read aloud and during reading group lessons, I invited several of them to explain how the strategy supported their reading. My hope was that those who were resistant to using the strategy independently would repeatedly hear the benefits from me and their peers.

A huge breakthrough occurred in April when Mary said, "I think I know why QtA is important and why you are doing all of this. [I'm holding my breath at this point.] I think it's because QtA helps us remember better because we stop and use stuff to figure out what the author means." A couple of knowing nods made this a memorable moment.

On May 31, I wrote the three QtA debriefing questions on the chalkboard and asked students to respond to them in their journals. This time, there were seven students who still weren't using the strategy, but 21 were using it on their own and finding that the strat-

egy helped them recall details and figure out big ideas. Ben's comment is representative of those students who were not using QtA at this point: "I find this strategy to not be very helpful. I prefer to analyze the story at the end." For some students, shaking old habits was difficult.

Madeline's journal entry contains most of the points made by students who started using the strategy (see figure 7.8). About half of the group in Madeline's camp also noted that they don't use QtA when they're reading a plot-driven book that's easy to read.

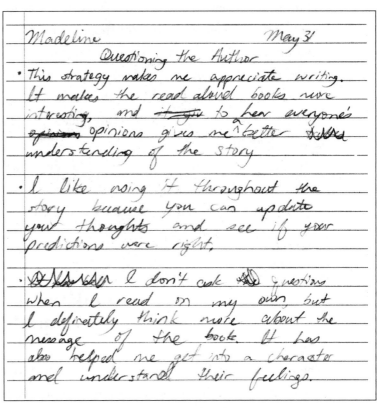

FIGURE 7.8: Madeline evaluates her use of QtA.

Using Students' Self-Evaluations to Differentiate

Recently, I was working with a fifth-grade teacher to help students figure out the personality traits of the person in the biography students were reading. Each fifth grader was reading a biography at his or her instructional reading level. Halfway through the study, as students were starting their second or third biography, their teacher asked them to think-pair-share about what they understood about figuring out the person's character traits, and then to write their thoughts on paper. We encouraged students to self-evaluate honestly. Our goal was to help them, not to punish them with a "bad grade," as several wondered. Three students could not explain anything about the strategy. They wrote four words: "I can't do it." So now the teacher and I would plan to meet one-on-one with each student to help him or her with this strategy. One meeting will most likely not be enough. Be prepared to meet several times. If at that point, a student still doesn't "get it," move on and make sure you review the strategy later in the year. I find that taking a breather and allowing time for the mind to work on a strategy often helps students better understand later on when the teacher repeats the lesson. That's why strategic reading should begin in kindergarten and continue through high school because repetition enables students to grasp the strategy and maturity helps students apply it with ease and depth (Allington, 2001. 2006; Pearson et al., 1992; Robb, 2000, 2008; Tierney & Readence, 2000).

You can also monitor students' understanding of a reading strategy as well as an issue by asking them to create bookmarks on which they write their responses to a query or queries, so that you can evaluate their level of absorption and whether they need your guidance or support from a peer.

Bookmarks Can Help You Assess Comprehension and Thinking

When teachers first began using bookmarks, it was to monitor students' application of reading strategies to independent and instructional texts (Crafton, 1991). At an IRA conference in 1992, I heard Linda Crafton, Carolyn Burke, and Dorothy Watson discuss this self-monitoring strategy. They recommended that students be given many opportunities to engage in teacher-led and student-led discussions about literature before introducing the bookmark strategy. In addition to monitoring the application of reading strategies, I have students use bookmarks to discuss issues and themes.

It's important for you to model during your read aloud the process of responding to reading using a bookmark, whether the focus is a strategy, an issue, or a theme and problem. When focusing on strategies, I make a list on chart paper of possible strategic responses: questions, predictions, confusing sections, visualization, emotions aroused, inferences, unfamiliar words or information, connections to other books, important information, evaluations of events and characters, and so on. For issues, or themes and problems, model responses that show your thinking about the issue.

Benefits to Teachers: Bookmarks make it possible to get inside a student's mind and follow that learner's thinking. This can help you identify which students would benefit from scaffolding or extra support from you or a peer. It also lets you know which students are starting to create mental images, converse with characters, or react to information while reading.

Benefits to Students: Using bookmarks enables students to develop and enlarge their conversations with authors and texts. This strategy can quickly let learners know if a book is too tough or if they lack the background knowledge necessary for them to connect to the topic and interact with the author. For example, Jesse, a sixth grader who read about two years below his grade level, chose Mildred Taylor's *Roll of Thunder, Hear My Cry* (Dial, 1977). Jesse's comments on the first 25 pages—"I can't remember stuff" and "I'm confused"—informed his teacher that the book was too difficult. I suggested that Jesse's teacher offer him three books to choose from—books he could read and enjoy—and suggest to Jesse that he save the Mildred Taylor novel for another school year. It's better to show students how to choose books successfully (see appendix page 262) than to have to ask them to change their selections.

I find that it's most beneficial to ask students to respond to a section of text, then reread and analyze their bookmarks to see what strategies they are using. This raises students' awareness of their interactions with a text. I like to do this in a three- to five-minute conference. Laura, a fourth grader, completed a bookmark for pages 92 to 111 of

Anastasia Again, by Lois Lowry (Houghton Mifflin, 1981) (see figure 7.9). When we conferred about this bookmark, Laura told me and her teacher, Ellen Benjamin: "I'm visualizing—I can see the tennis racket and draw it. I also make connections to my life and my cousin. On page 98, I make a prediction." Not all of your students will be as astute as Laura. For those who cannot categorize what they are doing, think aloud to show students how you figure out the strategy you're using.

In the next section, I've included examples of prompts you can offer students for bookmarks. You can adapt these prompts to create your own bookmark prompts that respond to your students' learning needs.

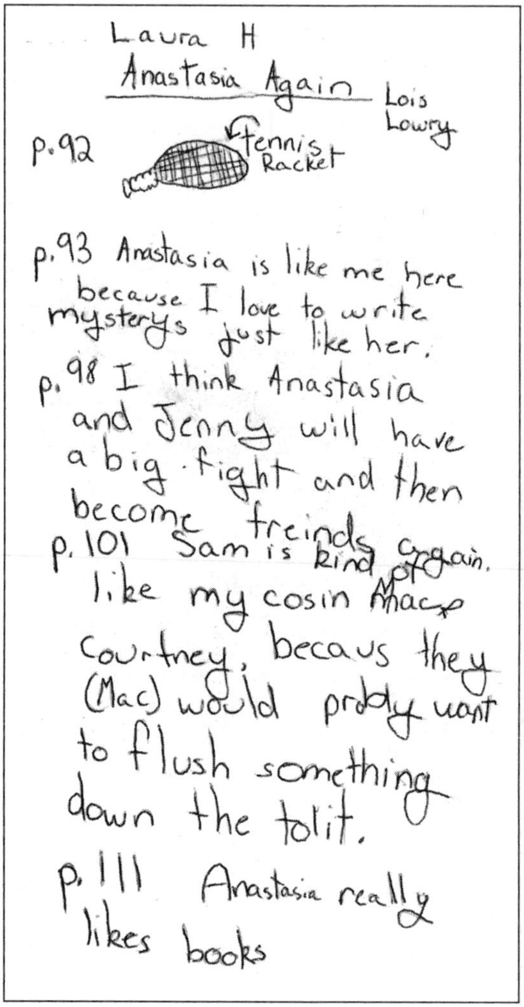
Laura H
Anastasia Again Lois Lowry
p.92 Tennis Racket
p.93 Anastasia is like me here because I love to write mysterys just like her.
p.98 I think Anastasia and Jenny will have a big fight and then become freinds again.
p.101 Sam is kind of like my cosin Mac & Courtney, becaus they (Mac) would probly want to flush something down the tolit.
p.111 Anastasia really likes books

FIGURE 7.9: Laura's bookmark.

MAKING AND USING A BOOKMARK

Making a bookmark for monitoring reading strategies is easy. Have students fold a piece of lined notebook paper or unlined standard-size copy paper in half. This gives students four sides on which to jot down their thinking while reading. If they need another strip, they can staple it to the original bookmark.

To make sure students understand how to set up their books for completing a bookmark, share these guidelines with them.

- Divide your text into three parts. Using three self-stick notes, place one after the second or third chapter, one halfway through the text at the end of a chapter, and the last note two chapters before the end.
- Put your name, the date, the title and author of your book, and the prompt you will

use at the top of the first column of your folded bookmark (see box on page 234 for bookmark prompts).

- Write the *same prompt* at the top of the second and third columns of your bookmark.

- When you reach a self-stick note, pause to reflect and then write your responses to the prompt on one of the three columns of the bookmark.

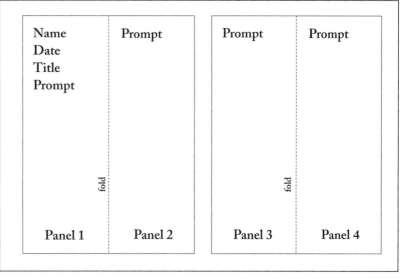

FIGURE 7.10: Here is a quick and easy way to set up a bookmark.

- Reread all of your responses. In the fourth column of your bookmark, choose one of these suggestions and write your ideas: *Pinpoint a big idea or a theme; explain what you learned about an issue or a problem; discuss how the text influenced the way you think about a topic or issues.*

USING BOOKMARKS TO MONITOR STUDENTS' READING AND DIFFERENTIATE INSTRUCTION

In my classes, students complete bookmarks for an entire book three times a year. I suggest that students monitor their application of strategies using bookmarks with part of a text. For example, students can use half of a picture book or three to four chapters of a fiction or nonfiction text. The goal, remember, is to get inside students' heads and observe their strategic interactions. Completing a bookmark for an entire text becomes tedious; if you overuse the strategy, you risk turning students off independent reading. Moreover, students who apply strategies while reading and have rich conversations with the text, do not need to frequently complete bookmarks to monitor their use of strategies. Used thoughtfully and sparingly, you can evaluate students' interactions and their

Bookmark Prompts

Prompts for the Application of Reading Strategies
- Predict and offer support from the text. In column four of your bookmark, adjust your predictions if necessary.
- Make personal connections to a character, specific problems, or conflicts.
- Question the Author by asking yourself: What does the author want me to understand with this information?
- Ask questions that pop into your mind, then jot down the answers as you come upon them while you read.

Prompts for Issues
- Show how the issue you're studying affects the main character.
- Explain how the issue you're studying connects to specific events.
- Explain the big ideas the author wants you to know by linking the issue you're studying to what happens in the book.

Prompts for Fiction
- Monitor the changes in the main character's personality traits. Explain what you believe is causing these changes.
- Show how the settings affect characters' decisions, interactions with others, and feelings.
- Identify key conflicts and evaluate how the main character deals with each one.
- Explain what you have learned about the historical period of your book.

Prompts for Biography
- Discuss the changes this person made that affected people's lives.
- Explain how others viewed and reacted to this person. How did the person cope with negative reactions?
- Discuss the influences that shape the life of this person. These can be people, events, places, and so on.

Prompts for Informational Texts
- Note fascinating facts and explain why this information is important to people.
- Note the connections you are making to this information. Show how this information affects your life and the lives of people in other age groups.
- Write down new information you are learning. Explain how this changes your thinking about this topic.

Differentiating Reading Instruction

USING BOOKMARKS TO REFLECT ON ISSUES AND THEMES

I find that students enjoy extending their knowledge of issues they've internalized from a unit of study by completing bookmarks that relate the issue or issues to their independent reading. Directions for this type of bookmark should be open-ended. Since these are free-choice selections, each text will have different themes. My directions to students are: *Make connections to issues in your life, in the lives of family members or friends, in school, or to world issues.* You can also invite students to discuss problems and conflicts and whether characters resolved them as well as why they were or weren't resolved. For informational texts, ask students to discuss an issue related to the topic: *How did this person, invention, information, or discovery change our lives?*

While I find that my students enjoy monitoring and connecting to an issue or issues that they understand in an independent reading text, I'm careful not to overuse the strategy. What follows are the bookmarks and follow-up

> I am the Greatest
>
> C.J.   April 16
>
> **World Issue:** A world issue that Muhammed Ali faces, is segragation. This effects his life, because he can't play with white kids or go into certain stores or restaurantes. He was also looked down upon in the white boxing comunity.
>
> **Family Issue:** A family issue for Muhammed, is the fact that his daughter, Laila Ali, is a pro boxer. In the book it says that he is worried that she might get brain damage from the sport. He is still happy that she is carrying on his dream.
>
> **Life Issue:** A life issue, is Muhammeds religon. He is Islamic, and he doesn't belive in fighting in a war. This effected him in 1971 when he refused to go and fight in the war. Muhammed was senteced 5 years in prison. After this sentece he started fighting again.
>
> **Big Idea:**
> - One big idea in this book is segragation and its setbacks. Segragation made it harder for Ali to become a pro boxer.
>
> - Another big idea in the book is speaking out. When Ali spook out he got in truble, but he had to do what he had to do.

FIGURE 7.11: C.J. uses his bookmark to link issues to his biography of Muhammad Ali.

application of strategies to texts and make decisions about the next steps you'll take for planning reading instruction.

conferences I had with two eighth graders. Note the variation in the level of students' responses. Expect this and use the responses to inform your interventions and scaffolds.

I always set aside time to confer with students about their bookmarks. This is the ideal time to support students who are retelling the text instead of using the information in a text to respond to an issue.

Finally, have students self-evaluate their bookmarks. When self-evaluations reveal that your modeling, conferences, and group lessons are making a difference in the personal reading lives of some students, the additional time invested in this kind of teaching feels beneficial and worthwhile. In February, when I read the self-evaluation of Hattie, an eighth grader, I inwardly cheered because she was beginning to experience the benefits of using bookmarks to build comprehension. Here's what Hattie wrote: "Since we have been connecting the read alouds in class, I have been making the same connections to my free-choice books. I have also discovered that I love reading for what I want to do in life. Last week I started volunteering as a docent for a Civil War museum. I need to love reading and connect to what I am reading to be a successful docent. (Especially since some of the nonfiction history books are a little dry!)"

As you read on, you'll explore the oral and written projects that grow out of the journaling students complete during reading class. These make ideal assessments and can be adjusted to meet students where they are with reading and writing.

Writing Projects and Assessments to Support Differentiated Reading Instruction

Whether you and your students negotiate the kinds of reading-related projects and writing tasks they'll complete, or your school district mandates specific writing assignments connected to reading, you can still make adjustments that meet each student's learning needs. For example, if an eighth or a ninth grader struggles to write a paragraph, then teach him or her to write a clear and organized paragraph, even though the district requires a fully developed essay on a piece of literature. Once the student learns to write a paragraph well, using that skill to write several paragraphs will follow.

Avoid the pitfall of thinking that all students must complete the same mandated assignment in order to pass a state test. If an eighth or a ninth grader can't write a paragraph, he or she won't pass the state writing test that year. However, if you and other teachers show a weak writer how to plan and write a paragraph, he or she might eventually pass the state test.

When you invite students to read their journals to find ideas or seeds to design writing, drama, and oral projects that relate to reading, you have begun to differentiate. I find that students tend to choose or design a project that's within their reach. It doesn't mean that one group does more thinking than another group. Students can infer, make connections, and address issues in a drama, an interview, a monologue, or an analytical essay. The point is to meet each student's needs, and this is one way to do just that.

NEGOTIATING ASSESSMENTS WITH STUDENTS

Several times in this book, I've suggested that teachers consider a range of assessments or projects that relate to students' instructional and independent reading levels. Your Big Picture Plans should reflect this range. However, you may have to make adjustments to your original plans as you observe students' strengths and talents because these will change throughout the school year as students improve their reading and thinking skills. I encourage you to have students complete projects that respond to their reading at school, where you can provide the continued support that your students will need, especially those who struggle with reading and writing (see scheduling suggestions on appendix pages 263–264).

Having the freedom to negotiate with your students about projects that emerge from their journal notes is ideal, so you don't have to ask students to complete tasks that will frustrate them—tasks such as organizing and writing essays that don't grow out of students' reading. I recommend that you involve students in creating a list of possible projects that tap into their journal writing but move beyond their entries. Involving your students in coming up with projects can result in a list of creative responses to texts that meets the diverse needs in your class.

What follows are examples of projects students and I negotiated—projects that permitted students to showcase their knowledge and understanding—in other words,

Figure 7.12: Danny's cartoon for "Shoes for Hector."

projects that courted success. For example, Danny, an eighth grader, devised this cartoon in response to "Shoes for Hector" by Nicholasa Mohr (see figure 7.12). Danny used this cartoon as a springboard for a dramatization of this short story, which he selected from *El Bronx Remembered* (HarperTrophy, 1975), a collection Danny read with a small group.

Julian, who entered my eighth-grade class at the end of January, decided to read Tony Medina's *Love to Langston* (Lee & Low, 2002) during differentiated whole-class instructional reading. Medina's book led Julian to Langston Hughes's poetry. For an oral presentation about what the poems taught him about racism, Julian created a poster. At that point, rather than completing a writing project, it was easier for Julian to talk about what he had learned by reading poems out loud, commenting on them, and using his poster. By April, daily journaling about read alouds and journaling about his instructional book, *California Blue* by David Klass (Scholastic, 2000), had enlarged Julian's writing confidence to the point where Julian chose to compare John, the main character of Klass's realistic novel, to a biography about Sam Clemens, *A Brilliant Streak: The Making of Mark Twain* by Kathryn Lasky (Harcourt, 1998) (see figure 7.13). During a conference, Julian's words reflected the ease he had gained with writing about reading: "I have lots of notes about John in my journal. I can use the queries you [Mrs. Robb] asked [for

California Blue] to think about Clemens." Julian and I celebrated this essay because it marked a breakthrough from oral presentations, which he still loved, to thinking on paper. To support Julian and other group members, I set aside time to generate discussions about possible connections between characters in realistic fiction and real people in biographies. These discussions, combined with some short conferences Julian and I had, offered the support Julian needed to experience success with a challenging writing-about-reading project.

You'll also find that pairs who read the same book during differentiated whole-class instructional reading may want to complete a response-to-reading project together. Let them. I find that partners share work better than groups, where it's easier for a student to slip through without completing much work. You can circulate while pairs work, offering support that brings

FIGURE 7.13: Julian's essay illustrates his newfound ability to think on paper.

Everyone is different

Everybody is different. Some people are considered different because the color of their skin, or their religion, or their gender. Have you ever seen a huge difference between you and another person? The character in the novel <u>California Blue</u> and the person in the biography <u>A Brilliant Streak</u> faced some of the same issues about being different.

The two books I read were very different. In <u>A Brilliant Streak</u>, Sam Clemens, Had a very exciting and fun childhood. He had lots of friends and had tons of adventures. Sam was a very crazy child and had to be watched constantly. The main character in the book <u>California Blue</u> John, was a very lonely kid, and very responsible. For example when his parents went away to a hospital out of town, they left him by himself. Sam was carefree and outgoing. He used to swim naked in Bear Creek because there were no rules about it. John, on the other hand, only went out in the woods to find butterflies, or out to school to run on the track. Sam and his friends set a long time goal to steamboat men. However John's only long-time goal was to get Miss Merrill to like him, this would not happen because she was a teacher and he was a loser.

Sam wasn't that good around water. He should have drowned at least eight times, but got lucky. One of the issues these too people had in common is that their dads didn't like them. John because he was too different, liked different things than his father did when he was little, and didn't play football. Sam's dad didn't like him because he was to wild and crazy, and he was always finding new ways to either kill himself (out of stupidity) or get in trouble with anyone he found. Another issue that Sam and John had in common that they both went on at least one big adventure in their life. John's was when he went to the hospital in San Diego to visit his dad. Sam had tons of adventures. For example: the time he wanted to be like Tom Sawyer and dressed up as a pirate hunted for buried treasure.

Everybody has their differences some are very drastic and some are minor. People can be very different, but underneath it all we are all just people with feelings towards different things. Overall my characters had lots of differences, but at least some similarities. If you try hard enough you can find a similarity in anyone.

students along. For example, two sixth graders, Colleen and Katie, had been reading picture books about Greek gods and goddesses. For their presentation, the pair just wanted to show stick puppets they designed. With extra support during three conferences, the girls also wrote scripts to use as they presented their puppet show for their peers.

Having total control over the kinds of writing-about-reading assessments you offer students is ideal because you are responding to the ever-changing needs of your students. However, I have partial freedom to negotiate responding-to-reading projects because my school's curriculum requires that all eighth graders write personal narratives and persuasive and analytical essays.

> ### Create Mentor Texts
>
> Each time students have to complete a written project, such as letters to a character or diary entries, create a mentor text for them to study, and/or invite them to study the writing of former students. Base mentor texts on your read aloud, the common student text. See appendix pages 285–286 for an example of letters between two characters that I created as mentor texts.

MANAGING DISTRICT-MANDATED REQUIREMENTS

You can still tailor required assignments to respond to what each student can accomplish. All students can complete an essay, for example, but your scaffolding, expectations, and grading criteria will differ depending on students' capacity to cope with such an assignment. Differentiation here also includes conferring with those students who require more support to successfully complete this task and learn from their experience. But remember, there are some tasks that will require you to make adjustments for students, such as having a student write an opinion paragraph about an event in a book instead of writing a persuasive essay.

During a six-week differentiated whole-class instructional reading unit in my eighth-grade class, individuals and some pairs chose an author to study. Differentiating instruction for the author study revolves around the number of books each student reads—some instructional and some at students' comfort level. All students read three to six books by an author of their choice. To support students' choices, I brought in a cart

Differentiating Reading Instruction

stacked with realistic fiction, historical fiction, fantasy, and science fiction by dozens of authors from the school's library and my class library. Students had two class periods to browse through books by their authors. I made it clear to students that if they disliked their choice after the first week of sustained silent reading, they could change their author. Four students did switch authors. I fully supported the changes because I want students to invest their time in books that they deeply care about because the genre and topics are motivating.

After each eighth grader completed two or three books—and this occurred at different times—I introduced the analytical essay to some students by sharing several essays from past years. Students' discussions of how they could improve weaker essays led them to the understanding that they needed specific examples from their books to support a point. Next, I gave students planning guidelines that asked them to compare their character's memories with their own memories. To assist their planning, I had students list the important memories a character in their book would have as well as their own important memories. In addition to having peers read students' notes and offer suggestions, I met with each student to discuss his or her plan.

Emily read all of Jacqueline Woodson's books, including Woodson's picture books, and chose *Maizon at Blue Hill* (Putnam, 1992) for her essay. Notice how Emily spent time planning this essay; during our two conferences, I worked with Emily on organizing her notes to include what she thought she needed in each paragraph of her essay. The detailed and thought-out plan enabled Emily to show her deep connection to Maizon, even though both girls lived in different worlds. Emily's plan made it possible for her to write a clear essay because she had ironed out her thinking before drafting. It's the connections, like those Emily made to Maizon, that show me the kinds of thinking students can do; it's these connections that make the reading memorable and motivating to students.

Those students who need more scaffolding than Emily receive additional support from me. Most of the support comes in the planning stage. I prefer to work with pairs to first review the mentor text. Next, I help students develop a thesis statement because the thesis enables them to find support from the text that proves their position. Then I help partners as they create detailed plans. Once a plan shows me that the thinking and support are rich and detailed (see figure 7.14), I know drafting the essay will be easier. Providing more support *before* students compose a draft helps them develop their thinking and notes, which can then be used to write a solid first draft (see figure 7.15).

To engage eighth graders in writing personal narratives, I have been reading aloud *Bronx Masquerade* by Nikki Grimes every year since its publication in 2002 (Dial). Students react in their journal to the personal narratives and poems that the high school students in Mr. Ward's class write and share every Friday during an "open mic" session described in the book. Halfway through the book, and again at the end, my students collaborate to discover the elements in these short narratives—elements that cause my eighth graders to beg me to read more

FIGURE 7.14: Emily's thorough planning enables her to craft her essay.

Memories

Emily

Title: Maizon at Blue Hill

Memories Maizon would have:
1. Meeting Charley in Hallway
2. Seeing the beautiful outdoors / Blue Hill
3. Cold winters in Connecticut on school grounds
4. Dinners in Cafeteria- clearing table- Seperation from whites tables ✓

My memories:
- When my friends and I showed up at the concert, a few of them were mumbling names such as "fags" and "prissies" because we were different, and went to Powhatan School. Maybe because we were in a large group, maybe because of our clothes or looks. Unlike them, we were dressed semi-nicely and we weren't huddled in a corner smoking cigarettes. I believe that maybe they were jealous of us for having opportunities, or maybe money, or friends.

Introduction - Sometimes my occasionally critical personality leads me to remembering the bad parts of my life. I tend to think about times when I was made fun of, or when a tragedy or accident occured.

Conclusion- "But of those memories, I am always able to derive the positives." "List positives of concert."

Third P - Alike - we both felt that we were awkward in the crowd. Maizon- black in whites. Me, Private schooler in Public schoolers. Makes me not want to relive these.... I felt awkward/weird during these memories.

each day. Here's what students noticed about Grimes's text:

- "These guys write about real issues like being abused or not wanting to live out their parents' dreams—dreams parents never made."
- "There's some dialogue."
- "They [the characters] look inside themselves honestly."
- "There's a story line—not a huge one, but it's there."
- "The poem kinda relates to the narrative. That's cool."
- "These are short because they show one thing or issue or feeling about a person or an event."
- "The voices are strong, like I can hear them talking to me."
- "They're written in first person."
- "They're all trying to find out who they are."
- "Each poem is different—some are shaped and some have stanzas."
- "The guys in the book make me think about myself."

> One in Infinity
>
> Emily
>
> Sometimes my occasionally critical personality leads me to remembering the negative parts of my life. I tend to think about times when I was made fun of or neglected, or when a tragedy occurred. For example, no matter how hard I try, I cannot erase the memory of my old home, and sometimes focus on the bad things about my new house.
>
> In the book, "Maizon at Blue Hill," Maizon feels awkward at her new school because she is one of the few blacks attending. If I were in Maizon's shoes, the memories that would stand out in my mind would probably begin at my first step through the door. As soon as she entered, Charley, one of the few other black girls immediately came up to her and introduced herself. I think that Maizon would remember this because it was the first time that she had met someone at her new school, and because it reassured her that she was not the only black girl there. Maizon would also probably remember her dinners in the Blue Hill cafeteria, because of the good smells of the hot food in chilly Connecticut. She would remember this also because her black friends chained her to sitting only with them, instead of turning into an "Oreo" and sitting with whites too. The last memories I think that Maizon would have cherished were the beautiful sun-drenched skies and icy winds of Connecticut. She loved to walk around the campus, and enjoy the lovely natural scenery. Of all of her memories, I think that Maizon would have remembered this one as her favorite, because it was such a delightful change from her urban New York home.
>
> On New Years Eve of 2005, my Powhatan School friends and I drove over to a Caydence Concert to celebrate. As soon as we got out of the car, there were a few guys mumbling names such as "fags" and "prissies" in our direction. I knew they didn't know we went to Powhatan School, and I didn't understand why they were calling us such obscenities. Could the reason for this treatment possibly be because of our clothes, or car, or maybe because we were in such a large group? I wasn't sure, and as weird as it felt to just keep walking by them, laughing joyously as we went, we did. Once we walked through the concert door, away from those judgmental guys, I realized that it wasn't us who were different, it was them. Sure we were from a private school, but we weren't the ones who were sitting around outside of a concert smoking cigarettes.
>
> Maizon and I have similar memories because they were both times when we felt left out, or different. However, maybe we remember the times when we felt depressed the most, because we have too many jovial memories to count, and it is so seldom that we are placed in an awkward position. I think that the moral of our memories is that, for every negative, there are infinite positives.

FIGURE 7.15: Emily's final draft.

This list showed me how much students had connected to this book's cast of characters—how much they had learned about the power that resides in personal narratives that are honest and introspective.

To meet school requirements, all students planned and wrote a personal narrative. To differentiate my requirements, if students had enough time, they could choose to add a poem to their narrative essay. Francesca's self-evaluation of this project shows how much she enjoyed hearing her classmates share during our version of "open mic." And Francesca shows her delight in this project when she writes, "Coming soon to an English class near you: Fashion design is to my life, as earth is to water!" Her narrative is as honest and open as the students in Grimes's fictional high school; her voice is strong because she cares deeply about these issues that shape her life and feelings.

I find that the longer I teach, the more freedom I offer students when responding to reading because this freedom can cultivate a joy in reading that the more traditional assignments such as book reports can't accomplish. And I hold dear the privilege of being able to get inside students' reading heads via journals and conferences.

Talk to Me

I just moved here. I guess that's why not many people in 8th grade really talk to me. It's like they all already have their own friends and problems. Well, I have problems too. I've wanted to fit in my whole life. Whether it's my hair or clothes, I've got to have what's "in". I mean, it's not that I don't like the stuff, just, that's the sole purpose of most of it. My Mom keeps saying, "Isn't this a lot better that it was at HDS?" I always say "Yeah, I guess", but I way disagree. I just say yes 'cause I don't want her to get concerned. This place is no better to me. I mean, Emalee seems like a great friend. So are all the really good friends I've made in 7th grade. But it's not the same as having more really good friends my age.

I want someone to share my sadness with. Someone who'll really understand me. I've been to at least 7 funerals, almost all of which were for family members. Especially Nana. Gosh, I'll never forget that week. The day after Easter, I get told my grandma died last night. I was only, like, 8. I didn't know how to handle it, so I just cried and cried. After that, I pretty much went into denial about her dying until Poppop got remarried. Alice is great. It's like I've got Nana back.

This is the kind of stuff I want to share with people. I now know that sharing sadness or depression with somebody close to you is better than just crying your eyes out. It feels good to let it all out, to share the sadness, to share the love. All I really want is someone to talk to me.

Figure 7.16: Francesca's personal narrative.

Pause, Reflect, and Consider Five Questions . . .

Both dipping into students' writing about reading in their journals and reading the assessments they complete during a unit of study arm you with important data that informs instructional decisions. You'll know if you should adjust the content of lessons or meet with students to scaffold their learning so you can gradually turn responsibility over to them.

Differentiating Reading Instruction

The questions that follow can help you reflect on your use of students' writing to differentiate their reading instruction. Reflect on them alone or discuss them with team or department colleagues.

- Is writing about reading an important part of my reading program?
- Do I know my students' reading levels and writing abilities well enough to provide a range of assessments?
- Do I keep a record of students' sharing of journal entries during read alouds and then reflect on my observations?
- Am I using students' writing to adjust my reading lessons?
- Am I using students' debriefings and writing about their reading to plan conferences and interventions?

Chapter 8

Professional Development and Differentiated Reading Instruction

Guidelines and Suggestions for Getting Started

A majority of the 14 English teachers in Lee High School in Staunton, Virginia, have shifted from one book or one basal anthology for all students to differentiating reading instruction. It has taken four years. In addition to working with me, these teachers meet regularly as a group and individually with Mary Ann Plogger, the high school differentiation specialist. Mary Ann facilitates study groups to build teachers' background knowledge on differentiation, using professional articles as well as Carol Ann Tomlinson's books. She also organizes and stocks, with the faculty's help, a reading resource room with texts from reading levels four on up, on diverse topics and genres. All administrators in Staunton city schools support this changeover to differentiation. In fact, every school in that district has a differentiation specialist like Mary Ann. The principal of Lee High School received funding from the central office to purchase books for teachers willing to differentiate reading instruction.

During the second year of workshops and professional study, Heather, a ninth-grade teacher, became the first English teacher at Lee High to implement a differentiated whole-class instructional unit. The third year, two more teachers, Brian and Katie, developed whole-class instructional units of study. Brian's tenth-grade class now studies science fiction, and Katie's ninth graders explore life in the South before civil rights legislation. Each time these three teachers shared their experiences with colleagues at meetings and workshops, they expressed not only the benefits of differentiation for students, but also

---

Supporting the Change to Differentiated Reading Instruction

Participate in ongoing staff development. Set aside enough time for teachers to learn more about the differentiation process and to exchange ideas and teaching experiences with colleagues. Administrators need to help teachers set up communication networks for meeting with one another and with teachers who are already differentiating reading instruction in their school or other schools. They can also discuss ways teachers can work with other staff members, such as the school librarian, resource teachers, and the differentiation specialist as they make plans for differentiating. Teachers can also help one another learn to use the information from assessments to get to know their students.

Gather materials. Administrators can offer support for teachers by (1) purchasing materials that help teachers learn more about differentiation and (2) by releasing funds for read-aloud texts and materials on diverse reading levels that pertain to the genre and the issue of the unit of study.

Set reasonable goals. Like the three teachers at Lee High School, if this is your first foray into differentiating reading instruction, then try one unit the first year. Avoid becoming overwhelmed. Don't let those discouraging and negative voices rule your mind.

their positive feelings about their units of study. All three felt that it had been helpful to begin by planning and implementing just one new unit that differentiated reading instruction during the first year.

By the fourth year, all but four teachers at Lee High School had designed and implemented at least one differentiated whole-class instructional reading unit of study. No administrator put pressure on the remaining four teachers. All of us understood that change takes time, and that these teachers required additional time to learn and observe colleagues' classes before taking the plunge.

As I look back at these years with teachers at Lee High School, and now with teachers I coach in other school districts, I see that there are core elements (see the box on page 248) that teachers and administrators should contemplate and address in order to differentiate reading instruction for all students.

Deepening Your Understanding of Differentiation

It's beneficial for all teachers and administrators to deepen their understanding of what differentiation means and how it can support their teaching and students' learning. Read articles in professional journals such as *Educational Leadership* (Association for Supervision and Curriculum Development), *The Reading Teacher* (International Reading Association), and *Language Arts* and *Voices From the Middle* (National Council of Teachers of English). In addition, stock your school's professional library with books about differentiating instruction. Teachers and administrators can organize themselves into small study groups, choose a book to read and discuss, and then share their findings with colleagues at faculty, team, or department meetings. In the box on page 250 are some book suggestions that can steer your differentiation journey and focus.

You can be the organizer of professional conversations about articles and books at your school (Routman, 2002). Grade-level teams, departments, or mixed groups of interested teachers can meet and converse to build their background knowledge and learn more about differentiation from other educators. Bimonthly or at the minimum, monthly, 45-minute conversations among groups of six to ten teachers can occur during common planning times, before the school day officially starts, during part of a faculty meeting, or during part of weekly or bimonthly early dismissal days. You and your colleagues prepare for these conversations by reading a professional article or part of a book about a week prior to the meeting date.

You or your reading or resource specialist can choose reading material for the first meetings. After the first two meetings, I turn the job of selecting reading materials over to group members by establishing a rotation roster so each member knows when to provide the group with reading materials.

It's helpful for the group to choose a facilitator. This person should be a volunteer who has the respect of colleagues and is an excellent listener who does not dominate discussions and can also keep the conversation going.

> ### Professional Resources on Differentiation
>
> *Differentiation in Action* by Judith Dodge. New York: Scholastic, 2006
>
> *How to Differentiate Instruction in Mixed Ability Classrooms* by Carol Ann Tomlinson. Alexandria, VA: ASCD, 1995
>
> *Multiple Intelligences: The Theory in Practice* by Howard Gardner. New York: Basic Books, 1993
>
> *The Differentiated Classroom: Responding to the Needs of All Learners* by Carol Ann Tomlinson. Alexandria, VA: ASCD, 1999
>
> *The Unschooled Mind: How Children Think and How Schools Should Teach* by Howard Gardner. New York: Basic Books, 1991

It's the facilitator's job to maintain the momentum of the discussion, to prevent one or two teachers from dominating the discussion, and to keep a positive tone. The facilitator does not join in the discussion but keeps ideas and sharing flowing.

Here are some prompts facilitators can use to move discussions forward:

- Does anyone have anything to add?
- Does anyone have a different idea? Opinion?
- Has anyone tried this strategy? How did it support differentiation?
- How might these ideas work in your classroom?
- Would you use all or part of the suggestions? Explain why.

During the last few minutes of the meeting, the facilitator summarizes the main points made and sets up the agenda for the next meeting. After two to three meetings, I recommend that a new facilitator be designated so that all participants have the opportunity to share ideas. Not only does this permit everyone to bring ideas to the conversation, but it also offers leadership opportunities to those who wish to try them.

I find that conversations are more productive if the facilitator sets these ground rules at the first meeting:

- Participants skim the text for a few minutes to refresh their memory.
- Every teacher shares one idea that resonated with his or her teaching style.
- Each participant initially shares for five minutes. If there's time after everyone has shared, people can say more.
- The focus of conversations is to consider whether the information read can be used by teachers and whether adjustments need to be made.

As teachers and administrators become knowledgeable about differentiation and make a commitment to bring this philosophy of teaching and learning to their schools, it's crucial to educate parents so that they understand the benefits of change. Your school might consider updating parents on its Web site or in a newsletter column devoted to differentiation. Your principal, perhaps with the help of the parents' association, might want to organize a series of morning breakfasts, at which administrators and teachers discuss differentiation with parents. Finally, you can build parents' trust and support by keeping them abreast of changes that affect their children's learning.

PARTNERING WITH ANOTHER TEACHER

It's helpful to partner with another teacher who has begun to differentiate reading instruction. You can pair up with a colleague in your school or one in your district. These meetings are informal and casual and can occur at a breakfast meeting, after school, or during common planning

Principal Evan Robb and Assistant Principal Griff Carmichael review multiple texts for a social studies class.

time if your partner is on your team or in your department. Arrange to have short meetings—15 to 30 minutes—when you have questions or need feedback on interpreting assessments. Having support from a peer who is on a similar teaching and learning journey can arm you with the encouragement and suggestions needed to succeed as you respond to the needs of all learners you teach.

In addition to shared conversations, you and your peer partner will benefit from observing each other as you differentiate reading instruction in your classrooms. Observations can lead to richer discussions and will provide each of you with mental models of what differentiating reading instruction looks like. I also urge partners to observe in other schools together, preferably, the same lesson. Such common experiences also lead to meaningful discussions and can enlarge your mental models of all aspects of differentiating reading instruction.

Examine and List Your School's Strengths and Needs

A school's faculty is its strength, especially if teachers are willing to study, grow, and revise their theory of the best way to organize their classes for instruction. Another strength, and a path to success with moving to differentiating reading instruction, is having the ongoing support for change from your principal and his or her administrators. It is also important to consider any needs your school may have. The suggestions that I list in this section relate to reading instruction in language arts and in content classes. They are just a starting point. Your school may have other needs for your to consider.

Possible Needs in Your School	Possible Solutions
• Take stock of your reading materials. Do you have materials that relate to your units of study on multiple reading levels?	• Use school funds and money raised by your parents' organization to purchase materials for units of study that represent a range of reading levels. • Place these multiple texts in a resource room so the materials are available to all teachers.

• Have each teacher order reading materials for one unit of study if funds are limited.	• Share materials with teachers of the same subject but who teach the unit at different points during the year.
• Study the way administrators group students heterogeneously. Remember, it's too difficult for a teacher to manage five to seven reading groups in one class.	• Keep the range of reading levels in a class diverse but not so wide that you have more than three reading groups. Make sure your groups include high, grade-level, and below-grade-level learners.
• Evaluate your class libraries in all subjects.	• Slowly build your classroom library so that you can support all reading levels for a rich independent reading program.
• Study the way you presently order reading materials.	• Avoid ordering class sets of 35 to 40 of one title. Instead, order 7 or 8 books around an issue or theme, written at reading levels that meet the needs of your students. Keep these in a resource room so others have access to the materials.
• Organize a committee to make sure that your report cards allow you to discuss the personal growth of each student.	• Create a checklist or a place with several lines so you can showcase each student's progress based on differentiation. For example, a checklist could include the range and variety of assessments you use, and students choose.
• Consider ways that teachers can build their mental models of what differentiation looks like in a classroom.	• Ask teachers to observe a colleague at his or her school who is differentiating reading instruction. Teachers can also visit schools where differentiation is thriving, and observe others. In addition, ask a teacher who differentiates reading instruction to model for colleagues what he or she does either during a professional day or a faculty meeting.

Review your needs and use them to set reasonable goals over two to three years. Starting small with goals you can achieve contributes to the success of this initiative and may prevent feelings of frustration, anxiety, and stress.

School Differentiation Specialists Provide Ongoing Follow-up and Support

A differentiation specialist, like Mary Ann Plogger of Lee High School, is a master teacher who can help teachers in all subjects differentiate instruction. It's beneficial if candidates for the position of differentiation specialist have taught several grade levels as well as more than one subject. These teachers should have demonstrated their ability to differentiate instruction in their classes. Having this practical experience base enables these teachers to model for colleagues and to gain the respect of colleagues because they have been teaching in response to diverse students' needs.

The differentiation specialist can model for teachers, gather resources for them to read and study, respond to questions, support teachers' use of assessments to plan instruction for classes of diverse learners, and teach demonstration lessons for teams, departments, and at faculty meetings. In some schools, this is a full-time position; in small school districts where money is tight, the differentiation specialist can teach one or two classes and spend the remainder of the day supporting colleagues.

Differentiation specialists are an important component of Staunton city schools in Staunton, Virginia. Assistant Superintendent of Instruction Dr. Sarah Armstrong, brought differentiation specialists to her school system during the 2000–2001 school year. She says this of her differentiation specialists: "They have been an invaluable resource in curriculum development and instructional modeling. I believe that all principals and teachers would tell you now that they couldn't do the important job of teaching diverse learners without them."

Start With Small, Reasonable Goals When Differentiating Reading Instruction

Like all teachers, when I learn new strategies at a conference or a workshop, or when I read a book filled with best practices, I want to do everything the next day at school. Over the years I've learned to enjoy these enthusiastic feelings, then to curb them and set goals I can meet, without anxiety and frustration. Give yourself the gift of time—three to five years to fully change from one anthology or class novel to using diverse, multiple texts. What follows are some suggestions for setting goals you can reach as you change your teaching style to differentiating reading instruction and respond to the needs of all your students.

The First Year
- Use your read alouds as a common text. Try two to three of the lessons in Chapter 3.
- Build a strong independent reading program. Have students keep book logs and discuss these every six to eight weeks, using the suggestions on pages 191–194.
- Practice taking observational notes on one or two students each day your class meets. Focus on students who might benefit from scaffolding and reteaching.

The Second Year
- Continue using your read-aloud texts to present lessons you tried during the first year; try two or three different lessons in Chapter 3.
- Maintain your independent reading. Invite students to present monthly book talks. Use the book-talk guidelines on pages 198–201 and also invite students to create their own guidelines.
- Design a four-week unit of study for a differentiated whole-class instructional reading workshop on a genre. Create Big Picture Plans (see pages 54–55) and gather texts from your school, classroom, and community libraries that meet the instructional needs of students in your classes. Review Chapter 4, pages 99–138.
- Work on observing students and taking objective notes; aim to observe two or three students who struggle and need your support first each time your class meets.

The Third Year
- Continue all the differentiation you have practiced during years one and two.
- Gather assessments and use these to inform your next teaching steps as well as for planning interventions and scaffolds for individuals and small groups (see pages 42–47).
- Take observational notes on five or six students each day.

The Fourth Year

- Continue all the differentiation you have practiced during years one through four.
- Design a second unit of study for differentiated whole-class instruction. Extend the unit to seven or eight weeks so students complete at least two instructional-level texts as well as a great deal of independent reading. Use assessments to inform your instructional decisions.
- Try strategic reading groups for a six-week unit of study if your teaching schedule permits this. Keep a week-by-week plan book for each of your two or three groups. Review Chapter 5.
- Continue taking observational notes and make it a goal to gather data on all students in a class in a four-week period. Make these notes an integral part of your grouping decisions.

The Fifth Year

- Continue with all the differentiation strategies you've practiced during the first four years.
- Develop a second small-group strategic reading unit. Plan for a six- to eight-week unit of study if your teaching schedule permits this. Keep a week-by-week plan book for each of your groups. Review Chapter 5.
- Use your observational notes as one assessment for grouping decisions.

A Closing Thought About Differentiating Reading Instruction

I know that when you teach each student at his or her instructional reading level and combine the power of instruction, interventions, and scaffolds with independent reading—time to read free-choice books at students' comfort levels at school and home—you can make a difference in your students' reading lives. Richard Allington pointed out that the teacher is truly important to students' progress and to developing the motivation to read to learn and to enjoy (2002).

There are no quick fixes or silver bullets when it comes to teaching reading. Progress takes time, but one of the most important tasks you and I have is to motivate students to choose to read on their own. In the figures on this page are two student self-evaluations of their reading progress. Both are in the same eighth-grade class, exposed to the same opportunities. Free-choice reading and my frequent read alouds have transformed Danny

> **My Reading Life**
>
> Justine   February 8
>
> I really hate reading. My reading life sucks. Read alouds don't really help me and talking about them don't really help me. I mean, I understand what you are talking about and I appreciate the effort but it doesn't help me very much. If I have to read, I'd rather read a magazine than a book. To me, reading is really boring and I really don't understand how people can sit down and read. ((no offense))

FIGURE 8.1: Justine reflects on her reading life.

> **My reading life**
>
> Danny   Febuary 8
>
> This year, wow. Reading a book has always been at the bottom of my list. Why not play video games or basketball? The answer for me is still unanswered. Right now, for some odd reason and really for the first time in my life, I'm confused.
>
> Lately, I've just randomly started reading, I've found out there are some good books in the world. Of course, I can still find myself shootin' hoops and hangin' out with my friends. But at night, when it's quiet and noone is there to do anything with, I'll read. My most recent book finished was Forest Gump. I've seen the movie and it's one of my favorites. But then I read the book. Unbelievably, the book's funnier!
>
> So is reading my favorite thing, no. Am I enjoying it though, yes. Until this year, I knew I could read fast, but I didn't know how many books that I could truly relate myself to. A book isn't just a forced thing now, it's almost, just might be, a hobbie.

FIGURE 8.2: Danny reflects on his reading life.

but not Justine. This is the reality of teaching. You and I want every student to be a Danny, but that doesn't happen. However, you and I need to teach well and differentiate reading instruction keeping the hope alive that we will reach all learners. Maybe not the year we have those students, but I always hope that the changeover will come in the future.

Pause, Reflect, and Consider Six Questions . . .

There is compelling support for differentiating reading instruction. By responding to each learner we teach we can meet their instructional needs and improve their reading comprehension, recall, and inferential thinking. Teaching to the middle only serves a small part of a class of students. Those who struggle because they can't read the texts are not receiving the instruction they require to improve and become better readers; these students slip backward from lack of practice and instruction. Above-grade-level readers who would benefit from challenges also suffer.

As you gradually move toward differentiating reading instruction, return to these questions, mull them over, and discuss your ideas and feelings with colleagues.

- Am I aware of the diverse reading levels of students in my classes? What have I done to gather this information?

- How am I differentiating reading instruction and helping every student become a better reader?

- Do I set aside time to review and interpret assessments, and then use this data to plan lessons that respond to students' needs?

- Have I begun to read and discuss professional materials about differentiating instruction with colleagues?

- Do I confer with students for short bursts of time in order to get into their minds and explore ways to help them learn and achieve?

- Am I building my classroom library so all students can practice reading at their comfort levels?

Appendix A

"The Party" by Pam Muñoz Ryan

It didn't take me long to figure out that I wasn't invited to the party. I got off the bus and saw my friends huddled under the tree where we all stood every morning before the first bell. There were six of us: Theresa, Becky, Barbara, Carol, Kim, and me. I can't even say that we were close friends. We had come from different elementary schools and never fit with the predictable middle school jocks, pops, or nerds. We were flotsam and jetsam that washed under a tree in front of the library and became an entity by default and by simply standing together.

The circle seemed tighter as I approached; the flittering of small white envelopes being hastily stuffed into backpacks and binders gave it away. I knew as well as the entire universe that Bridget's party was this weekend. Bridget was one of the pops, the popular ones and the antithesis of me. She was thin and wore clothes that looked like they came straight from the pages of magazines. She had that hair—red, and cut into a perfect page, smoothed into a bowl around her face, and every shade of shoes to match even her wildest outfits. She had a select group of followers who squealed and hugged each other between every class, as if they hadn't seen each other in years. We all wanted to be like her or them and being invited to her party meant elevation in the school pecking order. To not be invited meant standing in stagnant water.

My stomach churned, and I hoped that Bridget was still holding an envelope with my name on it to be delivered later. But my friends' shuffling feet and furtive glances guaranteed my fate. Their too-eager hellos told me that everyone already knew who was invited and who wasn't.

"Hi," I responded but that one word already sounded hollow with disappointment.

Becky, always the diffuser of uncomfortable moments, said, "Hey, did you get all the algebra homework done?"

"Everything but the last problem," I mumbled.

"Here, want to see the answer?" Eagerly, maybe out of guilt, she gratuitously flipped open her binder before I could tell her it didn't matter.

I pretended to be interested in her calculations but my head swam with that sinking feeling that there was something wrong with me. That I wasn't worthy.

Thankfully, the bell rang and I hurried toward English. When I passed the cafeteria, the impending lunch smells followed me, and I felt nauseous by the time I reached class, but I knew it wasn't from the aroma of creamed turkey and overcooked green beans. I couldn't concentrate on the short story we were supposed to be reading in class, but I had no trouble attending to the faux wood grain on my desk and wondering if I could dissolve into it and disappear.

Why hadn't she invited me? My feet were too big? No. Maybe. My face was broken out? Who wants someone with acne at her party? Why did she invite every person in my group except me? I tried to think of any interactions I'd had with Bridget recently. A few days earlier, we'd been partners during a sixth-period project. I was intent on getting the project done and impressing her with the grade we could get, and she was intent on looking at teen magazines. She barely spoke to me except to say, "You're so serious. You know, you should smile more."

By the end of second period, I had overheard all the details about the party. They were going bowling. It was a sleepover. There was going to be a scavenger hunt. They were renting scary movies and were going to stay up all night. Each time someone mentioned the party, I smiled weakly and nodded.

During third period, Meredith, one of the drama club girls, who wasn't invited and didn't care, asked me if I was going to Bridget's party.

Instead of saying no, I found myself repeating tidbits that I'd heard earlier. "Her dad is taking everyone to IHOP for breakfast. They're taking two big vans so everyone will fit." I said it with authority. As if I were going, too.

Meredith said, "I wish she'd invited me so I could tell her no. She's such a brat. And all that phony hugging. What's that all about, anyway?"

Where did Meredith get her confidence? I wondered.

At lunch, I sat with my group at our usual table, and they politely avoided the subject. When Kim got up to take her tray, she said, "I'm going shopping tomorrow after school. Anybody want to come?"

But I knew what they would be shopping for, so I said, "I can't. I'm busy."

Becky hung behind and walked with me to dump our trays.

"I heard Bridget could only invite so many people."

"Whatever," I said. "See you later." I didn't look at Becky. I couldn't look at her because if I saw any pity or kindness in her eyes, I'd start crying so I pretended to look for something seemingly important in my backpack until she left.

Maybe she didn't invite me because of my hair. It's so long and stringy. Maybe it's my coat. It is pretty ugly compared to some to the other girls' coats. I should have bought another color. But what does it really matter? None of my clothes match. I'm way too tall but there isn't anything I can do about that, and she couldn't not invite someone to a party because they were too tall, could she? Maybe I should smile and hug more but I just can't get into hugging people unless I know them really well. Probably if I'd smiled more, I would have been invited.

I hated Bridget. I hated her more for having the ability to make my life miserable. I wanted to go home. I felt sick. As I changed classes, I averted my eyes from everyone I knew so I wouldn't have to smile. So I wouldn't have to pretend that I was likable.

By fifth period, the news was out. Three girls that had been invited to the party couldn't go because of the overnight band trip. They rushed up to Bridget to tell her the sad news, and one of them cried, proving what a good friend she was and how much she wanted to go. They gave back their invitations. I passed the crier between classes and saw her injured, yet superior look.

After all, she had been invited.

Then, the whispers began, like tiny wisps of drifting clouds, about who might be chosen in their places. I walked to sixth period, trailing behind Bridget, hanging back and watching hopeful faces laughing a little too loudly as they passed her. I counted nine girls who smiled and said hello to her on the short walk between classes. They might as well have been saying, "Choose me. Choose me."

After school, Becky found me in the bus lines. Breathlessly, she said, "Bridget asked Barbara at lunch who else she should invite, and Barbara said you. And Kim just told me that she just heard Bridget say she was going to *maybe* invite you to her party. Call me, okay?" She held up both hands with fingers crossed, then hurried toward her bus.

There was still a chance. But what did Becky mean when she'd said Bridget was *maybe* going to invite me. Was there a condition?

Over all the heads, I could see the red hair bobbing toward the bus lines, then stopping. I heard Bridget laughing. She moved to another group and there was another little burst of laughter.

Kids began crunching forward to board the bus.

So what if I don't go the party. I'm still me whether I go or not. And it's just for one night. So what's the big deal? My thoughts were spinning. Bridget headed toward my line, weaving through the crowd, and it did seem as if she was headed toward me. I pretended to not notice and looked straight ahead at the bus.

I felt a hand on my arm.

I turned my head.

Bridget held out an invitation. "Will you come to my party?"

I looked at the small envelope, relishing the moment. But my mind was a jumble. Now she wanted me to come to her party, but she hadn't wanted me in the beginning. I am an afterthought. I am not on the A list. I'm just filling a space so the vans will be full. I need to smile more.

Take it, I thought. You know you want to go. Take it.

The crowd was moving me now, and I was only a few feet from the bus steps. Bridget moved with me as I inched forward, still offering the invitation. I looked at the envelope. The original name had been scribbled out but my name hadn't even been written in its place. If I didn't take it, I was sure that it would go to someone else.

I put my foot on the first step of the bus, then looked at her.

I hesitated.

Someone behind me yelled, "Get on the bus!"

I took a deep breath and gave her my answer.

And then, I smiled.

Appendix B

Choosing "Just-Right" Books for Independent Reading

Model with a think aloud how you use the three-finger method to choose a book. Jot down the four steps on chart paper so students can refer to them.

Use the Three-Finger Method to Find Free-Reading Texts	Is the Book a "Just-Right" Fit?
1. Open the text to a page near the middle. 2. Read the page silently. 3. Count words you can't say and those you don't understand. 4. If you don't know more than three words, set the book aside and find another.	• A book is too difficult if there are more than three words you can't say and don't know, and if you can't retell what you read. • A book is just right if you can say and understand all but two to three words, and you can retell what you read.

TIPS FOR HELPING STUDENTS CHOOSE TEXTS FOR INDEPENDENT READING

• Help those students who read far below grade level to select books. If a student who struggles chooses a hard book, don't take it away. Make a positive comment about the book and then offer them two to three other books to check out, just in case the student decides not to read the book she chose. It's important to be sensitive to the self-confidence and self-esteem of students who avoid reading.

• Encourage students, whenever possible, to pair up when choosing an independent reading book. Students can go through the three-finger process and support each other.

Appendix C

Sample Schedules for Whole-Class Instructional Reading

SCHEDULE FOR 45-MINUTE READING AND WRITING BLOCK

I suggest that you think of your schedule in a two-week block of time. The first week, you will have three reading and two writing classes. The second week you'll have three writing and two reading classes.

Reading Schedule

- Warm-up activity (3 minutes)
- Read aloud to build background knowledge, or for enjoyment (10 minutes)
- Choose from one of these (10–15 minutes):
  - a read aloud to model the application of a reading strategy
  - a read aloud to teach narrative story elements
  - a read aloud to teach informational text features
  - a read aloud to introduce a genre, topic, or an issue
- Independent reading of instructional-level books (15–20 minutes). During independent reading time, confer with a few students.

For homework: 30 minutes of independent reading each night

SCHEDULE FOR A 90-MINUTE READING AND WRITING BLOCK

Alternate instructional reading with two days of independent reading. With a longer block, you have the flexibility to extend your independent reading one week and the second week give more time to writing.

Reading Schedule

- Warm-up (3 minutes)
- Read aloud for fun (5 minutes)
- Choose from one of these (10 minutes):
  - a read aloud to model the application of a reading strategy
  - a read aloud to teach narrative story elements
  - a read aloud to teach informational text features
  - a read aloud to introduce a genre, topic, or an issue
- Independent reading of instructional-level books (20–30 minutes). During independent reading time, confer with a few students.
- Wrap-up (5 minutes)

For homework: 30 minutes of independent reading each night

Appendix D

Sample Schedules for Small-Group Instructional Reading

SCHEDULE FOR A 45-MINUTE CLASS

Because reading, writing, spelling, vocabulary, and grammar must be taught in these short, daily periods, I suggest you follow this schedule:

Teacher-Led Small Instructional Groups: the schedule remains the same for the length of the unit of study.

- Three days a week, meet with two groups a day
- Two days a week, hold writing workshop and teach language arts

For Homework: 30 minutes of independent reading each night.

SCHEDULE FOR A 90-MINUTE BLOCK THAT MEETS THREE TIMES A WEEK:

Students receive reading instruction each time the class meets.

Teacher-Led Instructional Reading Groups: there's time for instructional and independent reading.

- Lead two small reading groups a day; instructional and independent reading.
- Hold writing workshops and language arts 40 to 45 minutes each time the block meets.

SAMPLE READING BLOCK

- Warm-up (3 minutes)
- Read aloud for fun (5 minutes)
- Instructional read aloud or mini-lesson (10 minutes)
- Teacher-led small-group instruction: meet with two groups daily (25 minutes)
- Wrap-up (5 minutes)

For homework: 30 minutes of independent reading each night

OTHER SCHEDULING OPTIONS FOR WHOLE-CLASS AND SMALL-GROUP INSTRUCTIONAL READING

If you opt not to have an instructional read aloud or mini-lesson, then you have these options:

- Increase instructional reading to 35 minutes and complete extra conferences.
- Reserve 20 minutes for instructional reading and 15 minutes for independent reading.
- Invite several students to present book talks or an assessment project. You can also ask them to review and discuss their reading logs every four to six weeks.

Appendix E

Book Log

TITLE AND AUTHOR	DATE COMPLETED

Appendix F

Eleven Questions About Reading

Read the questions that follow. On a separate sheet of paper, take notes for each question. Then use your notes to write a paragraph in response to each question. If you can't answer a question, write, "I don't know."

1. Why do you read?

2. What benefits do you see in reading? How do you think reading helps you in your daily life?

3. What do you do well as a reader?

4. Do you read for pleasure at home? How often? What do you enjoy about reading?

5. How does reading make you feel?

6. How do you select a book to read for enjoyment?

7. What do you do with the book before you start reading it?

8. As you read, are you aware of any strategies you use when you don't understand a word? A passage?

9. When you finish a book, what do you do with it?

10. What are some of your favorite books?

11. Who is your favorite author? Why do you enjoy this author's books?

Appendix G

Interest Inventory for Grades 4 and 5

Name _____ Date _____

Complete this survey so your teacher and school librarian can help you find books you will want to read.

1. What do you enjoy doing most in your free time?

    _____

    _____

2. What sports do you enjoy playing? Explain why.

    _____

    _____

3. What sports do you love to watch? Explain why.

    _____

    _____

4. What is your favorite subject? Why do you enjoy it?

    _____

    _____

5. Do you have any hobbies? List a few, and then write about your favorite one.

    _____

    _____

6. What kinds of books do you enjoy the most when you read on your own? Name two or three titles as examples.

    _____

    _____

7. Who is your favorite author? Explain why you love to read his/her books.

    _____

    _____

Appendix H

Interest Inventory for Grades 6 and up

Name _____ Date _____

Complete this survey so your teacher and school librarian can help you find books you will want to read.

1. What do you enjoy doing most in your free time? _____
    _____

2. What sports do you enjoy playing? Explain why. _____
    _____

3. What sports do you love to watch? Explain why. _____
    _____

4. What is your favorite subject? Why do you enjoy it?_____
    _____

5. Do you have any hobbies? List a few, and then write about your favorite one.
    _____

6. Do you have a favorite author? If so, can you explain why you love to read his/her books?
    _____

7. If you could travel back in time, where would you go? Explain your answer.
    _____

8. Do you read comic books and magazines? Which ones do you enjoy most?
    _____

9. What kinds of music do you enjoy? Do you have a favorite group? Instrument? Musician?
    Name these. _____
    _____

10. What kinds of books do you enjoy the most when you read on your own? Use the list below
    to help you choose the genres you enjoy. _____

mystery	historical fiction	science fiction
romance	biography/autobiography	diaries
realistic fiction	series books	letters
information books	folktales	suspense
fantasy	short stories	myths and legends
funny stories	history	graphic novels

Differentiating Reading Instruction

Appendix I

Reading Strategy Checklist

Name _____ Date _____

Put a checkmark next to the strategies you use.

BEFORE READING . . .

_____ I skim, looking at and thinking about the pictures, photos, graphs, and charts.

_____ I read headings and captions.

_____ I read the book's back cover and/or print on the inside flaps of the jacket.

_____ I use the three-finger method to see if the book is just right for me.

_____ I ask questions.

_____ I make predictions.

WHILE READING . . .

_____ I make mental pictures.

_____ I identify confusing parts and reread these.

_____ I use pictures, graphs, and charts to understand confusing parts.

_____ I identify unfamiliar words and use context clues to figure out their meanings.

_____ I stop and retell to see what I remember. If necessary, I reread.

_____ I predict and then adjust or confirm.

_____ I raise questions and read on to discover answers.

_____ I jot down a tough word and the page it's on and ask for help.

AFTER READING . . .

_____ I think about the characters, settings, events, or new information.

_____ I discuss or write my reactions.

_____ I reread parts I enjoy.

_____ I skim to find details.

_____ I reread to find support for questions.

Comments:

Appendix J

Reading Strategy Lesson: Drawing Conclusions

PURPOSE: To deepen students' ability to use facts and details in their novels to discover the personality traits of characters and explore themes

MATERIALS: A realistic fiction read aloud; the realistic fiction books for your unit of study (This lesson is based on "The Party" by Pam Muñoz Ryan.)

TIME: About 10 to 15 minutes using the read aloud to model; 10 minutes for students to practice with their own books

PRESENTING THE LESSON

1. Use your read-aloud text to model how you draw conclusions. Here's my instructional think aloud for "The Party."

    I can conclude that peer approval is important to the narrator. I know this because the narrator says that her stomach churned waiting to see if an invitation would come her way. She tells us that Bridget is the most popular person in school and that the opposite is true of the narrator. So I can also conclude that the narrator is on the outside of the popular group. When the narrator says that "to not be invited meant standing in stagnant water," I can conclude that no invitation meant being even more isolated from the in-group. Isolation can cause loneliness and depression.

2. Ask students to tell you what they noticed. Here are the reactions of some seventh graders:

    - You gave a reason for what you said.
    - You used the story to show your conclusions were right.
    - You quoted part of the story to make a point.

3. Invite students to draw conclusions about "The Party." Here are two examples from that seventh-grade class:

    - I know that she [the narrator] has a bad image of herself. She wonders if the reason she wasn't invited was because her feet were too big and she had pimples on her face. She blamed herself and didn't look outside at the group.
    - I can conclude that she [the narrator] did not take the invitation. She smiles when she gets on the bus. She thinks if she should or shouldn't take it. I think she figured out what a snot and control freak Bridget is. So she got the invite, but turns it down.

4. Involve students in applying this strategy to their realistic novel. Allow pairs, who can work independently, to support each other.

5. Gather and work with students who read two or more years below grade level.

6. To discover a character's personality traits and a novel's themes, while at the same time

deepening your knowledge of how this strategy works and improves comprehension, together, you and your students will reflect on and determine what you learn about a character and theme by studying the following:

- dialogue between characters
- the inner thoughts of a character
- speaker tags such as "he shouted" or "she whimpered"
- decisions a character makes
- events a character lives through and how she handles these
- the motivation for a decision, an action, inner thoughts, or dialogue
- what others think and say about the character
- the character's actions and interactions
- conflicts between two or more characters

7. Use the list of personality traits on appendix page 283 as a resource.

Appendix K

Reading Strategy Lesson: Using Context Clues

PURPOSE: To develop students' ability to use text, photographs, and illustrations, to understand unfamiliar words

MATERIALS: A realistic fiction read aloud; students' realistic novels (I use "The Party" by Pam Muñoz Ryan.)

TIME: About 5–10 minutes of teacher modeling; 10 minutes of student practice

PRESENTING THE LESSON

1. Model, in a think-aloud, how you use context clues to figure out a word's meaning while reading. Here's my think aloud:

    The word is antithesis. *I'm not sure what it means. I'll reread the sentence: "Bridget was one of the pops, the popular ones and the antithesis of me." If being popular is the antithesis of the narrator, then the word* antithesis *must mean "opposite." The narrator is the opposite of popular.*

2. Invite students to share what they noticed about the think aloud. Here's what seventh graders said:

    • You reread the sentence.

    • You found clues.

    • You picked what you understood and connected it.

3. During teacher-led small-group lessons, show students how you use context clues to figure out a word's meaning, and then invite pairs in the group to try the strategy with a word you've selected.

4. Involve students in applying this strategy to their novels during group lessons.

5. Have students figure out the meaning of an unfamiliar word by doing the following:

    • If that doesn't work, read around the word by reading the sentences that come before and after the sentence that includes the word.

    • If that doesn't work, read the entire paragraph to discover the meaning from the situation or the description provided in the paragraph.

6. Sometimes there aren't any context clues, or not enough to help students figure out a word's meaning. If this is the case, have them try the following:

    • Ask a reading buddy or another student.

    • Jot down the word and the page number on a self-stick note to discuss during the next group meeting.

Appendix L

QtA Queries for Fiction and Nonfiction

Use the following queries to help students build comprehension while reading. Have students write two or three of the queries on a bookmark, made with half a sheet of notebook paper. Ask them to pause halfway through and at the end of a chapter, and use a query to think about meaning. You can also pinpoint specific pages during reading group sessions and invite students to use these queries for Questioning the Author.

QUERIES FOR NONFICTION

- What is the author trying to tell you about this person?
- What does the author want you to know? to understand?
- What's the big idea in this part?
- What does the author mean?
- Does what happened here make sense with what happened or came before?

QUERIES FOR FICTION

- How do things look for the character now?
- How does the author help you know that the character has changed?
- How does the author make you feel about this character? Explain.
- Why does the author put the character in a specific situation? What did you learn from this?
- What big ideas is the author trying to help you understand?

Appendix M

Explanations of Nonfiction Text Features

Knowing the purpose of nonfiction text features will support your students' reading of nonfiction texts. As students investigate these features, encourage them to compose explanations in their own words that you print on large chart paper. Help students understand that writers choose features that showcase their topic and the content of their books.

The Bibliography: This feature is found at the end of a book. It is a list of the other books and resources the author used to research information for his or her book.

Boldface Type: This is the darker printing type used for titles, headings, and key vocabulary. This feature calls readers' attention to words and phrases that are important.

Glossary: This alphabetic list at the back of a text contains the definitions of important and unusual words found in the text. Some glossary entries also include guidelines for pronouncing the word.

Index: This alphabetic list of key words, topics, and the names of people and places mentioned in the text comes at the end of the text. Next to each item is a page number or several page numbers that refer the reader to the place in the text where the topic or person is cited. The more page numbers an index entry has, the more details you'll find about that topic.

Introduction: This is a part of a text that is found at the beginning and can explain how the author conceived of his or her idea. This feature often recognizes others who helped the author gather information.

Maps: These representations help you locate places the author discusses in the text. Maps may also show you the path of an explorer, pilot, or rescue effort.

Photographs and Captions: Photographs are images of objects or people. They can also include information about a topic that's not in the text. Captions are one to two sentences that explain the photographs.

Quotations and Interviews: Quotations or interviews give the exact words of a person or expert. You'll often find quotes or interviews in sidebars or in a separate section of the page, outside of the text.

Sidebars: These boxes on a text page contain information that does not quite fit into the text's content but that the author wants to include. Sidebars can contain related information and quotations or parts of interviews, diary entries, letters, or newspaper clippings.

Table of Contents: This feature at the front of a text lists chapter titles and page numbers. It provides a quick overview of a text's subject matter and where it is located.

Timeline: This feature is a table that includes important dates, either in a person's life or from a historical period, such as the Middle Ages or the Civil War. Timelines may have photographs, illustrations, and short write-ups under each date.

Differentiating Reading Instruction

Appendix N

Open-Ended Genre Discussion Questions

The questions for each genre enable you to differentiate instruction for a class of students with diverse reading levels. Use these questions when students all read a different book, when partners read the same book, or when teachers or students lead small-group discussions of independent and/or instructional reading.

SUGGESTIONS FOR USING OPEN-ENDED QUESTIONS

Place questions on index cards; create enough card decks so each pair or group has a deck to use. To give students choice part of time, alternate between you choosing a specific question to discuss and them choosing a question card from the deck.

Make sure that students use details and/or inferences from the text to support their answers. Laminate card decks so you can reuse them annually. Bind each deck with a rubber band, or place them in a shoebox or a plastic crate.

ENCOURAGE STUDENTS TO PREPARE FOR DISCUSSIONS

Before students use the questions to spark conversations about their reading, ask them to think about their question(s), skim their book for support, and jot down in their journals all ideas they've collected. These notes should be in students' own words, as paraphrasing is one measure of understanding. This kind of preparation can create more thoughtful and effective discussions.

HISTORICAL FICTION

- What clues do you use to determine the time period and the place of this book?
- What does the book teach you about family life and relationships between family members?
- What does the book teach you about the role of men and women during these times?
- What kinds of struggles and problems does the main character face? List three and explain how the main character deals with and solves each one. If there is no solution, explain why you think the problem cannot be solved.
- Would you enjoy living during the time period of this book? Explain why or why not.
- What problems or conflicts does the main character face that you deal with in your life?
- How do the main character's problems differ from yours?
- How do people cope with economic problems such as a scarcity of food? Money? Jobs?
- How are minorities portrayed? Are they stereotyped? Offer examples.

FANTASY

- What are the settings? Explain the elements of fantasy that you see in the setting.

- How does the author enable you, the reader, to enter the fantasy world? Are there realistic elements? Discuss some of these and how they affect the story.
- How do trips to other times and worlds help the characters cope with the present time?
- Is there a struggle between forces of light and dark? Who wins? Offer support for the victory.
- What special powers does the hero possess? For what purposes does he or she use these powers?
- What does the hero learn about himself/herself? About life?
- What personality traits do you have in common with the hero? Discuss two of these.
- How do ideas and themes in this book connect to other fantasy books you've read?
- Does the story deal with values and themes about death?
- How has this book changed your thinking?

SCIENCE FICTION
- What scientific advances do you see in the society? How do these advances in technology affect the characters' decisions and actions?
- Are the problems the characters face in the story similar to or different from the ones that people face today? Explain with examples.
- Does the author deal with present-day issues such as population, food supplies, ecology, and technological advances? Compare the author's views with your own.
- Does the story offer hope for humanity, or is it a warning? Explain your conclusion.
- How do people fit into this futuristic society? Are they subordinate to machines? Has democracy vanished? See if you can identify the changes and offer reasons for each one.
- Would you like to live in this society? Are there advantages and disadvantages? Offer reasons from the text for your decisions.

REALISTIC FICTION
- What problems does the main character face? Do you feel these problems are realistic? Why? Why not?
- Describe three or four settings and show how each one influences the events and characters' actions and decisions. Would similar settings have influenced you in the same way? Explain.
- How realistic is the main character compared with your own experiences?
- What about two or three minor characters is realistic in terms of your experiences?
- What problems and conflicts in this book are realistic?
- What problems do you and the main character or a minor character have in common? Compare how you deal with these problems with how the character deals with them.
- What are the realistic themes and issues in the book? Are they about growing up, peer pressure, friendships, family relationships, survival, divorce, stereotyping? Discuss three themes the book explores.
- In real life, events and people can change a character. How does an important event or person change the main character at the end of the book?

MYSTERY

- How does the author build suspense and excitement? Find two to three passages and discuss how the author accomplishes this. Is it through description? Characters' thoughts and actions?
- What is the mystery that must be solved? How does setting affect the mystery?
- What are some clues that the author includes to lead you away from solving the mystery?
- What traits does the main character possess that enables him or her to solve the mystery?
- Why does the main character become involved in the mystery?
- How does danger affect the decisions and actions of the main character/detective?
- At what point in the book are you able to solve the mystery? What helps you do this?
- What part do you consider the most suspenseful? Share it and explain why.

NONFICTION

- Why did you select this book?
- What new information did you learn?
- What questions did the book raise but not answer?
- What did you learn from photographs? From charts and diagrams? From illustrations?
- Did this book change your thinking on this topic? How?
- Did the author weave opinions into facts? Can you find some examples?

FOLKTALES AND FAIRY TALES

- Can you classify your folktale or fairy tale and explain why you selected the category? Is it a cumulative, circular, realistic, wonder, beast, numskull, giant, or quest tale?
- Does the tale revolve around magic numbers? If so, explain the role of these magic numbers in the story and how they affect the adventures and characters.
- Why must heroic tasks or deeds be accomplished?
- How do the adventures, the magic, and the minor characters change the life of the hero or heroine?
- What are two difficult decisions characters make? What influences these decisions? How do their decisions change their lives?
- What human characteristics do the animals, flowers, and toys have? How are their qualities similar to yours?
- What is the clash and struggle between good and evil? Who wins? Offer support for your opinion on the victory.
- Who is the hero? The heroine? What qualities make him or her heroic?

Appendix O

Book Review Guidelines

Length: One handwritten page, or three-quarters of a double-spaced typed page.

Heading:
- Write your name and the date at the top of the page.
- Skip a line and write the title and author.

First Paragraph:
- Write an introductory sentence that includes one of these elements:
  - a short quotation from the book or magazine selection
  - a statement that gives the book either a thumbs-up or a thumbs-down evaluation, and a reason to support your position
- Write, from notes you've taken, a short summary of your selection and identify the genre in the introduction: fantasy, science fiction, realistic or historical fiction, biography, autobiography, poetry, photo-essay, informational chapter, magazine story, play, or article.

Second Paragraph:
- Choose one to three of the questions for forming opinions about fiction or nonfiction and use these to inform readers about the strengths and weaknesses of your book or magazine article.
- Use specific examples from the book or magazine to support each question you choose to respond to in your book review.

Closing Paragraph:
- Reread your second paragraph and decide who would enjoy this book or magazine selection.
- Offer one or two reasons why the book is either a great read or a boring read.

Appendix P

Book Review: Fiction

Use these questions and prompts to prepare for your written book review.

- Was the book a page-turner? Why, or why not?
  - Briefly, give an example of how the events, or what happened in the book, created excitement and kept you interested.
  - Or, discuss why a conflict or problem the character faced held your interest.
- Was it hard to concentrate on the story? Why or why not?
- Was it boring? Explain why.
  - Discuss one or more of these issues: the story contained little or no action; the events or plot did not make sense to you; you could not connect with the character's problems, friends, or family.
- Did you personally connect with one character, event, or conflict? Explain why.
  - Explain how you and the character are alike. Do you have the same feelings? Worries? Problems? Hopes? Dreams? Thoughts?
  - Have you lived through similar events? Explain how your reaction to a similar event was the same as the main character's reaction.
- What about this book made you enjoy or dislike the genre?
  - Think about why you enjoy and usually choose a specific genre. Explain how this book or magazine selection met or did not meet your standards.
  - Were there surprises in the story that held your interest? Explain one.
    - Show how the plot or the events contained twists and turns you did not expect. Was the author good at leading you along one path, then suddenly changing?
    - Explain how a character solved a problem or reacted to a conflict in a way that was different from what you thought this character would do.
  - Did any chapters end with cliff-hangers? Briefly discuss one.
    - Think about how each chapter left you wanting to go right on to the next chapter to find out what happened.
    - Explain why you do or do not enjoy cliff-hangers, using the one you chose to discuss.
  - Was the plot or the events believable or unbelievable?
    - Give one or two examples that show that the plot, or the events that happened, was realistic and could have happened to you or your friends.
    - Give one or two examples that show that the plot was not believable and explain why you feel this way.
  - What new understanding about life, people, or a historical period did you develop?

- Think about what the author was trying to tell you about how people, such as parents, friends, brothers, sisters, teachers, or relatives, behave and feel.
- Show what life was like for children, soldiers, the rich, the poor, or adults during a specific historical period or in an imagined world.
- Did you enjoy the fantasy and magic? Discuss one example.
- Describe one example of magic or fantasy that made the piece exciting for you. Explain why it was exciting.
- Show how the fantasy was part of a reality that helped you connect with the fantasy and magic elements.

From *Writing Advantage*, Level F, by Laura Robb, Great Source, 2006

Appendix Q

Book Review: Nonfiction

Use these questions and prompts to prepare for your written book review.

- Did you enjoy specific nonfiction features?

- Discuss something terrific or unusual you learned from a sidebar, a photograph and caption, or a diary or journal entry.

- Was the writing interesting or boring? Was it hard for you to concentrate on the reading?

- Point out whether the author included stories or anecdotes to hold your interest. Briefly retell one of these.

- If the book or article is a list of facts, explain how you feel about this, and include whether it held your interest.

- Explain how the author used a story or a photograph to explain a tough concept.

- What new understandings about the topic did you develop?

- Discuss how your book or article gave you more information about the topic. Explain one or two things you learned.

- Explain one change you experienced in how you see and think about the topic.

- With biography or autobiography, did you connect with the person's experiences? What did you find fascinating about your subject's life and achievements?

- Explain what the person did that had an impact on history and/or the lives of other people.

- Explain why you admire or dislike this person. Discuss one to two characteristics of this person to help you respond.

- Show how other people affected and/or changed this person's life.

- Choose one key decision this person made and discuss how the decision affected the person's life.

- Were the photos or illustrations effective?

- Choose a photo or an illustration that you enjoyed, briefly describe it, and explain why it appealed to you. You might want to explain what you learned from it, or if it showed you something you never saw before or could imagine.

- Did you make any personal connections with the photos or illustrations?

From Writing Advantage, Level F, by Laura Robb, Great Source, 2006

Appendix R

Sample Journal Entries

JOURNAL ENTRY 1: DRAW CONCLUSIONS ABOUT A CHARACTER

Name _____ Date _____

Title and Author _____

Directions: Discover what the personality of a character in your novel is like by making inferences based on that character's conversation, actions, decisions, thoughts, or the reactions of other characters.

1. Name the character.
2. On the left-hand side of your journal page, list a personality trait you discovered.
3. Now "Prove It!" by giving support from the book.

Name of the Character: _____

Personality Trait   Prove It!
1.   1.

2.   2.

JOURNAL ENTRY 2: INVESTIGATE RELATIONSHIP ISSUES

Name _____ Date _____

Title and Author _____

Directions:

1. On the left-hand side of your journal page, write the names of two characters from your realistic novel.
2. Explain their relationship in the story.
3. Discuss an event, decision, or person that either spoiled their relationship or strengthened their relationship. Explain why.
4. Do this for two sets of characters. You may repeat one character for each set.

Characters and Relationship   What either spoiled or strengthened the relationship? Explain why.

1.

2.

Appendix S

Guidelines for Summarizing Fiction and Nonfiction Texts

WRITE A SUMMARY OF A FICTION TEXT

Introduce students to the summarizing scaffold *Somebody Wanted but So* to support summary writing of fiction or biography. Write each word and its explanation on chart paper so students can refer to it.

Somebody: Name an important character, or the person in your biography.

Wanted: State a problem the character or person faced.

But: Explain some forces that worked against the character.

So: Without giving the ending away, show how the character/person resolved the problem.

WRITE A SUMMARY OF A NONFICTION TEXT

Introduce this framework for an informational text: *Topic, Fascinating Facts, How the Facts Changed My Thinking*. Write each phrase and its explanation on chart paper so students can refer to it.

Topic: Explain what the topic is.

Fascinating Facts: Choose two facts that you found fascinating. For each fact, explain why it fascinated and/or interested you.

How Facts Changed My Thinking: Show how the information in the book changed the way you think about this topic. Did it add knowledge to what you already knew? Did it make you rethink your ideas? If so, explain.

TIPS FOR STUDENT SUCCESS

- Have students take notes using the summary scaffold.
- Help struggling students take notes, and support them through this process.
- Read students' notes before they write their summaries so that you can meet with any students who require extra support before they begin writing.
- Tell students that you want the title and author mentioned in the first sentence.
- Explain to students that the notes under each scaffolding term can be turned into one or two sentences. A summary should be short—about five to seven sentences.

Appendix T

List of Words That Describe Personality Traits

The following list of adjectives can support students as they try to figure out a character's personality traits by using what a character says, does, and thinks. This is a starter list. Encourage your students to add additional character trait descriptors. Remember that thinking about characters' personality traits can broaden students' vocabulary.

RESOURCE LIST OF ADJECTIVES THAT DESCRIBE CHARACTERS' PERSONALITIES

adventurous	cruel	humble	naughty	spiteful
aggressive	daring	imaginative	nosy	stubborn
aloof	determined	impatient	obnoxious	suspicious
anxious	dignified	impish	optimistic	timid
assertive	distrustful	impulsive	overbearing	treacherous
bitter	evil	innocent	pessimistic	tyrannical
bloodthirsty	fierce	insincere	practical	unfaithful
boisterous	foolish	inventive	rational	ungrateful
bossy	friendly	joyful	realistic	unhappy
brave	fussy	kind	reasonable	unique
brutal	gentle	knowledgeable	rebellious	unpopular
capable	grouchy	lazy	reckless	unruly
careful	gullible	lively	rowdy	unwise
careless	harsh	loving	sarcastic	vain
cheerful	haughty	loyal	secretive	villainous
clever	helpful	modest	silly	vivacious
confident	heroic	moody	sincere	weak
confused	hopeful	morbid	snobby	wise
cowardly	humane	mysterious	sociable	witty

Appendix U

Mentor Text for Letters Between Two Characters

For these letters to be successful, both characters in your book need to have lived through the same experiences.

- Write two exchanges between the characters, using two or more different experiences they shared.
- Show each character's point of view and perspective on the lived-through experience. What would each character remember the most? Explain why. What would each character feel? What caused these feelings? How would each character feel about the person he or she is writing to? Show whether the experience changed one character, or both, and explain your position.

Sample letters between Seth and Adam, from "On the Bridge" (Dell, 1987):

Dear Adam,

I can't wait until we can hang out together tomorrow. I keep thinking about all your cool stories: dating older girls. Wow! That's on my radar screen now. It's cool smoking cigarettes, especially when you get away with being underage. I watched how you buy packs from vending machines so you don't have to show an I.D. That's something I can try tomorrow. Then, we can both smoke and feel like we're the top of any group at school.

 I almost forgot to tell you. I bought a jean jacket and washed it a zillion times. It's not totally cool yet; it's got no blood or rips. But hanging out with you will give me a chance to make it look cool. Tomorrow we get cigarettes and meet on the bridge.

 Your friend,

 Seth

Dear Seth,

Hey, thanks for the note. You're right; I'm cool and tough. Don't forget those guys I beat up and my talent for making truck drivers honk when I signal. Don't get your hopes up with older girls. They dig me, but they won't dig you. Good that you got a jacket so we can both look tough. Make sure you get patches of blood, dirt, and some neat-o rips. Tomorrow, you'll get some cigarettes, and you can watch me smoke and learn what to do. We'll be mean and tough and show everyone that Adam is in charge, and Seth is his buddy.

Adam

Dear Adam,

I thought you were cool, man. Not anymore. My nose is broken and bled all the way home. I can't believe you blamed me for flicking that cigarette onto the Camaro's windshield. Man, I'd never rat on you, especially when it wasn't even true. And that bull about the guys pointing a knife. You're chicken, man, face it. And I took everything you should have gotten from those thugs. What for? To be your friend? No thanks! I dumped my bloodied and torn jean jacket in the garbage can outside my garage. My mom was upset when she saw me. But I told her that I was fine. And I am because I intend to be me—Seth—and not try to be you.

Seth

Bibliography of Professional Books

Adler, M., & Rougle, E. (2005). *Building literacy through classroom discussion: Research-based strategies for developing critical readers and thoughtful writers in middle school.* New York: Scholastic.

Allington, R. (2001). *What really matters for struggling readers: Designing research-based programs.* New York: Longman.

Allington, R. (2002). What I've learned about effective reading instruction. *Phi Delta Kappan*, 83(10): 740–747.

Allington, R. L. (2006a). Fluency: Still waiting after all these years. In S. J. Samuels & A. E. Farstrup (Eds.), *What research has to say about fluency instruction.* Newark, DE: International Reading Association.

Allington, R. L. (2006b). "Intervention all day long: New hope for struggling readers." *Voices from the Middle*, 14(4): 7–14.

Allington, R., & Cunningham, P. M. (2002). *Schools that work: Where all children read and write.* (2nd ed.) Boston: Allyn & Bacon.

Alvermann, D. E., Hagwood, M. C., Heron, A. H., Hughes, P., Williams, K. B., & Jun, Y. (2000). *After-school media clubs for reluctant readings.* Final Report (Spencer Foundation Grant #199900278).

Alvermann, D. E., & Phelps, S. E. (1998). *Content reading and literacy: Succeeding in today's diverse classrooms.* (3rd ed.) Boston: Allyn & Bacon.

Anderson, R. (1984). Role of reader's schema in comprehension, learning, and memory. In R. Anderson, J. Osbourne, (Eds.), & R. Tierney, *Learning to read in American schools.* Hillsdale, NJ: Lawrence Erlbaum Associates.

Anderson, V. (1992). A teacher development project in transactional strategy instruction for teachers of severely reading-disabled adolescents. *Teaching & Teacher Education*, pp. 391–403.

Anderson, R. C., & Freebody, P. (1983). Reading comprehension and the assessment and acquisition of word knowledge. *Advances in Reading/Language Research, 2*: 285–303.

Anderson, R. C., Wilson, P. T., & Fielding, L. G. (1988). Growth in reading and how children spend their time outside of school. *Reading Research Quarterly, 23*: 285–303.

Applebee, A. N., Langer, J. A., Nystrand, M., & Gamoran, A. (2003). Discussions-based approaches to developing understanding: Classroom instructions and student performance in middle and high school English. *American Educational Research Journal*, 40(3): 685–730.

Armbruster, B. B., Lehr, F., & Osborn, J. M. (2001). *Put reading first: The research building blocks for teaching children to read.* (Eds.) Washington, D.C. The National Institute for Literacy.

Atwell, N. (1987, 1999). *In the middle: Writing, reading, and learning with adolescents.* Portsmouth, NH: Heinemann.

Aukerman, M. (2006). Who's afraid of the big "bad answer?" *Educational Leadership*, 64 (2): 37–41.

Bamford, R. A., & Kristo, J. V. (Eds.) (2003). *Making facts come alive: Choosing quality non-fiction literature K–12*. Norwood, MA: Christopher-Gordon.

Barrentine, S. J. (Ed.) (1999). *Reading assessment: Principles and practices for elementary teachers*. Newark, DE: International Reading Association.

Beck, I. L. & McKeown, M. G. (1991). Social studies texts are hard to understand: Mediating some of the difficulties. *Language Arts*, 68(6): 482–490.

Beck, I. L., McKeown, M. G., Hamilton, R. L, & Kucan, L. (1997). *Questioning the author: An approach for enhancing student engagement with text*. Newark, DE: International Reading Association.

Beck, I. L., & McKeown, M. G. (2006). *Improving comprehension with questioning the author*. New York: Scholastic.

Beck, I. L., McKeown, M. G., Hamilton, R. L, & Kucan, L. (1997). *Questioning the author: An approach for enhancing student engagement with text*. Newark, DE: International Reading Association.

Beck, I. L., McKeown, M. G., & Kucan, L. (2002). *Bringing words to life: Robust vocabulary instruction*. New York: Guilford Press.

Beers, K. (2002). *When kids can't read: What teachers can do*. Portsmouth, NH: Heinemann.

Blachowicz, C. L. Z., Fisher, P. J. L., Ogle, D., Watts-Taffe, S. (2006). Vocabulary: Questions from the classroom. *Reading Research Quarterly*, 41, 524–539.

Black, P., & William, D. (1998). Inside the black box: Raising standards through classroom assessment. *Phi Delta Kappan*, 80(2): 139–148.

Block, C. C., & Mangieri, J. N. (2002). Recreational reading: Twenty years later. *The Reading Teacher*, 55(6): 572–586.

Block, C. C., & Reed, K. M. (2003). *Trade books: How they significantly increase students' vocabulary comprehension, fluency, and positive attitudes toward reading* (Research Report No. 1734–004). Charlotte, NC: Institute for Literacy Enhancement.

Bowers, R. S. (1995). Early adolescent social and emotional development: A constructivist perspective. In M. J. Waverling (Ed.), *Educating young adolescents: Life in the middle* (pp. 79–109). New York: Garland.

Braunger, J., & Lewis, J. P. (2006). *Building a knowledge base in reading* (2nd ed.). Newark, DE: International Reading Association.

Brown, R., Pressley, M., Van Meter, P., & Schuder, T. (1996). A quasi-experimental validation of transactional strategies instruction with low-achieving second graders. *Journal of Educational Psychology*, 88: 18–37.

Buehl, D. (2001). *Classroom strategies for interactive learning*. Newark, DE: International Reading Association.

Calkins, L., & Harwayne, S. (1991). *Living between the lines.* Portsmouth, NH: Heinemann.

Carnevale, A. P. (2001). *Help wanted . . . college required.* Washington, D.C.: Educational Testing Service, Office of Public Leadership. Available online at http://www.ets.org/research/public/pubs.html.

Clay, M. (1993). Marie Clay responds . . . In *Reading in Virginia,* vol. XVIII: pp. 1–3.

Crafton, L. K. (1991). *Whole language: Getting started . . . moving forward.* Katonah, NY: Richard C. Owen.

Culham, R. (2003). *6 + 1 traits of writing: The complete guide, grades 3 and up.* New York: Scholastic.

Damico, J., & Riddle, R. (2006). Exploring freedom and leaving a legacy: Enacting new literacies with digital texts in the elementary classroom. *Language Arts,* 84(1): 34–44.

Davies, M. A. (1996). Age-appropriate teaching strategies. In M. J. Waverling (Ed.), *Educating young adolescents: Life in the middle* (pp. 187–201). New York: Garland.

Day, J. P., Spiegel, D. L., McLellan, J., & Brown, V. B. (2005). *Moving forward with literature circles: How to plan, manage, and evaluate literature circles that deepen understanding and foster a love of reading.* New York: Scholastic.

Dodge, J. (2006). *Differentiation in action.* New York: Scholastic.

Dowhower, S. L. (1999). Supporting a strategic stance in the classroom: A comprehension framework for helping teachers help students to be strategic. *The Reading Teacher,* (57): 672–688.

Duke, N. K., & Bennett-Armistead, V. S. (2003). *Reading and writing informational text in the primary grades: Research-based practices.* New York: Scholastic.

Duke, N. K., & Pearson, P. D. (2002). Effective practices for developing reading comprehension. In A. E. Farstrup & S. J. Samuels (Eds.), *What research has to say about reading instruction.* Newark, DE: International Reading Association.

Flippo, R. F. (1999). *What do the experts say?" Helping children learn to read.* Portsmouth, NH: Heinemann.

Fountas, I. C., & Pinnell, G. S. (2001). *Guiding readers and writers grades 3–6: Teaching comprehension, genre, and content literacy.* Portsmouth, NH: Heinemann.

Galda, L., & Cullinan, B. E. (2003). Literature for literacy: What research says about the benefits of using trade books in the classroom. In J. Flood, D. Lapp, J. R. Squires, & J. M. Hensen (Eds.), *Handbook of research on teaching the English language arts* (2nd ed.) (pp. 640–648). Mahwah, NJ: Erlbaum.

Gambrell, L.B. (2007). Reading: Does practice make perfect? *Reading Today.* 24(6): 16.

Gardner, H. (1991). *The unschooled mind: How children think and how schools should teach.* New York: Basic Books.

Gardner, H. (1993). *Multiple intelligences: The theory in practice.* New York: Basic Books.

Gee, J. P. (2000). Teenagers in new times: A new literacy studies perspective. *Journal of Adolescent & Adult Literacy,* 43, 412–420.

Gillet, J. W., & Temple, C. (2000). *Understanding reading problems: Assessment and instruction.* New York, NY: Longman.

Graves, M. F. (2006). *Vocabulary book: Learning & instruction.* Urbana, IL: National Council of Teachers of English.

Grolnick, W. S., & Ryan, R. M. (1987). Autonomy in children's learning: An experimental and individual differences investigation. *Journal of Personality and Social Psychology,* 52(5): 890–898.

Guice, S., Allington, R. L., Johnston, P. Baker, K., & Michelson, N. (1996). Access?: Books, children, and literature-based curriculum in schools. *The New Advocate,* 9(3): 197–207.

Guilfoyle, C. (2006). NCLB: Is there life beyond testing? *Educational Leadership,* 64(3): 8–13.

Guthrie, J. T. (2004). Teaching for literacy engagement (Vol. III, pp. 403–422). *Journal of Literacy Research,* 36, 1–30.

Guthrie, J. T., Schafer, W. D., Wang, Y. Y., & Afflerbach, P. (1996). Relationships of instruction to amount of reading: An exploration of social, cognitive, and instructional connections. *Reading Research Quarterly,* 30 (1): 8–25.

Guthrie, J. T., & Wigfield, A. (2000). Engagement and motivation in reading. *Handbook of reading research.* M. L. Kamil, P. B. Mosenthal, P. D. Pearson, & R. Barr (Eds.) Mahwah, NJ: Erlbaum.

Guthrie, J. T., Wigfield, A., Metsala, J., & Cox, K. (1999). Motivational and cognitive predictions of text comprehension and reading amount. *Scientific Studies of Reading,* 3(3): 231–256.

Hall, L. A. (2006). Anything but lazy: New understandings about struggling readers, teaching, and text. *Reading Research Quarterly,* 41, 424–426.

Harvey, S., & Goudvis, A. (2000). *Strategies that work: Teaching comprehension to enhance understanding.* York, ME: Stenhouse.

Hernandez, A., Kaplan, M. A., & Schwartz, R. (2006). For the sake of argument. *Educational Leadership,* 64 (2): 48–52.

Hiebert, E. H. (1983). An examination of ability grouping for reading instruction. *Reading Research Quarterly,* 18: 231–255.

Huck, C. S. (1992). Literacy and literature. In *Language Arts,* 69(7): 520–525.

Ivey, G., & Broaddus, K. (2001). "Just plain reading": A survey of what makes students want to read in middle school classrooms. *Reading Research Quarterly,* 36, 350–377.

Ivey, G., & Fisher, D. (2006). When thinking skills trump reading skills. *Educational Leadership,* 64 (2): 16–21.

Jongsma, K. (1991). Grouping children for instruction: Some guidelines. *The Reading Teacher,* 3(2): 610–611.

Jordan, M., Jensen, R., & Greenleaf, C. (2001). Amidst familial gatherings: Reading apprenticeship in a middle school classroom. *Voices From the Middle,* 8(4): 15–24.

Kommer, D. (2006). Considerations for gender-friendly classrooms. *Middle School Journal*, 38(2): 43–49.

Krashen, S. (1993). *The power of reading: Insights from the research*. Englewood, CO: Libraries Unlimited.

Kucer, S. B. (2005). *Dimensions of literacy: A conceptual base for the teaching of reading and writing*. (2nd ed.) Mahwah, NJ: Erlbaum.

Laminack, L. L., & Wadsworth, R. M. (2006). *Learning under the influence of language and literature*. Portsmouth, NH: Heinemann.

Lenters, K. (2006). Resistance, struggle, and the adolescent reader. *Journal of Adolescent & Adult Literacy*, 50, 136–146.

Liben, D., & Liben, M. (2004). Learning to read in order to learn: Building a program for upper elementary students. *Phi Delta Kappan*, 86(5): 401–406.

Marzano, R. J. (2004). *Building background knowledge for academic achievement: Research on what works in schools*. Alexandria, VA: Association for Supervision and Curriculum Development.

McKeown, M. G., Beck, I. L., & Worthy, M. J. (1993). Grappling with text ideas: Questioning the author. *Reading Teacher*, 46(7): 560–566.

McTighe, J., & O'Conner, K. (2006). Seven practices for effective learning. *Educational Leadership*, 63(3): 10–17.

Michaels, J. R. (2001). *Dancing with words: Helping students love language through authentic vocabulary instruction*. Urbana, IL: National Council of Teachers of English.

Morrow, L. M., Gambrell, L. B., & Pressley, M. (Eds.) (2003). *Best practices in literary instruction* (2nd ed.). New York: Guilford Press.

Murray, D. M. (1984). *Write to learn*. Portsmouth, NH: Heinemann.

Nagy, W., & Anderson, R. (1984). How many words are there in printed school English? *Reading Research Quarterly*, 19: 304–330.

Neuman, S. B. (2006). No is for nonsensical. *Educational Leadership*, 64 (2): 28–31.

NCTE Principles of adolescent literacy reform. Urbana, IL: National Council of Teachers of English.

Neuman, S. B., Delano, D. C., Greco, A. N., & Shuel, P. (2001). *Access for all: Closing the book gap for children in early education*. Newark, DE: International Reading Association.

Nicholson-Nelson, K. (1998) *Developing students' multiple intelligences*. New York: Scholastic.

O'Flavahan, J., Stein, S., Wiencek, J., & Marks T. (1992). *Interpretive development in peer discussion about literature: An exploration of the teacher's role* (Final report to the trustees of the National Council of Teachers of English). Urbana, IL: National Council of Teachers of English.

Opitz, M. E. (1998). *Flexible grouping in reading*. New York: Scholastic.

Paratore, J. R., & McCormack, R. L. (2007). *Classroom literacy assessment: Making sense of what students know and do*. New York: Guilford Press.

Pearson, P. D., & Gallagher, G. (1983). The gradual release of responsibility model of instruction. *Contemporary Educational Psychology*, 8: 112–123.

Pearson, P. D., Roehler, L. R., Dole, J. A., & Duffy, G. G. (1992). Developing expertise in reading comprehension. In S. J. Samuels & A. E. Farstrup (Eds.), *What research has to say about reading instruction* (2nd ed.). Newark, DE: International Reading Association.

Pressley, M., Gaskins, I. W., & Fingerety, L. (2006). Instruction and development of reading fluency in struggling readers. In S. J. Samuels & A. Farstrup (Eds.), *What research says about fluency instruction* (2nd ed). Newark, DE: International Reading Association.

Reis, S. M., & Fogarty, E. A. (2006). Savoring reading, schoolwide. *Educational Leadership*, 64 (2): 32–36.

Reutzel, D. R., & Hollingsworth, P. M. (1991). Reading time in school: Effect on fourth graders' performance on a criterion-referenced comprehension test. *Journal of Educational Research*, 84: 170–176.

Robb, L. (2000a). *Grammar lessons that strengthen students' writing*. New York: Scholastic.

Robb, L. (2000b). *Teaching reading in middle school: A strategic approach to reading that improves comprehension and thinking*. New York: Scholastic.

Robb, L. (2001). *35 must-have assessment & record-keeping forms for reading*. New York: Scholastic.

Robb, L. (2002). Multiple text: multiple opportunities for teaching and learning. *Voices From the Middle*, 9(4): 28–32.

Robb, L. (2003a). *Teaching reading in social studies, science, and math: Practical ways to weave comprehension strategies into your content area teaching*. New York: Scholastic.

Robb, L. (2003b). *Literacy links: Practical strategies to develop the emergent literacy at-risk children need*. Portsmouth, NH: Heinemann.

Robb, L. (2004). *Nonfiction writing from the inside out: Writing lessons inspired by conversations with leading authors*. New York: Scholastic.

Robb, L. (2007). *Teaching reading with think aloud lessons*. New York: Scholastic.

Robb, L. (2008). *Teaching reading: A differentiated approach*. New York: Scholastic.

Roller, C. (1996). *Variability and disability*. Newark, DE: International Reading Association.

Rosenblatt, L. (1978). *The reader, the text, the poem: The transactional theory of the literary work*. Carbondale, IL: SIU Press.

Routman, R. (2002). Teacher talk. *Educational Leadership*, 60(7): 32–35.

Ruddell, R. B., & Unrau, N. J. (1997). The role of responsive teaching in focusing reader intention and developing reader motivation. In J. T. Guthrie & A. Wigfield (Eds.), *Reading Engagement: Motivating Readers Through Integrated Instruction*. Newark, DE: International Reading Association.

Schunk, D. H., & Zimmerman, B. J. (1997). Developing self-efficacious readers and writers: The role of social and self-regulatory processes. In J. T. Guthrie & A. Wigfield (Eds.), *Reading engagement: Motivating readers through integrated instruction*. Newark, DE: International Reading Association.

Self, J. (Ed.) (1987). *The picture of writing to learn*. In *Plain talk: About learning and writing across the curriculum*. Richmond, VA: Virginia Department of Education.

Shallert, D. L., & Reed, J. H. (1997). The pull of text and the process of involvement in reading. In J. T. Guthrie & A. Wigfield (Eds.), *Reading engagement: Motivating readers through integrated instruction*. Newark, DE: International Reading Association.

Shefelbine, J. (2000). *Reading voluminously and voluntarily*. New York: Scholastic Center for Literacy & Learning.

Shepard, L. A. (2006). Linking formative assessment to scaffolding. *Educational Leadership*, 63(3): 66–71.

Sizoo, R. (2001). *Teaching powerful writing*. New York: Scholastic.

Snow, C. E., & Biancarosa, G. (2004). *A report from the Carnegie Institute of New York: Reading next: A vision for action and research in middle and high school literacy*. Washington, D.C.: Alliance for Excellent Education.

Snow, C. E., Burns, M. S., & Griffin, P. (1998). *Preventing reading difficulties in young children*. Washington, D.C.: National Academy Press.

Sousa, D. A. (2001). *How the brain works*. Thousand Oaks, CA: Corwin Press.

Spencer, B. H., & Guillaume, A. M. (2006). Integrating curriculum through the learning cycle: Content-based reading and vocabulary instruction. *The Reading Teacher*, 60 (3): 206–219.

Staples, B. (2006). How schools pay a (very high) price for failing to teach reading properly. *New York Times* Op-Ed, Monday, June 19, 2006.

Tierney, R. J., & Readence, J. E. (2000). *Reading strategies and practices: A compendium*. Boston: Allyn & Bacon.

Tomlinson, C. A. (1995). *How to differentiate instruction in mixed ability classrooms*. New York: Basic Books.

Tomlinson, C. A. (1999a). *The differentiated classroom: Responding to the needs of all learners*. Alexandria, VA: ASCD.

Tomlinson, C. A. (1999b). *Leadership for differentiated classrooms. The School Administrator Web Edition*. http://www.aasa.lrg/publications/sa.1999_10/tomlinson.htm.

Tomlinson, C. A. (2002, September). Different learners, different lessons. *Instructor Magazine*.

Tomlinson, C. A., & Cunningham, E. C. (2003). *Differentiation in practice: A resource guide for differentiating curriculum—grades 5–9*. Alexandria, VA: ASCD.

United States Department of Education. (2003). *Nation's report card: Reading 2002*. Washington, D.C.: National Center for Education Statistics. Available online at http://nces.ed.gov/pub search/pubsinfro.asp?pubid=2003521.

Vaughan, J., & T. Estes. (1986). *Reading and reason beyond the primary grades.* Boston: Allyn & Bacon.

Vygotsky, L. (1978). *Mind in society: The development of higher psychological processes.* Cambridge, MA: Harvard University Press.

Ward, C. C. (2006). *How writers grow: A guide for middle school teachers.* Portsmouth, NH: Heinemann.

Wells, G. (1986). *The meaning makers. Children learning language and using language to learn.* Portsmouth, NH: Heinemann.

Wigfield, A. (1997). Children's motivation for reading and reading engagement. In *Reading Engagement: Motivating readers through integrated instruction,* J. T. Guthrie & A. Wigfield (Eds.), Newark, DE: International Reading Association.

Wilhelm, J. (2001). *Improving comprehension with think-aloud strategies.* New York: Scholastic.

Wilhelm, J. (2005). *Reading is seeing.* New York: Scholastic.

Wormeli, R. (2005). Tiering: Adjusting the level of challenge. *Middle Ground,* 9(1): 25–27.

Worthy, J., Moorman, M., & Turner, M. (1999). What Johnny likes to read is hard to find in school. *Reading Research Quarterly,* 34(1): 12–29).

Zarnowski, M. (1998). It's more than dates and places: How nonfiction contributes to understanding social studies. In R. A. Bamford & J. V. Kristo (Eds.), *Making facts come alive: Choosing quality nonfiction literature K–12.* Norwood, MA: Christopher-Gordon.

Zellmer, M. B., Frontier, A., & Pheifer, D. (2006). What are NCLB's instructional costs? *Educational Leadership,* 64 (3): 43–37.

Zinsser, W. (1988). *Writing to learn.* New York: Harper & Row.

Bibliography of Children's Books

Arnosky, J. (2003). *All about sharks*. New York: Scholastic.

Arnosky, J. (2004). *Following the coast*. New York: HarperCollins.

Atwater, R., & Atwater, F. (1966). *Mr. Popper's penguins*. New York: Time Warner Book Group.

Avi. (1993). *Nothing but the truth*. New York: Avon.

Biesty, S. (2004). *Egypt: In spectacular cross-section*. New York: Scholastic.

Bishop, N. (2004). *Forest explorers: A life-size field guide*. New York: Scholastic.

Blackwood, G. (2001). *The Shakespeare stealer*. New York: Penguin.

Bradbury, R. (1990). "The fog horn" in *The vintage Bradbury*. New York: Vintage Books.

Brenner, B. (2004). *One small place by the sea*. New York: HarperCollins.

Bridges, R. (1999). *Through my eyes*. New York: Scholastic.

Brown, C. (2002). *Barn raising*. New York: HarperCollins.

Cleary, B. (1977). *Ramona and her father*. New York: Morrow.

Coles, R. (1995). *The story of Ruby Bridges*. New York: Scholastic.

Cormier, R. (1974). *The chocolate war*. New York: Pantheon.

Cyrus, K. (2005). *Hotel deep: Light verse from dark water*. New York: Harcourt.

Dahl, R. (1959). "The landlady" in *Kiss, kiss*. New York: Knopf.

DeCamillo, K. (2001). *Because of Winn Dixie*. Cambridge, MA: Candlewick.

Deedy, C. A. (2000). *The yellow star: The legend of King Christian X of Denmark*. Atlanta, GA: Peachtree.

Delacre, L. (2000). *Salsa stories*. New York: Scholastic.

Dorros, A. (1991). *Follow the water from brook to ocean*. New York: HarperCollins.

Elliot, L. M. (2001). *Under a war torn sky*. New York: Hyperion.

Esbensen, B. J. (1993). *Sponges are skeletons*. New York: HarperCollins.

Evslin, B. (1975). *Heroes, gods, and monsters of the Greek myths*. New York: Bantam.

Faustino, L. R. (1998). *Dirty laundry: Stories about family secrets*. New York: Viking.

Frank, A. (1952). *The diary of a young girl*. New York: Doubleday.

Gallo, D. R. (Ed.) (1997). *Visions: Nineteen short stories by outstanding writers for young adults*. New York: Bantam.

Gipson, F. (1956). *Old Yeller*. New York: Harper.

George, J. C. (1960). *My side of the mountain*. New York: Dial.

Giovanni, N. (2005). *Rosa*. Illustrated by Bryan Collier. New York: Henry Holt.

Grimes, N. (2002). *Bronx masquerade*. New York: Dial Books.

Hanlin, M. (2003). *Smart robots*. New York: Scholastic.

Harness, C. (2003). *Rabble rousers: 20 women who made a difference*. New York: Dutton.

Harrison, D. L. (2003). *Oceans: The vast, mysterious deep*. Honesdale, PA: Boyds Mills Press.

Harrison, D. L. (2004). *Connecting the dots: Poems of my journey*. Honesdale, PA: Boyds Mills Press.

Hemingway, E. (1952). *The old man and the sea*. New York: Charles Scribner's Sons.

Jiang, J. L. (1997). *Red scarf girl: A memoir of the cultural revolution*. New York: HarperCollins.

Jiménez, F. (1997). *The circuit: Stories from the life of a migrant worker*. New Mexico: New Mexico University Press.

Jones, L. (2000). *Great black heroes: Five brilliant scientists*. Illustrated by Ron Garnett. New York: Scholastic.

Karr, K. (2005). *Mom went to jail for the vote*. New York: Hyperion.

Klass, D. (2000). *California blue*. New York: Scholastic.

Korman, G. (2000). *No more dead dogs*. New York: Hyperion.

Kronberg, R., & McKissack, P. C. (1990). "Tante Tina" in *A piece of the wind*. New York: HarperCollins.

Krull, K. (2003). *Harvesting hope: The story of Cesar Chavez*. San Diego, CA: Harcourt.

Krull, K. (2000). *Wilma unlimited: How Wilma Rudolph became the world's fastest woman*. San Diego, CA: Harcourt.

Lasky, L. (1998). *A brilliant streak: The making of Mark Twain*. San Diego, CA: Harcourt.

Lauber, P. (1996). *Hurricanes: Earth's mightiest storms*. New York: Scholastic.

Lee, H. (1960). *To kill a mockingbird*. Portsmouth, NH: Heinemann.

Lewis, J. P. (1999). "The many and the few" in L. B. Hopkins (Ed.), *Lives*. New York: HarperCollins.

Lowry, L. (1981). *Anastasia again!* Boston: Houghton Mifflin.

Mannis, C. D. (2006). *Snapshots: The wonders of Monterey Bay*. New York: Viking.

Marshall, E. (1983). *Fox on wheels*. New York: Dial.

Martin, R. (1998). *The brave little parrot*. Illustrated by Susan Gaber. New York: Putnam.

Maruki, T. (1980). *Hiroshima no pika*. New York: Morrow Junior Books.

McCully, E. (1992). *Mirette on the high wire*. New York: Putnam & Grosset.

McGovern, A. (1970). *The Defenders*. New York: Scholastic.

McNulty, F. (2006). *If you decide to go to the moon*. New York: Scholastic.

Medina, T. (2002). *Love to Langston*. New York: Lee & Low.

Melmed, L. K. (2003). *CAPITAL! Washington D.C. from a to z*. New York: HarperCollins.

Mohr, N. (1975). "Once upon a time . . ." In *El Bronx remembered*. New York: HarperTrophy.

Mohr, N. (1975). "Shoes for Hector." In *El Bronx remembered*. New York: HarperTrophy.

Myers, W. D. (1992). *Somewhere in the darkness*. New York: Scholastic.

Myers, W. D. ((2001). *The greatest: Muhammad Ali*. New York: Scholastic.

Naylor P. R. (1992). *Shiloh*. New York: Atheneum.

Nelson, M. (2001). *Carver: a life in poems*. Ashville, NC: Front Street.

Paterson, K. (1977). *Bridge to Terabithia*. New York: Crowell.

Paterson, K. (1978). *The great Gilly Hopkins*. New York: Crowell.

Paterson, K. (1991). *Lyddie*. New York: Dutton.

Paterson, L. (1992). *The king's equal*. New York: HarperCollins.

Paulsen, G. (1977). *The foxman*. New York: Viking.

Paulsen, G. (1988). *Hatchet*. New York: Bradbury.

Peacock, L. (1998). *Crossing the Delaware: A history in many voices*. New York: Simon and Schuster.

Peck, R. (2004). *Past perfect, present tense: New and collected stories*. New York: Dial.

Rawlings, M. K. (1966). *The yearling*. New York: Scribner.

Robinson, S. (2004). *Promises to keep: How Jackie Robinson changed America*. New York: Scholastic.

Sachar, L. (1985). *Sideways stories from Wayside School*. New York: Avon.

Shange, N. (1997). *White wash*. New York: Walker.

Singer, I. B. (1994). *Zlateh the goat and other stories*. New York: HarperCollins.

Smith, J. (2005). *Out of Boneville*. New York: Scholastic.

Soto, G. (1990). "Seventh grade" in *Baseball in April and other stories*. San Diego, CA: Odyssey Books.

Speare, E. G. (1983). *The sign of the beaver*. New York: Dell.

Spinelli, J. (1996). *Crash*. New York: Random House.

Steele, P. (2005). *The world of castles*. Boston: Kingfisher.

Strasser, T. (1987). "On the bridge" In *Visions*, Donald Gallo (ed.). New York: Dell.

Taylor, M. (1977). *Roll of thunder, hear my cry*. New York: Dial Books for Young Readers.

Taylor, M. (1987). *The friendship*. New York: Dial Books for Young Readers.

Taylor, M. (1987). *The gold Cadillac*. New York: Dial Books for Young Readers.

Van Leeuwen, J. (2004). *Oliver the mighty pig*. New York: Dial.

Walker, A. (2002). *Langston Hughes: American poet*. New York: HarperCollins.

Whelan, G. (2004). *Chu Ju's house*. New York: HarperCollins.

Woodson, J. (2000). *Miracle's boys*. New York: Penguin-Putnam Books.

Woodson, J. (1992). *Maizon at Blue Hill*. New York: Putnam.

Index

abandoning books, 196
Allington, R., 12–13, 14, 23, 175, 176, 256
Alvermann, D., 19, 29, 37, 173
Anderson, V., 13, 22, 171, 172, 173
assessment charts, 43–47
assessments, 24–25, 38–41, 115–138
   book conferences and, 121–125
   conferences and, 40–41
   criteria for writing, 42–47
   eleven questions about reading, 38–39
   formative, 13, 38
   forms for assessing students for differen-
      tiated instruction and, 47–49
   independent reading and, 180
   interest inventory, 39
   negotiating ideas from journals and,
      237–240
   ongoing, 19
   ongoing performance, 42–49
   oral reading, 41
   peer book conference, 127–129
   reading conferences, nonfiction, 124
   reading strategy checklist, 40
   retellings and, 115–121
   small-group reading instruction, 165–168
   standardized test scores and, 40
   strategy conferences, 126–127
   what's easy, hard exercise, 39

background knowledge, read alouds and, 69
Beck, I., 16, 18, 29, 58, 172
Biancarosa, G., 15, 42, 57
Big Picture Plans, 26, 54–56
biography differentiated whole-class instruction
   unit, 107–114
biography questions, 108–109
   guidelines for students, 109–111

prompts and questions for, 108
schedule, week-by-week, 111-114
book conferences. *See conferences*
book logs, independent reading, 191–201
   discussion topics that work with any texts,
      193
   reviewing, discussing, to foster self-
      evaluation, 194–195
   snippets of book log discussions, 192
   suggestions for involving students in
      discussions, 193–194
bookmarks
   assessing comprehension, thinking with,
      230–236
   benefits to students and, 231–232
   benefits to teachers and, 231
   issues, themes and, 235–236
   making, using, 232–233
   monitoring reading, differentiating
      instruction with, 233–235
book talks, 131, 197–198
   diverse reading levels and, 198–201
brain research, 21
bridging learning gaps, 65–67

cartoon making, 135
catalyst read alouds, 85–86
   following up and, 88
   how, helps, 87
   lesson planning, 86–90
   preparing, lessons, 87
   presenting, lessons, 87
cause/effect/infer strategy, 100
choice, 14, 175–176
classroom libraries, 176-178
   book displays, 178
   funding, 177

motivational benefit of, 178–179
comfort levels, 26–27
    student book presentations and, 195
comprehension, 29
conferences, 40–41, 115–138
    assess, retellings and, 115–121
    assessing with books and, 121–125
    peer book, 127–129
    reading, fiction and, 123
    reading, nonfiction and, 124
    strategy, 126–127
    strategic reading and, 128
contemplation, comprehension and, 29
criteria for writing, 42–47

daily class schedules, 34
diagrams, making labeled, 135
differentiated instruction
    brain research and, 21–22
    defined, 13–14
    key principles of, 13-14
    multiple intelligences research theory and,
        20–21
    research base for, 20–24
    schema theory reading research and, 22
    supporting research on, 14–15
    ten practices of, 17–20
    texts about, 19
    Tomlinson, C. A. and, 20
differentiated reading instruction, 57–64
    having students working in pairs, 62–63
    my QtA think aloud, 59–60
    QtA journal responses and, 60–62
    sample lesson plan, QtA, 58–59
    self-evaluation, QtA and, 63–64
    small reasonable goals and, 254–256
    three-part framework, 28–29
differentiated whole-class instruction, 99–102
    activities, 106
    assessments, 103–104
    biography unit and, 107–114
    books, finding, 103

conferences, 103
consequences, what to do about, 104–105
groups and, 106–107
multiple texts and, 104
number of books to assign and, 105–106
organizing around a theme and, 100–101
differentiated whole-class instruction
    assessments, 129–139
    book talks and, 131
    creating Web sites and, 135–136
    designing posters and, 135
    dramatic monologues and, 131–134
    essays, 137–138
    journals, 131
    making cartoons and, 135
    making labeled diagrams and, 135
    making movies and, 135
    preparing PowerPoint presentation and,
        136–137
    presenting dramatic monologues and, 134
    tests, 137
discussion, 26–27, 36–38
    encouraging, 18–19
    internal, 37–38
    paired, 37
    small-group, 37
    teacher's role and, 36–37
diverse learners, 13–14
diverse materials, teaching with, 18
diverse reading levels, book talk guidelines,
    198–201
dramatic monologues, 131–134

eleven questions about reading, 38–39
English language learners, 15, 57
essays, 137–138

forming groups, 144–148
    See also small-group reading instruction
framework, planning units of study, 49–56
    assessments and, 50
    goals of lesson and, 50

learning experiences and, 50
Frustration Zone, 23

Gardner, H., 20–21
group work, 14
Guthrie, J., 26, 129, 175, 179

independent practice reading, 18
independent reading, 35–36
    assessing students who read different texts, 180
    choice, time and, 175–176
    importance of, 169–170
    motivation and, 173–175
    research on, 172–173
    student-led discussion groups and, 181–187
    student presentation of comfort level books, 195–201
inferential thinking, 16
informational text lesson plans, 83–88
instructional learning levels, 23
instruction reading level, 27–28
interest inventory, 39
introducing issues for unit of study read alouds, 90–92
    planning a lesson, 91–92
issues, core questions and reading texts, 92–97
issues, organizing instruction around, 27–28

journal entries and read alouds, lesson plan
    following up and, 90
    how it helps, 88
    preparing the lesson and, 89
    presenting the lesson and, 89
journaling
    analyzing student responses to read alouds and, 222–224
    differentiating expectations and, 208–209
    differentiating in response, about small-group lessons, 226–227

differentiating response to read alouds and, 224–226
    management tips for student response, 209–219
    managing journal sharing and, 216–220
    self-evaluations and, 228–233
    sharing and, 214–216
    student feedback about, 207–208
    teacher read alouds: grade five, 220–227
journals, 131

Kindig, J., 172

Laminack, L. L., 68
Lenters, K., 173, 174

McKeown, M. G., 16, 18, 29, 58
mandated requirements, 240–244
meaningful discussion, 22–23
memorization, 28–29
motivation
    classroom libraries and, 178–179
    independent reading and, 173–175
movies, making, 135
multiple intelligences, 20–21
multiple texts, 17

narrative story elements, lesson plan, 80–82
    follow-up and, 82
    how it helps, 80
    preparing the lesson, 80
    presenting the lesson, 80–82
narrative story elements, read alouds, 76–80
    follow up and, 79–80
    how it helps, 77–78
    lesson planning, 76–77
    presenting lessons and, 78–79
nonfiction text lesson plans, 83–85
    following up, 85
    how helps students and, 83
    preparing lessons and, 84
    presenting lessons and, 84–85

observational notes, making, using, 161–165
oral reading assessment, 41

paired discussion, 37
partner think alouds, 73–75
Pearson, P. D., 22, 49, 69
peer book conferences, 127–129, 130
Phelps, S. E., 19, 29, 37
planning, 26, 49, 54–56, 107
posters, designing, 135
PowerPoint presentations, 136–137
problem solving, 14
professional development, 247–249
    differentiation, deepening understanding
        of and, 249–251
    differentiation specialists and, 254
    goal setting and, 254–256
    partnering with teachers and, 251–252
    schools strengths, weaknesses and, 252–253
professional journals, 249
Project CRISS, Creating Independence
    Through Student-owned Strategies, 180

QtA, 205–206
    my QtA think aloud, 59–60
    sample strategy lesson plan, 58–59
    self-evaluations, journaling and, 228–233
    students self-evaluate, 63–64
Questioning the Author (QtA). *See* QtA

read alouds, 16–17, 17–18, 35, 67–69
    background knowledge and, 69
    narrative story elements, teaching, 76–80
    power of, 68
    strategic, 70–75
    See also strategic read alouds
readers theater scripts, 165–168
    guidelines for writing, 166
reading accommodations, 12–13
reading conferences, fiction, 123
reading conferences, nonfiction, 124
reading levels, organizing instructions for, 18

Reading Next, (Snow and Biancarosa), 15, 42
reading strategies, 16–17
reading strategy checklist, 40
reading workshops, 15–17
    concerns about, 31
    differentiation blocks and, 32
    experiences to include in, 32
research
    brain research and, 21–22
    differentiated instruction and, 14–15
    multiple intelligences research theory and,
        20–21
    schema theory reading research and, 22
response journals, 34–36
retelling
    assessing through, 115–121
    checklist: informational texts, 120
    checklist: narrative texts, 119
    scaffolding, differentiating and, 118–121
Robb, L., 16, 22, 29, 32, 49, 69, 146, 176, 208
routines, 33, 147–148
    daily class schedules, 34
    differentiated instruction and, 34–36
    independent reading, 35–36
    response journals, 34–35
    warm-up activities, 35

scaffolding, 23–24
scaffolds, retellings and, 118–121
schema theory reading research, 22
self-discussions, 37–38
self-evaluations
    differentiation, journaling and, 230
    journals and, 228–233
small group discussions, 37
small-group reading instruction, 139–141
    assessments and, 165–168
    big picture plans and, 149–150
    book selections and, 144
    classroom overview and, 142–143
    forming groups and, 144–146
    instructional reading levels and, 148–149

key tips for, 150–151
observational notes and, 161–165
preparing groups for books and, 151–152
routines, success and, 147–148
sample lesson plans, 155–161
teacher-led discussion groups and, 158–159
teacher-led groups and, 148–151
three diverse groups and, 154–155
tips, focusing and differentiating lessons, 153–154
Snow, C., 15, 42, 57, 173
Sousa, D., 26
brain research and, 21–22
How the Brain Works, 21
standardized test scores, 40
strategic read alouds, 70–75
following up and, 72
preparing the lesson and, 71
presenting the lesson and, 71–72
strategic reading conference, 128
strategies, 16
strategy conferences, 126–127
struggling readers, 15
student-led discussion groups, independent reading, 181–187
assessing students' agenda notes and, 190–191
management tips for student-led discussions, 184–185
open-ended questions and, 181–183
scaffolding discussions, agendas, notes and, 185–187
student created questions and, 183–184
student-led reading partnerships, groups in action and, 187–190
student presentation
advertising independent reading books, 197–198
guidelines for, 198–201
student presentations independent reading and, 195–201
student's writings, 16–17

talk show interviews, 167–168
teacher's role, discussion and, 36–37
tests, 137
think alouds, 73–75
three-part framework, 28–29
tiered assignments, 18
tiering, 25–26
timelines, making illustrated, 135
Tomlinson, C. A., 12–13, 15, 18, 19–20, 23, 25, 42, 248
research on differentiated instruction and, 20

units, planning and, 19–20
U.S. Department of Education struggling readers, notes about and, 15

Vygotsky, L., 22–24
instructional learning levels and, 23
learning research and, 22–24
meaningful discussion and, 22–23
scaffolding and, 23–24

Wadsworth, R. M., 68
warm-up activities, daily, 35
Wigfield, A., 179
writing
comprehension and, 19
criteria for, 42–47
importance of, 203–204
plans, 47
writing projects, 236–237

Zone of Actual Development, 23
Zone of Proximal Development, 23